PRAISE FOR THE RESULTS OF *THE PROFESSIONAL PROFILE*™ *PROCESS*

What are real job seekers and solopreneurs saying about the results they achieved with the first edition of *Résumés That Resume Careers* and the Professional Profile™ Methodology?

Imagine how you'll rave about *your* results with the expanded second edition, this very book.

JOB SEEKERS

Convention is to put as much as possible in a résumé and follow the boilerplate herd. Courageous approaches focus on simplifying a résumé to only those items that are important. Don's wisdom is to consider the things that may not yet even be on the page! And that has made all the difference.
- *Brent Ward. Business Development. Raleigh, NC*

Don Burrows has put a spin on the traditional résumé which, unlike so many others out there, actually works! I've been with my current employer since 2007 and recall during my interview my "new" boss telling me that my résumé format provided great insight into what I could bring to her team. I'm happy I invested my time, in me! - *Jennifer B. Haga. Digital Media Sales Specialist. Raleigh, NC*

I tried for three months on my own after graduation to have meaningful contact with companies that might be interested in a recent college graduate with a physics / mathematics degree. I was getting nowhere fast. Don helped me put together a Professional Profile. I have submitted it to several companies and while they have not had entry level positions available, they were interested enough after reading it to meet with me. I know that the time and effort will pay off soon. – *Kyle Margolies. Recent College Graduate. Issaquah, WA*

My final interview was with the CEO of the company. He said that I was at the top of his list to have interviewed for one reason: *"I had to meet the engineer who thinks like this. This resume (really, my Professional Profile) demonstrates that you are not a typical engineer, but an engineer who will be disruptive. I need that in my company."* ... He chose to speak with me because of my profile! A week later I received a letter with an offer – for an opportunity to work with a company that fit me!
– *Greg Pease. Director of Engineering. Division of a high tech company*

There is no one I have ever met that brings as much of himself, his humanness and his humanity, to his work as Don Burrows. This is neither conjecture nor hyperbole ... this is a personally experienced fact. Don is the kind of person you want to work with, to learn from, to know ... for selfish reasons, because you know in doing so you will get so much more than you could ever give.
– *Jon Scott Williams Organizational Generalist; OD Consultant.*

Being a transitioning military officer who did not want your typical defense consulting job I found it very difficult to find a job I wanted. Don helped me create profile of transferable skills that any employer would love to see in an applicant. Also, I found that I have a possible career path that may be different than what I originally planned. Don really opened my eyes to all the possibilities in the world.
– *Billy Duke. Court Coordinator. Renton, WA*

A day after I finished my professional profile and sent it out I received several calls within a few hours for job interviews. A few weeks later I got a job in which my manager received over 500 résumés for the position. Still until this day my manager talks about my professional profile. If you want to get your dream job, work with Don.
- *Eric Castaneda. Reservations Agent. Avalon Transportation*

Don's Professional Profile process will not only provide you with a resume that will ring your phone, it will prepare you for the follow-up interviews. You'll be on the path to your next adventure, the one YOU want, by your targeted profile that fits the job you want the most. By following the steps of the Professional Profile, you will be amazed at the impact you've had on your employers, and yourself. The Professional Profile helped me understand my true strengths and what I can do to improve a company's bottom line, and my own.
– *RSB. Manager, Customer Voice at Lulu.com. Raleigh, NC*

I read the book and Don worked with me one-on-one! He provided me with the confidence to really look at myself, my achievements, be proud of them, brag about them, and keep a discipline of entries to my Database of Accomplishments as they occur. I highly recommend the book to anyone searching for a job, looking at changing careers or just simply searching for a new tool to reformat their current résumé . Today's professional world is always changing so providing a different way to stand out – this is the key. Have doubts about yourself? Take a good look at your Database of Accomplishments. The positive effects are incredible!
– *Lourdes Tsukada. Alderwood Manor, WA*

SOLOPRENEURS

This is something every entrepreneur should do. This process not only brings a clear vision of who you are to your customers, but you will amaze yourself by re-discovering all of the gifts and talents you bring to your business and customers. This process will put YOU into you business and attract the type of customers you've always wanted.
- *Gerald Grinter, The Twelfth Power Consulting, Business Mentor. Seattle, WA*

Don, I went from tongue-tied to fluently speaking, from *"I don't know what I have to offer"* to *"this is what people gain when they work with me."* The process of getting from one to the other was challenging! It was so difficult to make the shift – but it was so worth the effort! I am much more confident talking about my services than before. *Thank you so much!* -*Leona Rehm, Simply Effective Coaching, LLC. Mountlake Terrace, WA*

My experience came with mixed emotions, some sad, some mad at myself and some, frankly mad at Don. *"Just who was this guy and why was he making me think about painful things? I haven't done anything worthy of noting!"* I kept going through the process and discovered more than I had ever thought possible. There I was writing these things about this person, that just happened to be me. Don's method is intense, the process gut wrenching, but the results are truly amazing. You may not know what result you want going into the process, but when you come out the other side you will see you are a better person for it.
-*Susan Straub-Martin, Strauberry Studio Designs. Bellevue, WA*

Don Burrows gets you the attention you deserve by showing hiring managers exactly why they should hire YOU! A Professional Profile will get your phone ringing and will get you that interview. Don's targeted strategies put your name, skills and accomplishments right in front of the people that you need to talk to. Turning your résumé into a Professional Profile will snap you out of the job search doldrums; you're going to remember all of the amazing things you have achieved, and you're going to showcase what you can achieve for your future employers.
– *Scott Bell, Media Design Seattle, Creative Director / Producer. Redmond, WA*

Don's help in putting together my Professional Profile was invaluable in helping me understand what was needed to really help a person get a position in today's economy. Don offered tons of help and insight into what accomplishments really were in life and work and not simply what job did you do.
– *Mike Margolies. Sport Psychology Consultant. Issaquah, WA*

Burn Your Résumé!
You Need a Professional Profile™

Winning the Inner and Outer Game of Finding Work or New Business
IS the name of the game we invite you to play and win.

Donald M. Burrows
Deborah Drake

PO Box 1800
Marysville, WA 98270
www.YourProfessionalProfile.com
800.597.9972

© 2012
Acorn Consulting Inc.
All Rights Reserved

Burn Your Résumé. You Need a Professional Profile™ (Winning the Inner and Outer Game of Finding Work or New Business)
Copyright © 2012 by Acorn Consulting Inc.
All Rights Reserved.

Address inquiries to either:
Donald M. Burrows
Deborah Drake
C/O Acorn Consulting Inc.
PO Box 1800
Marysville, WA 98270
Telephone: 800.597.9972
www.YourProfessionalProfile.com

ISBN: **978-1-935586-62-3**
Library of Congress Control Number: **2012933021**
Publisher: Aviva Publishing, Lake Placid, NY www.avivapubs.com
Associate Editor: Jennifer Haga
Guest Editor: Christopher Burrows
Graphic Typesetting: Mike Margolies www.headwaterspublications.com
Cover Design & Interior Layout: Jon Knight/Sound Design Solutions www.soundpnp.com

The authors have made every attempt to provide accurate information and to properly attribute all sources. Both the authors and publisher have applied their best efforts in the creation of this book. It is sold with the understanding that no one is rendering legal, medical, financial, or any other professional advice or services. Should you require expert advice or services, you should contact a competent professional. No warranties, expressed or implied, are represented, and neither the publisher nor the authors shall be liable for any loss of profit or any other financial or emotional damage in the use of this book

Printed in the United States of America
First Edition 2 4 6 8

a life can change in a tenth of
a second
or sometimes it can take
70
years.

Charles Bukowski
you tell me what it means
The Flash of Lightening Behind the Mountain

Having a social media profile
And not bothering to put anything in it
Is like going to a networking meeting
With a paper bag over your head.
And then staying in the rest room.

Pete DiSantis
http://peterdisantis.com

Dedication

I dedicate this edition to the unemployed and underemployed in America, and to President Barack Obama for his efforts to help them regain their economic footing.

Through no fault of their own, some thirteen million Americans - intelligent, competent, hard-working, possessed of the values and virtues of the American work ethic, and committed to doing things right as well as doing the right things . . . find themselves on the outside looking in.

Consequently employers seem to have the pick-of-the-crop from which to interview.

Or do they? I believe they have the pick-of-the-crop *of those who know how to effectively present themselves as specific solutions to specific opportunities.*

Our intention is to help those who still present themselves generically through mass mailings and Internet postings to learn and use a more effective strategy to STAND OUT in their efforts to find jobs or new business.

Donald M. Burrows, Marysville, WA

"Affluence, unboundness and abundance are our natural state. We just need to restore the memory of what we already know." ~ Deepak Chopra, *Creating Affluence: The A-to-Z Steps to a Richer Life.*

I have always loved this quote. In fact, I have anchored myself with it since 1993. Its message resonates with me to this very day.

I believe we all deserve a rich life that is comprised of both meaningful work we can enjoy as defined by us individually and a work/life balance that allows for us each to also "live all the days of our life" with family and friends and loved ones as we would choose.

I dedicate this 2012 edition to you the reader who perhaps seeks to remember what makes you tick professionally and better still, what lights you up from the inside-out. I dedicate this book to all who commit to working and living on purpose and happily so. To know our talents and have our vocation align is entirely possible. We simply need claim it wholeheartedly.

With your **Professional Profile™** may you be both memorable and unstoppable. Trust the process and enjoy the journey!

Deborah Drake, Bellevue, WA

SPECIAL DEDICATION TO MYRTLE FORD (1912 – 2011)

Karin is my wife. Myrtle is her aunt.

A Seattle native and deeply committed historian and lover of all things Seattle, Myrtle lived a full-to-overflowing 99 years before passing on her own terms on September 15, 2011.

I knew her for only 22 of those 99 years. In that time I came to love her dearly, and was always in awe of her quick wit, humor, love of life, and flat-out spunk.

For over 70 years, Myrtle was the family photo-historian. She was legendary for hauling around a camera bag with more equipment than an AP staff photographer, and in later years, a small pocket camera. She documented every family event, and on the back of any photo she took, she religiously noted those present, date and location and anything else that was photo-pertinent.

When Karin first brought me home to meet the family, it took Myrtle all of about 6 ½ seconds to make me feel we'd known each other since forever. For me, hooking up and hanging out with her was always the highlight of any family gathering.

Myrtle was a Registered Nurse, graduating from Seattle General Hospital in the Class of 1934. In 2008 she was honored as one of Washington State's early professional nurses.

Here she is at her best professional self - - caring, competent, dependable, unflappable. Over the decades, she was the rock upon whom many built the foundations of their lives.

And today – radiant in a different way.

What a life she made for herself between Seattle, Mercer Island and Bellevue. What a role model for a life well-lived. And how I would have loved to help her write her Professional Profile™.

She would have just said, "Oh, go on!" And laughed.

Thank you, Myrtle, for my last hug and kiss.

Love, Don –

Gratitude. Gratitude. Gratitude.

To **Deborah Drake**, my writing and business partner, for her writing skills, insightful vision, and commitment to her firm belief that *'authentic writing provokes.'*

To **Marie Baptiste, Lisa Smith** and **Gerald Grinter** my Goals Mastermind partners, for their unfailing weekly encouragement, and the occasional boot in the butt to get back on track and "Keep It Moving."

To **Jennifer Haga**, my daughter, for taking what I taught her about writing Professional Profiles™ to a completely new level and then sharing her ideas with me.

To **Chris Burrows**, my son, for letting me help him with his technical résumé, then improving on what we created, and sharing his format with me.

To **Scott Bell,** our videographer, for filming the supplemental information videos we'll direct you to on www.YourProfessionalProfile.com.

To **Rachel Braynin**, my entrepreneurial friend who encourages wide distribution of this book and its companion workshop.

To **JonScott Williams**, my wise counselor and articulate supporter of this book and of Mr. Obama.

To Marie Baptiste, Greg Pease, Kyle Margolies, Billy Duke, Aaron Urban, Eric Castaneda, Scott Bell, Gerald Grinter, Taye Cook, Susan Straub-Martin and JonScott Williams for granting us permission to use the cover letters and Professional Profiles™ we created with you and for you.

Finally, to **Karin Burrows**, my wife, who took care of home, hearth, health and happiness while I took care of the book. ~ **Donald Burrows**

To **Don Burrows**, my business partner, mentor and friend, for his tell it like it is attitude, his enthusiasm, and commitment to helping others find work they want, and for his tenacious and feisty way of drawing out the best in a person.

To **Jon Knight**, for his creative agility, enthusiasm, and his team attitude as we co-created a cover and interior layout that honored the content of this book.

To **John Calvin Dotson**, my lifetime friend and creative and writing mentor since 9th grade English who awakened in me a love of Authentic Writing that has served me over 30 years and counting.

To **Bronte**, my daughter, who at 12 years of age surpasses my memory of 12 year old me, in self-confidence and self-awareness, wise beyond her years and clear on what her talents are and what dreams may come true—as defined by her. ~**Deborah Drake**

Table of Contents

Introduction — 1
How to Get the Best Out of You Using this Book — 4
Why We Have Earned the Right to Advise You — 4
Origins of an Inner Game: The Game Really Starts Here — 5

Chapter 1: Introduction to the Professional Profile™ Process — 11
Still Using a Reverse-Chronological Résumé? Our Twelve Predictions — 15
The Inner Game Starts Now and Sets the Tone — 16
Elements of a Professional Profile™ — 17

Chapter 2 Your Accomplishments — 19
What Have You Actually Accomplished? — 20
Converting Activities and Job Duties into Accomplishments — 25
Using Power Words — 27
Exercise: Getting to the Essence of Your Accomplishments — 44

Chapter 3: Your Accomplishments Data Bank — 51
Organizing Your Accomplishments: Subcategories and Key Words — 55

Chapter 4: Your Special Skills and Abilities — 57
Special Skills and Abilities — 58
How to Identify Your Special Skills and Abilities — 62
Special Skills and Abilities Data Bank — 67
Sample: Client Special Skills and Abilities Data Bank — 68

Chapter 5: Customize Your Objective — 71
Exercise: Writing Objectives — 76

Chapter 6:
"Part B" – The unchanging second half of your Professional Profile™ — 79
How to Present this Information — 80
How Do You Handle the "Age" Thing? — 81
Your Job History Can Do You In — 84

Chapter 7:
Working with Your Special Skills and Accomplishments Data Banks — 89
The Narrative Style of Professional Profile™ — 89
Exercise: Selectivity / Using Your Data Banks — 90

Chapter 8: The One-Page + Addendum Style — 115

Chapter 9: The Technical + Narrative Style — 125
Summarizing the Three Styles of Professional Profiles™ — 130

Chapter 10: The Bonus Section — **131**

Using Your New Professional Profile™ in Ways that
  Make You Stand Out — 131
Introduction to Cover Letters — 132
Elements of Targeted Cover Letters — 133
Strategy for Exploratory Letters for Mass Mailing — 136
Be Bold: The Spaghetti or the Meatball? — 136
Four Magic Sentences for Your Cover Letter — 139
In Closing — 143

Appendix of Professional Profiles — **145**

The Authors:
Donald Burrows — 147
Deborah Drake — 153

Job Seekers — **159**
Technical Trainer / Financial Services — 159
Director of Engineering / High Tech Manufacturing — 164
New College Graduate (Physics) / Entry-level engineering position — 170

Military to Civilian — **176**
US Army Officer Transitioning into Civilian Job Market — 176

Transitioning from Solopreneur to Employee — **183**
Self-Employed Journeyman Carpenter / Home Maintenance Expert
  to Employed Carpenter — 183
Commodity retail sales clerk to boutique Reservations Agent — 188

Solopreneurs — **192**
Contract Producer of Educational and Training Videos — 192
Serial Entrepreneur (Start-up Specialist) — 198
Graphic Artist — 202

Baby Boomers — **208**
Laid off Organization Development Manager repurposes
  contents of Professional Profile™ to become University Lecturer — 208
Laid off HR Manager in a for-profit company repurposes
  contents of Professional Profile™ to secure interview as
  HR Manager for municipal city government. — 218

The Epilogue — **223**

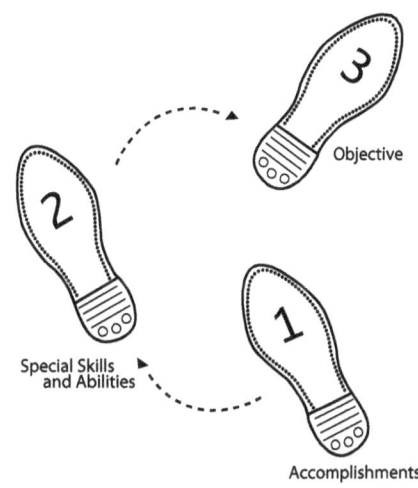

Introduction

THIS IS NOT A ONE-SHOT-AND-YOU'RE-DONE-WITH-IT RÉSUMÉ-WRITING BOOK.

If that is what you are seeking, please look elsewhere.

WITH THIS BOOK, YOU WILL LEARN TO CREATE A PROFESSIONAL PROFILE™.

Your Professional Profile™ is based on Data Banks you create that reflect your RELEVANT PROFESSIONAL ACCOMPLISHMENTS and your SPECIAL SKILLS AND ABILITIES.

Your Data Banks will grow and evolve as you and your career do. Your Professional Profile™ --maintained and updated--will continuously reflect the most current and accurate professional story you can tell about yourself.

Keeping your Data Banks current will enable you to easily customize the credentials you submit (cover letters, Professional Profiles™) as you present yourself as the "ideal candidate" in your search for new work or new customers.

The Truth is…

Having a strong working résumé be it chronological or functional in style will not help you actually get the desired position or assignment or project if you can't also talk intelligently about what lives in that document and who you are and what you bring. And if that is a confronting statement to read, please consider the following:

What is most important when it comes to finding work? Is it having a strong résumé that reflects great experience? Is it knowing the right contacts? Is it the ability to win the job offer because you could talk intelligently about your career goals? Or is it about something else?

Ask yourself the following questions:

- Are you clear on what you like to do where work is concerned?
- Are you aware of what you are naturally skillful at and what challenges you?
- Are you able to talk about yourself like you understand your strengths and your career goals--presuming of course you have identified what they are?
- Have you ever really taken an in-depth personal inventory on what you want where work and career are concerned?
- When you succeed at interviews and gain the new position or assignment, does the same person who interviewed show up for work on day one with the same confidence and enthusiasm?

What if you could not only apply for work with confidence but also enthusiasm--knowing well what you bring to the world of work, the team you would become part of and knowing you were well suited for the work you'd be doing?

This working book is about creating all of that for you. This process we call developing one's Professional Profile™ is about letting professional you get to know yourself well. It is about masterfully presenting yourself on paper as well as in person (with ease and confidence.)

We call it the "Inner and Outer Game of Finding Work You'll Love." It is a journey taken by those who work for others and those who work for themselves. It will be a journey through the archive of stories that make up your personal and professional life.

Some who have taken on developing their profile tell us first they got angry and frustrated for it was a rigorous, revealing, and confronting process. In pushing through, they got to know themselves better, they discovered wonderful parts of themselves they had forgotten and not thought about for a long time. They discovered that even as young people, long before working for pay, they had ideas about what they really wanted to do for a vocation, what they enjoyed doing and what talents they innately possessed. They got reacquainted with early dreams and their natural instincts.

As a young girl, I wrote ALL the time. I journaled as early as nine years old. I don't have that first Hallmark Diary with a lock and key (oh so secure!) but I have all the others! 35 years of Deborah, in boxes, journals fancy and plain documenting my ups and downs and ever changing perspectives as I evolved personally, academically then professionally.

Now as a Writing and Communications coach and looking back on what I always loved doing for business or pleasure, *I can connect the dots*. I see the talents and characteristics that I have used *in every position I have ever held*! Everything I have done professionally in journalism, publishing, advertising, sales, business development and training is in the mix of who I am professionally now. I know that staying current on my professional achievements will pay off in more than one way.

Whether the economy is challenged or booming, Don and I believe we all deserve to be doing work we want to be doing. What does it take to get that work? I am of the belief that when we are clear and intentional in telling our professional story, we stand a much better chance of standing out to a potential employer or client.

Confidence is felt within ourselves and by the people we talk with. **Enthusiasm** also is sensed as present or missing. Simply put, these qualities are present in our writing and our speaking, or they are not. Conversely, the absence of confidence and enthusiasm is also felt. **Authenticity** cannot be feigned. How do you want to be experienced from the start?

We want you to develop a story about yourself that reads well, tells well, keeps well and grows well. We want it to be one you happily can tell with both passion and humility as many times as is required. This would be Professional Storytelling at its best. May you be as confident to tell your professional story as you naturally are when you introduce yourself! After years of saying, "Hello, I am Deborah Drake," I have yet to forget WHO I am even under pressure or when in a hurry! (smile)

Our hope is that as you are reading this book, you have an important goal for yourself: To capture a rich COLLECTION OF YOUR professional STORIES that REFLECT your core values and skills, your achievements, your contributions, and SET you up to be the one who easily gets the interview desired and ultimately the work you want.

Let us also be clear about a few things. Direct experience matters a great deal. Gaining competence takes time and there are also talents we seem to be born with that simply need cultivating. Some people seem to be born sales people, yes? Others are more organized than I will ever be, no matter how hard I work at it! And still others have an eye for artistic compositions, while others understand numbers and complex technical concepts.

As for the array of talents we need on the job, many can be learned through direct experience and mentoring and synthesized by some high quality reflection on our part. We believe this book gives you the opportunity to do just that: To reflect on what you can do well, what you love to do, and even reveal what you prefer not to do. It's all good to know.

Whether you are in transition professionally, seeking work that matches more with your sense of purpose or simply staying ahead of the game SO that you can respond rapidly to new professional opportunities, we hope that you both read all of this book and build your profile.

Yes, it is true, many times we invest in books intending to read them, take them to heart, take action and then we don't. We hope you stay committed to reading all of this labor of love. We hope you invest the time in getting to know your professional STORIES.

We encourage you to take on crafting your Professional Profile™. Do the work. Trust the process. And trust the process even when you want to stop. Get support and an accountability partner or three to work with you. Like Nike ads declare, "Just Do It." We want for you, be you job seeker or entrepreneur, to be able to create stunning profiles that capture your essence and skills and most current accomplishments. Why?

So that you are working at work you enjoy and thriving in the best sense of the word.

And you know it!

How to Get the Best Out of You Using this Book

Creating a Professional Profile™ is like driving from the west coast to back east. It is not like taking a drive to the beach and being home for dinner.

Some people like to read a book like this from cover-to-cover so they get an overview of the process, and then come back and methodically follow the process. When these people undertake a cross-country drive, they plan their route, know the sites they want to see along the way, and have an idea where they will stop each night.

Others prefer to do the exercises as they come. When they do the cross-country drive, they gas up and head out, willing to take detours and make some wrong turns, and trusting that they will ultimately get to their destination.

Whether you are reading this as a download or in an actual book, we strongly recommend you read it cover-to-cover so you get an overview of the process, then come back and work the process.

If you have the download, please print it out because you will have many opportunities to make notes and copy-and-paste what you have written.

And finally, as you read the book for the first time, keep a notebook handy to capture questions, ideas and sudden flashes of brilliance.

We are certain you will have all three.

And to give you a little taste of the journey you are about to undertake with us, we invite you to visit www.YourProfessionalProfile.com/DonsVideos. **Please scroll down to** Interview with Don Burrows, author of *Résumés that Resume Careers*.

Why We Have Earned the Right to Advise You

Simply put, clients credit our Professional Profiles™ with getting them more interviews, sooner, than when they used traditional chronological résumés.

When the recession hit and President Obama urged us to volunteer our abilities to help others, I (Don) created and offered a series of free two-hour workshops to teach others how to write their own Professional Profiles™. The workshops resulted in interviews and sometimes jobs. Participants encouraged me to create a website to share the course.

Writing Professional Profiles™ has been an avocation for over 30 years. I have written hundreds of them, for people who have suddenly found themselves laid off, without funds and in desperate need of an effective résumé. Others I have written for money, between $1,500 and $2,000 per résumé, in Spanish and English.

My Human Resources management experience spans over 30 years. For twenty of those thirty years, I have recruited, hired and fired employees from entry to executive levels throughout the United States, Latin America, Europe, Australia, New Zealand and the Asia-Pacific Rim.

In my corporate and consulting careers, I worked in: hospitality, metal-cutting, financial services, agri-business, transportation, global accounting, chemical manufacturing, and concrete production. All of my corporate positions included recruiting, outplacement, candidate assessment, and job search counseling.

Here's something to keep in mind: based on the accomplishments a candidate presented, it was not uncommon for me to interview them for one position, only to end up considering and then hiring them for a higher-level position. Often these were the very positions for which I was having difficulty finding qualified candidates.

I did this any number of times over my career. Moreover, because I used a functional résumé when I was in the job market, the same thing happened to me when I was hired for my last corporate job; I applied for one position and was hired for another I did not know existed!

Bottom line: *HR's responsibility is to fill jobs with candidates who meet as many of the hiring qualifications as possible. They do that by screening out as many applicants as possible.*

Knowing that fact, doesn't it make a whole lot of sense to customize your résumé for each position and present yourself as a match for each of their unique qualifications?

In my experience, people who shotgun their résumés doom themselves to a very long job search. After months of no recruiters calling, a silent telephone gets pretty depressing, doesn't it?

Please visit www.YourProfessionalProfile.com/DonsVideos and watch *Opening Remarks: "Judge By Results. Often Harsh. Always Fair."*

Let's make your phone ring.

Origins of an Inner Game: The Game Really Starts Here

Playing an effective INNER GAME is the foundation of your Professional Profile™

When you stop and think about the first time you wanted a job (that you might earn some spending money) to supplement your allowance if you got one, what is your first potent memory? How young were you? And how easy or difficult was it?

Did you work for your parents or go and apply at the local fast food or coffee house or a retail business? Or did you create your own "small business" offering your services to mow lawns, babysit the neighbor's young ones or wash cars? Were you the one with the lemonade or Kool-Aid stand on the corner on Spring and Summer breaks? Perhaps you cut your entrepreneurial teeth on Girl Scout cookies or a magazine drive for school that won you "valuable prizes" and best of all status as a rockstar at sales? What if I suggested right now, these things matter even now?

Or perhaps it goes back even further and you earned your first quarters and dollars by doing your chores without being asked? Or did your parents rewarded you with cold hard cash and bonus experiences to movies and shopping sprees and your favorite requested meals?

Somewhere in our early years our first lessons about working were given to us (both directly and indirectly). We developed ideas about what we were worth and our potential for getting promoted and being given more responsibility. **The origins of our current day work ethics and sense of self existed long before our first post-college job.** Affected by these early experiences a little or a lot, we decided how hard we would be willing and have to work for the fruits of our labors. And maybe, you had a good role model who encouraged and rewarded you?

How much encouragement did you receive as you earned more responsibility growing up? These are your first accomplishments in one sense. How important was getting good grades to you once you started getting grades in Middle School? Did you see yourself as succeeding when you were consistently on time turning in homework, getting good grades, giving well received oral reports, and contributing to extracurricular activities like Year Book, Safety Patrol, Model U.N., any number of sports teams or, community service before it was required to graduate from High School? Stop and think about those early years differently please!

What is my point? **We all internalized ideas about what mattered and what didn't long before we started college and got our first "real" jobs in the "real" world.** As "grown-ups" we bring our "inner selves" to the world of work and that inner self contains our collective experiences and the meanings and the values we assigned them.

Speaking for myself, I developed a work ethic based on working for privileges and a small allowance from the age of seven onward. It began just before my parents would divorce. Chores were tracked on a chart and TV time and $2 a week were earned as beds were made daily, dishes were washed and put away, laundry was done and weeds were pulled bi-monthly.

At 12, I was "allowed" to work for an hourly wage of $2.50 at my stepmother's mother's second-hand consignment store, *Dress for Less*. In a single summer I grew to forever despise organizing by color and item all the clothes tried on but not purchased. I literally vowed NEVER to work in retail clothing. And, I NEVER have. Nor do I organize my own closet as I was forced to organize that "boutique" when I was 12. I decided from that point that if I had to work in retail it would involve anything but clothing: No folding t-shirts into neat squares at The Gap for me.

In subsequent summers, I opted for "messier" and more satisfying manual labor with people I liked. There was the summer I worked with my dad, painting contractor that he was, masking off second story windows on tall ladders and painting apartment stairwells all day long. And then there were the summers I worked as a Certified Nurse's Aide to elders by day and at my uncle's restaurant by night as a bus-person and when lucky as hostess.

In college, I dreamed of working at the campus coffee house, but I landed work as a typesetter for the college newspaper which allowed for me to write feature stories, do layout and shoot images for the copy camera. When becoming a paid editorial staff member stayed out of reach, I opted for another line of work after 18 months. Intelligent and artistic and lover of all things journalistic, I applied to become a food server. So here I was seven years after my first retail work experience opting to take orders, schlep food, clear dirty dishes and pinch hit as dishwasher. I opened and closed and opened and closed. It was honest work that I actually liked.

But, of course I wanted to earn more money than I was. Getting free meals was great but it didn't make up for the minimum wages and the meager tips that college students offered when they would even bother to tip.

Why we take work that we do still interests me. I know I liked the flexibility of restaurant work and the social aspects and the diversity of who came in now and then and who came in every day. It was a mix of both steady and ever changing. At one point I took an office job as a leasing agent in the complex I lived in and hated it so much I went back to restaurant work. The pay was better but the company I got to keep and the work itself was not. **It became clear to me that liking what we do is critical for our well being. And I wish I had taken that lesson to heart much sooner than I did.**

I have suffered through more years of work I didn't like for the sake of money, benefits, supposed security and the great promised opportunities spoken of in the interview process. The greatest by-product of all that "grunt work" (as in work I did with waxing and waning levels of resentment) is how it impacted my self-confidence and sense of self.

We all have talents and skills. When these are applied to the right line of work we are more likely to experience success, gain responsibility and earn more income over time. If we are among those in the minority who identify early their future vocation and occupation, we are doubly blessed.

We all know the teacher, the doctor, the counselor, the artist, the musician, the lawyer, the engineer who can tell the story of knowing young and staying enthusiastic for many decades. With time they get better and more respected and have more opportunities to make a lasting impact on their world. All of which enhances their confidence and mastery of the inner game of succeeding where it matters most.

Many have quite the opposite experience. Some spend years misdirected, in a constant search of what if, what about, what next, maybe this, maybe that, chasing the trending pipedream of getting rich quick and in some cases investing precious resources be it time and money to get trained, certified, accredited, and accepted as the professional they think they want to be.

Don't we also know the teacher who got burned out after a few years, the lawyer who very quickly got disillusioned, the real estate agent who gave up after a few seasons of low sales. Are they all examples of confidence lost or confidence not quite firmly rooted in the first place? **Ask yourself, was there ever a time you were clear on what work you wanted to do?** Did you or did you not pursue that dream vocation?

Self-mastery and deeply rooted confidence take time to gain through experience. And some early experiences may need to be acknowledged, examined and then discarded. Our collective personal and professional experiences both matter a lot. And we don't always assign as much value to the personal experiences that shaped our characters when we are focused on our professional pathways,

This book and the process of crafting a Professional Profile™ is really about shedding light on how important and inter-related the combined set of experiences is. We need to learn how not to discount either channel when it comes to portraying ourselves on paper and in person.

Above all we must BELIEVE in ourselves, our abilities, first and fully recognize our own talents. Why? That we might be a congruent and consistent applicant professionally for one thing. **Imagine having a résumé that gets you an interview but giving an interview that makes them wonder why they invited you in?** How many go into interviews essentially unable to talk of themselves with the right mix of confidence and storytelling and poise and humility?

> *It is not what you say as much as it is the TONE and MANNER in which you say it that makes a lasting impression.*
>
> *It naturally follows, therefore, that sincerity of purpose, honesty and earnestness must be placed back of all that one says if one would make a lasting and favorable impression.*
>
> *Whatever you successfully sell to others, you must first sell to yourself.*
>
> ~ **Law of Success**, Napoleon Hill (from the chapter on Enthusiasm)

The most important advice I could ever give a job seeker or solopreneur in search of new business is about as simple as can be:

Master the inner game long before you arrive for the meeting. Bring not only your knowledge of your skills and accomplishments and professional history. Bring also your awareness of who you are and what you bring to the world of work as a member of the team, an individual contributor and as a person.

We do business with real people. Therefore, we hire real people. And hopefully you are hired for the real person you are as well as the skill set you bring to the organization you join. So if you are searching for work, be it a new internal position or a new client to serve, we believe it is critical and valuable to be clear on who we are both professionally and personally.

Really knowing yourself creates natural confidence that others can sense and will experience.

Getting to know your personal and professional Self in both ways is a valuable experience for many reasons. For some it is easier than others. Where your career aspirations are concerned: Maintaining a sense of who you are and how you are evolving is the equivalent of working SMART. If you have not maintained a detailed CV that tells professional stories about you vividly and honestly, you may be short changing your future.

Unless you have a professional angel or fairy godmother, we believe you will need to develop the ability to be your own best advocate. The Professional Profile™ process is designed to make you GLAD to be your own best advocate, and is best begun with a commitment to work on your Inner Game as you design your Outer Game.

**Winning the Inner and Outer Game of
Finding Work or New Business
IS the Big Game we invite you to play and win.**

And interestingly, when you become your own best advocate from an enthusiastic and humble place of deep knowing, others become your advocate as well.

To your success in getting to know you, getting to know all about (professional) YOU!

~ Deborah and Don

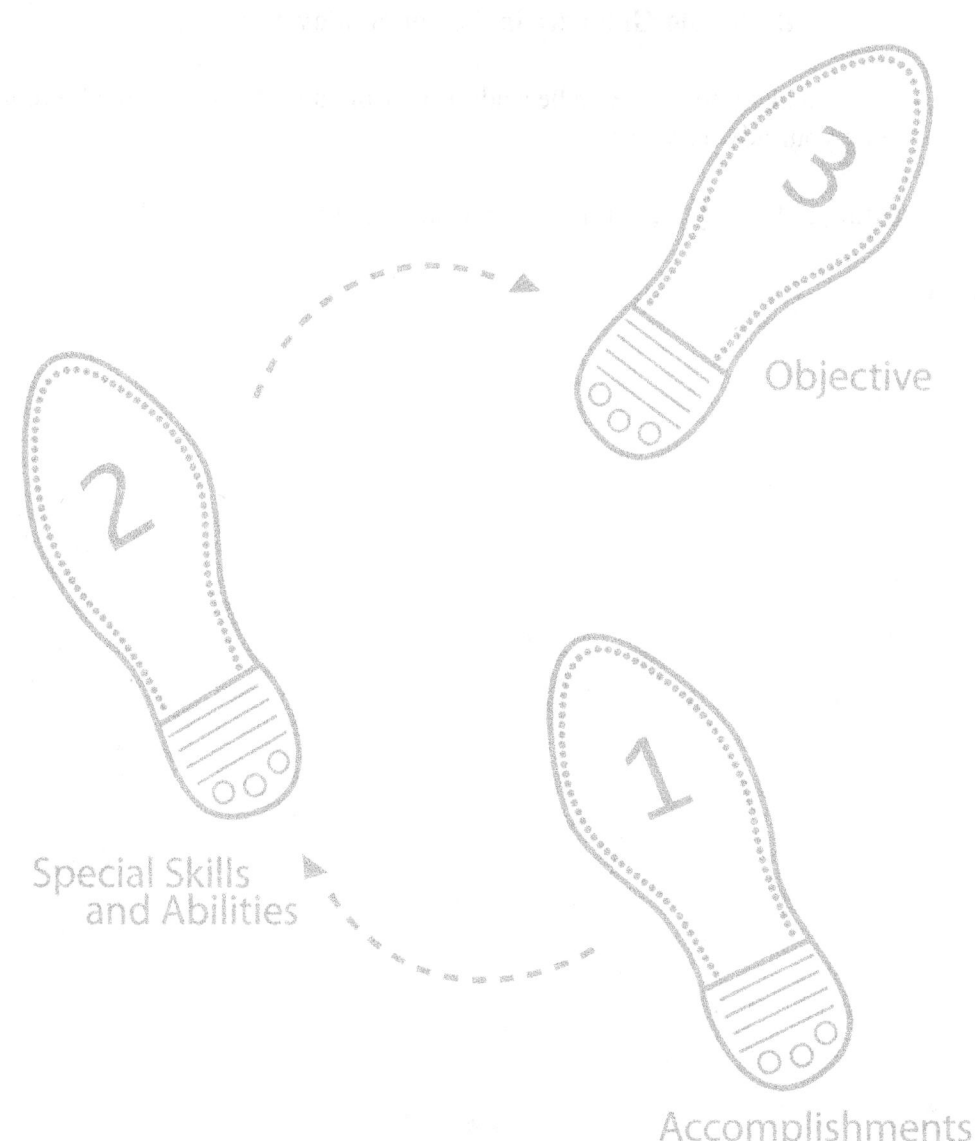

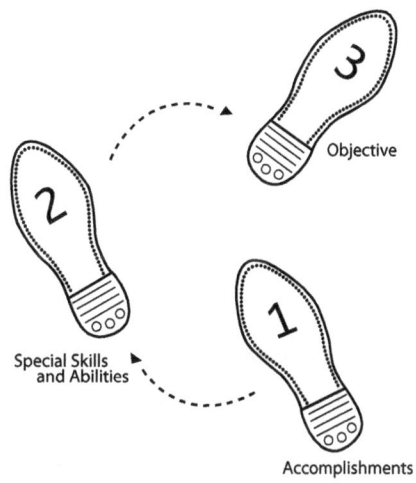

CHAPTER 1

Introduction to the Professional Profile™ Process

Hello! We're glad you are finally here!

The sooner we get started and you complete your Professional Profile™, the sooner you'll STAND OUT so an interviewer can call you or new business can find you.

What's a ***Professional Profile*™**? It is our term for a functional- or accomplishments-based résumé.

Why "Professional Profile™" not "résumé?" Because when we hear the word "résumé" we think of a mass-mailed chronology based on "dates and duties." Because that's not how we do it, we wanted a different term for our product.

Our **Professional Profiles™** are never the same twice. They are custom-made, up-to-date and always-evolving documents that will enable applicants to present themselves as "IDEAL CANDIDATES" each time they apply for a position for which they are qualified.

As you proceed through this book, please keep paper or notebook handy to jot down sudden thoughts.

You are about to learn a unique process. Once you have mastered it, you will be able to present yourself as a well-qualified vendor to service a prospective client's needs or an ideal candidate for any job for which your experience supports your application.

If you are thorough in your preparation, you may even be able to present yourself as the unique solution to an employer's or client's needs currently going unrecognized and unmet.

Said another way, you may be able to create business or a job for yourself. It is always easier and more expeditious to sidestep the competition than to beat it.

However, like so many things that are unique and special, effort is required before success can occur.

Whether you are looking for a new job or want to attract new business, you must satisfy the needs of your potential employer or customer. To do that, you must customize three elements of your Professional Profile™ - based on the unique requirements of your potential employer or client.

Essential Element 1: Representative Professional Accomplishments. Selectively, include only your most relevant Representative Professional Accomplishments. Do this to customize your Professional Profile™ to the experience requirements demanded by your potential new employer or client.

Essential Element 2: Special Skills and Abilities. Selectively, include only your most relevant Special Skills and Abilities. Do this to customize your Professional Profile™ to meet the established skills requirements set by your potential new employer or client.

Essential Element 3: Objective. Customize your OBJECTIVE to match the title used by your perspective client or potential employer.

We are going to take the steps in sequence. By the time we are done, we believe you will agree that tailoring your Professional Profile™ to present yourself as a uniquely-qualified candidate is not that hard.

> **JOB SEEKER OR SOLOPRENEUR**
>
> Remember: YOU are the product.
>
> If you want the buyer to pick YOU,
> **customize yourself**
> to be the unique solution to their specific needs.

Through a thought-provoking exercise, you will have an opportunity to work with an actual Narrative format Professional Profile™ that a client used to get the interview and the job.

Once you have a brand new and unique Professional Profile™, we prefer you use a new set of strategies to search for new business or employers. You'll find more information in the Bonus Section.

There we will show you how to create a straightforward, targeted cover letter that will enable you to present yourself as the best possible ideal match for the job or consulting assignment you are seeking, in a manner that complements and highlights the strengths in your new Professional Profile™.

We will also share job search strategies to help you come to the attention of decision-makers – strategies that have paid off handsomely for Don and for clients. We will end the Bonus Section with some absolutely magical words for your cover letters.

And finally, in the Appendix you will find thirteen real examples of targeted cover letters, Professional Profiles™ (including our own) and an analysis of each person's situation in these categories:

Each benefitted from the work we did for, and with, them.

Here's what you'll find in the Appendix:

Our Professional Profiles:
- Don's
- Deb's

And then you'll find these summaries, cover letters and Professional Profiles™:

Job Seekers:
- Technical Trainer / Financial Services
- Director of Engineering / High Tech Manufacturing
- New College Graduate (Physics) / Seeking entry-level engineering position
- US Army Officer Transitioning into Civilian Job Market

Transitioning from Solopreneur to Employee:
- Self-Employed Journeyman Carpenter / Home Maintenance Expert to Employed Carpenter

Career Transitions:
- Commodity retail sales clerk to boutique Reservations Agent

Solopreneurs:
- Contract Producer of Educational and Training Videos
- Serial Entrepreneur (Start-up Specialist)
- Graphic Artist

Baby Boomers:
- Laid off Organization Development Manager repurposes contents of Professional Profile™ to become University Lecturer
- Laid off HR Manager in a for-profit company repurposes contents of Professional Profile™ to secure interview as HR Manager for municipal city government.

Let's get to it.

We Begin with this Basic Premise:

No matter what credentials you use – custom cover letter and Professional Profile™ or generic Dear Sir or Madam cover letter and reverse-chronological résumé – their function is never to get you a job or new clients.

Rather, they are to show as many relevant facets of you until you can speak on your own behalf, and they are to generate enough interest that someone will call YOU for an interview or more information.

Until someone contacts you, nothing much happens.

Meatball or Spaghetti?

Please look only at the spaghetti. Does any single strand stand out from all the others? You could pick any one; they all look alike.

That's how it is with a computer-full or pile of one-size-fits-all résumés, or a static website, or a "stealth" social media profile: like each look-alike strand of spaghetti on a plate.

The odds that YOU will be contacted are minimal, at best.

Now, please consider **the meatball**.

That meatball is part of the pile of spaghetti and you can't miss it, can you?

And it's the same for a Professional Profile™: IT STANDS OUT.

So really, it's up to you.

The prize is an interview and possibly a job offer or a new customer.

Is it worth the effort to learn how to create a unique Professional Profile™ so **you stand out** *like the* **meatball**, or are you satisfied with the results you are getting?

Asked another way, could it be that recruiters or new clients are not calling you because you appear no different than everyone else?

If your credentials or website or social media profile are bland and generic, like everyone else's, we believe that is a problem worth resolving.

Still Using a Reverse-Chronological Résumé? Our Twelve Predictions

If you are in the job market, we believe that sending out the same ***generic*** résumé when applying for a number of ***unique*** positions prolongs your job search.

NOTE: If you are a Solopreneur, are not in the job market and think this information does not apply to you, think again. These predictions are just as applicable to websites and social media profiles as to résumés.

We predict your job search will be long, frustrating and disappointing if your current résumé:

1. Looks like everyone else's résumé. If it does, what would make a recruiter pick yours out of a pile of similar résumés? Not much.

2. Simply lists your job duties and activities. Pretend for a moment that you are the recruiter or hiring manager: As you are thinking about the work problems the new-hire will be expected to fix, you are evaluating two résumés side-by-side. One lists the applicant's job duties and activities; the other presents the applicant's accomplishments - the problems that person has faced and fixed -- and the problems they have fixed are similar to the ones you need fixed. As they say in the movie, *"Who You Gonna Call?"*

3. Does not present your ACCOMPLISHMENTS or the successful PROJECTS in a compelling, authentic, straightforward, meaningful manner. There is no question which résumé will be read more closely and which will be quickly skimmed and tossed into the TBNT (Thanks-But-No-Thanks) pile. You absolutely **must** get clear on what you have accomplished, select the accomplishments most relevant to the position, and then tell the recruiter about them.

4. Focuses on <u>what you want</u>, not on what you can do for the company. Companies are recruiting to fill a specific need THEY have; they are not socially-motivated organizations there to satisfy your needs. Tell them what you have done for other companies and what you will do for them, <u>not</u> what you want them to do for you.

5. Shrieks of desperation with an OBJECTIVE that suggests, "I'll do anything." Referring back to the previous point, unless it is a company's mission to provide employment to people in difficulty, employers generally shy away from hiring desperate people.

6. Is boring and fails to catch and hold the recruiter's attention. When I (Don) was a recruiter, it was not unusual for me to go through a foot of résumés in a day, and more at home after dinner. Nothing has eased up. You have about the first ¾ of page one (maybe seven seconds) to catch the attention of a tired and overworked recruiter. If you want to be the one they call, give them quality information that is of interest and matches their needs.

7. *Reads like assembly instructions for a desk*. Most people don't enjoy reading product assembly instructions. YOU are the product. You must tell the recruiter why you are worth their investment – what <u>benefits</u> will they get when they "buy" you.

8. *Is generic, not customized for each position.* You know how you feel when you get a letter addressed to "Dear Sir or Madam?" It generally hits the trash. The same applies when you are applying for a position. Don't be lazy. Personalize your cover letter and customize your résumé for every single position for which you apply. Sound like a lot of work? How much do you want to get back to work or attract a new client?

9. *Forces the recruiter to figure out what you are applying for*. Recruiters are not mind readers. <u>Tell the recruiter</u> what position you are applying for, and then make certain your cover letter and résumé prove you are qualified. This is the time to focus like a laser, not spray like a garden hose. Lasers cut to the chase; hose water evaporates.

10. *Calls the reader's attention to your inconsistent work history by prominently presenting it on the first page.* How many employers do you think will jump at the chance to hire someone who has built their career bouncing from job to job to job?

The correct answer is NONE. When I (Don) first started out in HR, the managers I supported made it abundantly clear to me that my primary reason for being there was to make sure they *always* had responsible, dependable employees, and more in the pipeline.

Leading with impressive and relevant accomplishments that are effectively presented can often compensate for an inconsistent work history, so that the recruiter will at least call you and do a phone interview.

11. *Raises more questions than it answers.* The content of your résumé may cause a ripple of interest, but if your words are unclear and raise more questions than answers, it's very likely the recruiter will pass on you and look elsewhere. You may be qualified, but filling in all the holes, sorting through all the inconsistencies, and getting answers to all of their questions can feel like more trouble than it's worth.

12. *Buries relevant information about your skills, abilities and experiences so deep within the résumé that the recruiter never gets to it* because of any of the preceding eleven items.

As you look back over these twelve predictions, which ones resonate with you? Probably more than one – yes? We invite you to visit www.YourProfessionalProfile.com and click on *"BLOG."*

The Inner Game Starts Now and Sets the Tone

Are you a job seeker or a Solopreneur? Regardless of which category you put yourself into your main objective is essentially the same: to create a clear professional story about yourself to present to others that reflects who you are. And as good as your Professional Profile™ will be, your attitude and your ability to tell your story is ultimately what matters at the end of the day.

We don't always think or remember to visualize the results we seek, but it is a good practice to make part of your process as you apply for work or submit proposals. Visualization is like mentally practicing winning before we start. To learn how to coach yourself into a positive and truly confident mental space will affect the results of your work search.

Before getting started, take a few minutes and prime your mind by imagining what you want this exercise to accomplish for you. And if during the process you find yourself losing steam from time to time, stop, step back, take a break, reset your internal temperature to one that is grounded in the Big Agenda as determined by you.

Our intention is that you enjoy this exercise and the process from start to finish, and we know that somewhere in the middle you too may experience resistance and want to take a short cut. Each of us is different in how on point we can stay. Some of our clients produced their first drafts of profiles in a single weekend, while others took weeks to complete. Your process will take the time it takes, and remember to honor that. And if you are on a real deadline, use that as a reason to stay positively motivated.

Suggested Videos to watch that can be found on the website are:

www.YourProfessionalProfile.com/DonsVideos (*"To Be Successful, Play a Stronger Inner Game"*)

www.YourProfessionalProfile.com/DonsVideos (*"What a Crock! There's No Work. Nobody's Hiring"*)

Elements of a Professional Profile™

When I was a recruiter screening résumés, applicants had the first ¾ of the first page to hook my interest. (I know I am repeating myself, but this point is critically important.) If they did, it did not matter how many pages were in the résumé. So long as the content was interesting and relevant to a job I needed to fill, I read every word on every page. If the content was boring or irrelevant to my open positions, TBNT (Thanks But No Thanks file).

Don't forget: the first ¾ of the first page. Applicants had seven to ten seconds for their career in my company to maybe start or surely die.

SOLOPRENEURS AND JOB SEEKERS:

Don't forget:

the first ¾ of the first page.

As a recruiter, applicants had seven to ten seconds for their career in my company to maybe start or surely die.

Remember, think "MEATBALL," not "spaghetti." Customizing these three elements of your Professional Profile™, each time you apply for a position, *will enable you to create a unique document that will stand out because it will be <u>tailored to each position:</u>*

- *Representative Professional Accomplishments*
- *Special Skills and Abilities*
- *The Objective*

Tailoring these three elements of your Professional Profile™, each time, for each position for which you are applying, is absolutely critical. No more using a *generic* résumé for *specific* positions.

If that sounds like too much effort, here's that question again: *how soon do you want to get back to work?*

As personal development expert Brian Klemmer says, ***"Judge by results. Often harsh; always fair."***

Before going to the next chapter, please step back and take stock of what you just read. Are you clear on the concept, or what questions do you have? How do you feel about what you read? Any "Ah-Ha's?" Please make your notes here.

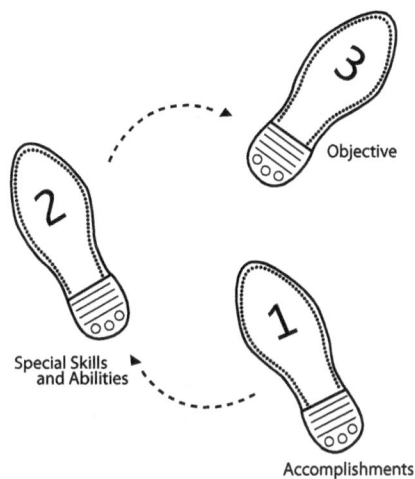

CHAPTER 2

Your Accomplishments

<u>JOB SEEKERS AND SOLOPRENEURS:</u>

Where do they belong? On your résumé. On your social media profile. On your business website.

Potential employers and potential customers have some interest in a list of your job duties, responsibilities or generic services BUT what do they really want to know?

They want to know what you have accomplished.

They want to know what problems you have faced and fixed for other employers or customers.

In this chapter, you will create a Data Bank of Accomplishments that you would be wise to use on your business website, your social media profiles, and in your résumés (which we call a Professional Profile ™

When talking about your accomplishments, this is not the time to be shy or modest. If you are looking for work or customers, recruiters and potential clients are interested in YOU, in what YOU have accomplished, and in what problems YOU have faced and fixed. And we hope you will discover that you have faced and fixed more problems than you are remembering--as you will find out soon.

It's time for you to become comfortable using **"I"** a lot.

What Have You Actually Accomplished?

This may be a difficult question to answer. You may even feel uncomfortable just thinking about it for many of us are taught and told not to brag or boast BUT to get to the core of what you are skilled at requires acknowledging what you have done. We must first acknowledge ourselves. In the course of honestly assessing ourselves and professionally so for our profile, we'll honestly get to know ourselves again and perhaps remember some forgotten golden moments that shaped what we bring to the world of work. This activity builds true confidence and future employers like true confidence, so claim yours!

> *Consider for a moment how well you play what we call the* **Inner Game.** *The Inner Game is the conversation you are having with you. The Inner Game is either you encouraging and supporting yourself or you being the first one to tell yourself you can't or won't or aren't suitable. Depending on your Inner Game, you can either take a compliment or you can't. The status of your Inner Game sets the tone you convey in cover letters, phone calls, screening interview, and face to face meetings. It is how you show up and affects how people experience you. From day to day our confidence may ebb and flow but what matters is your baseline. Do you know what your baseline of true confidence is where professional skills and accomplishments are concerned?*
>
> *Ask yourself on a scale of 1-10 how much do you believe in your competencies? Do you need a pep talk and a reality check? If you are planning on writing your profile you are about to experience one. I predict looking back at what you used to think and see and believe about your abilities, you will be a jumble of feelings and reactions: and ultimately you will see more transparently and authentically who you are. We hope that with a little self-prescribed "tough love" and "get it done" and our virtual support (as you are reading this book), you will come to understand yourself more, AND talk openly and with confidence like you do when the time is right to do so. Opportunities are waiting for those ready to respond (Deb).*

In our workshops, people often say things like, *"I have no accomplishments. I'm just a ..."* fill in the blank. "Or *"I haven't accomplished anything. I was just doing my job."*

If you are one of those people, please stop right here, read those quotes again, and really think about what holding those beliefs says about you, how it will impact your job search or if you are selected by a new client as the "chosen one."

This section is the **essence** of the process, so we want to make sure you embrace it fully and uncover the very best about you professionally and personally. Some will belong in your profile and some may not BUT you will benefit from acknowledging it (and yes, that applies to you humble people too!).

This is important:

White collar, Blue collar, Office Administrative, Service worker, Minimum Wage, Military transitioning to civilian, Student looking for your first job . . . Whatever your position: If you have done volunteer work or been paid for your work, or earned a diploma or certificate,

YOU HAVE ACCOMPLISHMENTS.

Did you find yourself saying, *"Yeah, right"* when you read that last sentence? If so, we encourage you give yourself a break, see yourself in a new light, and consider that these words may be the truth.

Shortly we will show you how easy it is to convert *"just doing my job"* into ACCOMPLISHMENTS.

First though we want to convince you to never, ever again say *"I was just doing my job"* unless you're in a cowboy movie and you preface it with *"Aw, shucks, ma'am…"*

Let me (Don) emphasize this point with a story.

Some years back, I remember reading that Stephen Covey (author of *Seven Habits of Highly Effective People*) got into a taxi in New York, expecting it to be the usual unsanitary and uncomfortable experience.

He was astonished to find the interior spotless, the driver neatly and professionally attired in a suit and tie, offering an array of business services and niceties right there in his cab.

If a passenger needed to send a fax, or make a cell phone call, a professionally-lettered sign announced that he could do both. Thirsty? Another professionally-lettered sign told passengers he had a cooler with cold drinks and a thermos of hot coffee, with cups, cream and sugar. Racks on the backs of both front seats held current magazines and neatly folded newspapers. To complete the service, two umbrellas were available and there were two reading lights for passengers to use, just like in a limo.

After an engaging conversation, Covey apologized for asking an indelicate question: *"Given how you run your cab, what do you earn in comparison to your counterparts?"*

"I earn double," was the driver's answer.

Cab drivers drive people from point A to point B. Cab rides are a commodity service, and if you spoke with fifty drivers, my guess is that, *"I'm just doing my job"* would be how most would summarize what they do, with very little to differentiate one from the other.

And yet this man defined *"just doing my job"* very differently, and he was rewarded for it.

Viewed proactively, and with a little help, everyone can convert *"just doing my job"* into ACCOMPLISHMENTS that will make you money, earn you the interview, or gain you a new client.

And in case you are wondering, the Professional Profile™ process is not just for managers. I'd absolutely love to write that cabbie's Professional Profile™!

A woman in one of our workshops had been a waitress in the same Interstate exit restaurant for 28 years and from one day to the next was laid off when the owner closed the place. She was in her 60s. She absolutely needed work, and as more doors closed to her, her anxiety and sense of desperation increased. It was clear she was losing her Inner Game.

When we began the part on Accomplishments, she said, *"I've got no accomplishments. I'm just a waitress."* What kind of Inner Game do you think she was playing?

Beyond the obvious self-putdown, her statement was just plain untrue. I asked her if she had experienced guests who came in happy, got angry at something, were ready to storm out upset and she had to salvage them as future guests? *"Of course,"* she said. *"All the time. It was part of the job."*

She was astonished when I told her that each time she resolved a conflict, it was a separate and unique accomplishment, and companies paid for that kind of skill. When she realized she had 28 years of accomplishments, she was speechless. And just like that, she began to win her Inner Game.

She came to another workshop three weeks later and told that class she had applied to the region's newest and most prestigious casino, where she went up against some 500 applicants for only a handful of food service jobs. She focused her cover letter and Professional Profile™ on her customer service skills and success at guest retention accomplishments.

In only three weeks, she was interviewed twice, hired and back to work. Her tips were three to four times what she made before. As she shared this, it was clear to see she has absolutely won her Inner Game.

Remember she was in her 60s. For more on this particular situation, please see the video www.YourProfessionalProfile.com/DonsVideos (*"Stop Saying, 'I'm Just a ...'"*)

Another workshop participant, also in her 60s, was a woman who had retired after a thirty-year career in administration. She thought she had retirement under control but the 2009 recession forced her back to work. She was dreading returning to her former field of employment; what she really wanted to do was tend the flowers in the garden shop of one of the big-box home improvement stores.

She had tried to get interviews there but was denied because she had no formal education or experience in the field, and was using her old administrative résumé.

However, she had an astounding home garden. She followed the process and reapplied. She also took my suggestion to include photos of her garden. Five weeks later she wrote to tell me she got the interview and the job. Her happiness and self-confidence were through-the-roof. *Please recall that she too was in her 60s.*

When you focus on your accomplishments, age becomes much less of an obstacle.

In these two examples and many others, the people who completed the process experienced a significant and unexpected benefit: a huge spike in self-confidence and self-esteem.

Talk about playing a new and improved Inner Game. . .

Exercise: Thinking About Your Accomplishments

We'd like to ease you into the identification of accomplishments by asking you to sit back, close your eyes and recall things you have done that made you proud. **Made you proud.** That's the primary criteria.

Please do not limit your thinking only to work-related accomplishments. **Made you proud.**

Make a quick list of them in the space below – no details; just three or four words to describe each one.

Let me give you an example of a big one for me (Don): *successfully managing the shut-down and outplacement of a ninety-person office – on time, within budget, with no discrimination lawsuits, and helping everyone find jobs equal to or better than the ones they lost.*

I would write *"Outplacement 90 people"*

Please make your list here, now. Work it! Aim for all 20!

1.
2.
3.
4.
5.
6.
7.
8.
9.
10.
11.
12.
13.
14.
15.
16.
17.

18.

19.

20.

That was the first pass, just to get you thinking about your accomplishments.

Now let's get more precise. From the above list, identify between seven and ten that are the major ones. In addition to being most proud, the selection criterion are these:

- They moved your reputation, career, department, company or organization furthest along
- If you died next week, these are the Biggies you'd want on your headstone.

    Please write them here:

    1.

    2.

    3.

    4.

    5.

    6.

    7.

    8.

    9.

    10.

    11.

    12.

All right. Maybe that went smoothly, or perhaps you had difficulty getting beyond your job duties and responsibilities and into thinking about the net result of your accomplishments.

If that was the case, don't worry. What we are about to do will take care of it.

Converting "Activities" and "Job Duties" Into "Accomplishments"

If you have always thought in terms of job responsibilities (*inventory control, manage a staff of ten*) or generic services you provide to your clients (*QuickBooks training, weight loss coaching*), this may be a new experience for you.

Let's turn our attention to converting activities and job duties into **ACCOMPLISHMENTS.**

Here are examples of regular job duties and activities that can easily be converted into ACCOMPLISHMENTS. These are not made up; we've had personal experience with people in each of these categories.

SECRETARY Reorganized files Improved accuracy of phone message Improved boss's productivity: * Repetitive tasks * Some meetings * Gatekeeper * Calendar management * Budget analysis	**CUSTOMER SERVICE** Reduced average call time Reduced escalations Transitioned customer service calls into sales Number of customer compliments to my boss Resolved customer objections without conflict
LAWN KEEPER Suggest design ideas and materials owners had not considered Cost-conscious on owners' behalf Suggest ways to reuse materials vs. haul away Completed project on time and under budget Brought in water specialist to solve drainage problem Gave homeowners before and after photos of final project Personal enthusiasm On time and brought good help	**MANAGER** Supported company in community Created and maintained environment of personal motivation for staff Committed to making contributions Shared knowledge Actively mentored others Saw needs going unmet / problems going unsolved: Took initiative Developed and implemented plan Championed plan with persistence Measurably achieved goals
HOME REPAIR Perfectionist If my work does not meet MY standards, will redo at no charge My work is my reputation Check back after work done: All working OK / to your satisfaction? Recommend most appropriate materials, not most expensive or cheapest Clean up daily Once fixed, it stays fixed	**INTERIOR HOUSE PAINTER** Offer color suggestions, rather than "whatever" Recommend best paint for job Meticulous care at wall and ceiling edges Critical eye for evenness Come back and do touch-ups after moving in. No Charge Genuinely happy person Follow-up call months later. Is everyone still happy?

"So What?"

We don't mean *"So What?"* in a flip, dismissive or combative tone. Rather, *"So What? Tell me more."*

The bulk of those items are *activities (general)*. Each of them can be converted into an *accomplishment (specific)*. We need to convert *general* into *specific*.

Here's how.

First, select an activity from the list. and then ask **"SO WHAT?"** several times.

With each *"SO WHAT?"* your answers will become more and more specific.

Think of the process as a funnel – going from wide-open and general down to very specific. Or maybe it's like descending a flight of steps until you get to the bottom.

When you find yourself repeating yourself or you have no more answers, you have arrived at your ACCOMPLISHMENT.

Let's look at an example. The question is, *"What do you do?"*

ACTIVITY:

"I do home repairs for people"	**"SO WHAT?"**
\ *"Well, I work fast. I get in, get out and get to the next job."*	**"SO WHAT?"**
\ *"The faster I work, the more focused I am. The more attention I pay, the more money I make. My number of NC (No Charge) calls to come back and redo my work dropped to zero. I have not had to do an NC redo in over eleven months."*	
That's how to go from ACTIVITY to ACCOMPLISHMENT.	☺

This is the **ACCOMPLISHMENT** that would go in your Accomplishments Data Bank and on the Professional Profile™:

"The faster I worked and more focused I was, the more attention I paid and the more money I made. My number of No Charge (NC) calls to come back and redo my work dropped to zero. I have not been called back for a redo in eleven months."

Assume you needed a home repair specialist and you saw two social media profiles or websites. One says, *"I do home repairs."* The other says, *"The faster I work and more focused I am, the more attention I pay to the details and the more money I make. My number of No Charge (NC) calls to come back and redo my work dropped to zero. I have not been called back for a redo in eleven months."*

Which will you call first? Do you think there will be a second call?

Do you see how that worked? We have yet to find an activity that could not be converted into an accomplishment. There may be one out there, but we haven't met it yet.

Here's a chance to try practice *"SO WHAT?"* to convert an activity into an accomplishment. Pick one of the activities from above and use your imagination, or select one from your own experience.

Use this space.

Whether you are a CEO in Seattle or a taxi driver in Taos, New Mexico or something someplace in between, please know that the *"SO WHAT?"* game will enable you to transform any ACTIVITY into an ACCOMPLISHMENT. Play on!

SOLOPRENEURS AND JOB SEEKERS:

Accomplishments are worth more than Activities

Pretend there is a *"SO WHAT?"* SUPER BOWL
And YOU WON IT!

Using Power Words

One more thing before you begin writing your accomplishments. We'd like you to consider **Power Words.**

We're sure you *know*, but we want you to move beyond *knowing* and become <u>very aware</u>, that the words you use to describe your accomplishments tell discerning people a lot about how you see yourself. We're certain you remember the waitress who said, *"I'm just a waitress. I have no accomplishments."*

When you think about your achievements, are the words you use *powerful and confident*, or are they *weak and passive*? There are many ways to express a thought. Some words (like *Helped, Participated in* and *Assisted*) are not very active. In fact, they are passive and weak, and for our purposes, let's avoid them.

The words in the following table are active, strong and vibrant and are appropriate for use in your ACCOMPLISHMENTS and throughout your Professional Profile™.

The list is not exhaustive, but it will certainly get you going. Feel free to add to the list with words of your own.

POWER WORDS LIST:

Accelerated	Developed	Launched	Resolved
Accomplished	Devised	Learned	Reviewed
Achieved	Drafted	Managed	Revised
Approved	Eliminated	Mentored	Saved
Assembled	Exemplified	Measurably	Streamlined
Authored	Facilitated	Monitored	Supervised
Authorized	Formulated	Negotiated	Taught
Coached	Gained	Operated	Tracked
Collaborated	Generated	Organized	Trained
Committed	Guaranteed	Overcame	**DON'S FAVORITE**
Constructed	Implemented	Presented	*Got 'er done!*
Completed	Improved	Produced	**DEB'S FAVORITE**
Created	Increased	Raised	*Cultivated*
Critiqued	Influenced	Reached	**WHAT OTHERS?**
Debugged	Initiated	Recovered	
Decreased	Innovated	Reduced	
Dedicated	Installed	Replaced	
Designed	Inventoried	Researched	

SOLOPRENEURS AND JOB SEEKERS

How did you feel as you read those Power Words -

uncomfortable or perhaps suddenly more aware of new ways to describe your accomlishments?

A word of caution: It is very easy to overload your Professional Profile™ and cover letter with power words, to the point that it becomes comical. With attention and practice, you'll develop a sense of when the balance is right. Until you get to that point, before you send out your first cover letter and Professional Profile™, we recommend you get feedback from people whose experience and judgment you trust.

Exercise: Identifying Powerful Words that Describe You

Here is the list again. In the small boxes to the left of the columns of words, put a little check by each of the words that accurately describe you in a work situation.

	Accelerated		Developed		Launched		Resolved		
	Accomplished		Devised		Learned		Reviewed		
	Achieved		Drafted		Managed		Revised		
	Approved		Eliminated		Mentored		Saved		
	Assembled		Exemplified		Measurably		Streamlined		
	Authored		Facilitated		Monitored		Supervised		
	Authorized		Formulated		Negotiated		Taught		
	Coached		Gained		Operated		Tracked		
	Collaborated		Generated		Organized		Trained		
	Committed		Guaranteed		Overcame		**DON'S FAVORITE**		
	Constructed		Implemented		Presented		*Got 'er done!*		
	Completed		Improved		Produced		**DEB'S FAVORITE**		
	Created		Increased		Raised		*Cultivated*		
	Critiqued		Influenced		Reached		**WHAT OTHERS?**		
	Debugged		Initiated		Recovered				
	Decreased		Innovated		Reduced				
	Dedicated		Installed		Replaced				
	Designed		Inventoried		Researched				

When you create your custom cover letters and Professional Profile™, use ONLY those words you can substantiate with examples.

Let's assume you checked "Innovated" and in the **Special Skills and Abilities** part of your Profile said you were "Innovative." The recruiter or potential client would have every right to say, *"Tell me about a time when you were particularly innovative in solving a business problem."* If you cannot support the claim, you are dead in the water.

Anything you include in your credentials is fair game for the interviewer or potential customer. You definitely don't want to get caught in an overstatement or an unjustifiable accomplishment. (We hesitate to use the word "lie" and know you get the point.)

Introduction to Exercise: Writing your Accomplishments

All right!

By this point, we trust you have:

- Identified your seven to ten **ACCOMPLISHMENTS**
- Learned to convert activities into accomplishments using *"SO WHAT?"*
- Considered **POWER WORDS** and identified the ones that pertain to you.

Now it's time for you to get very focused and ready to do some real thinking and writing.

This next point is absolutely critical. *If you miss this point, you miss both the purpose and the power of all that we are doing.*

We said *"write about. . ."*

We did NOT say *"think about"* seven to ten ACCOMPLISHMENTS essays.

This exercise is the guts of the course, and if you are going to get your money's worth, you must do it.

You don't need to be an expert writer to benefit from this exercise.

You don't need to have gotten A's in school when you had to write essays.

ALL you need to know how to do is write.

Not necessarily write well. Start writing.

If writing paragraphs makes your head explode, use bullet points.

If that does not work, find someone who will write or type your words as you say them.

Please do not skip this step. Do this.

Seven to ten accomplishments essays is the minimum, just to get started. As you get the hang of it, you will want to do more later. You may even get enthusiastic about it (and better and quicker) over time. One client didn't slow down until after 25 essays!

We would be thrilled if you would be an over-achiever, go 'way beyond the suggested minimum and write 15 or 20 accomplishments essays so you would have a bunch on deposit in your **Accomplishments Data Bank.**

WHY? Because the more accomplishments you have in your Accomplishments Data Bank, the greater flexibility you will have to present yourself as the *ideal solution* to an employer's needs or expectations of a potential new customer.

That's pretty great!

The step-by-step process you will follow is this:

1. Write your accomplishments essays. The target is 250 words per essay. (That's about a one-page essay from high school English class.) No one needs to see this essay; it is only for you. More on this later.
2. Distill each essay into a short paragraph, what we call your **"accomplishment statement."**
3. Once you have the accomplishment statement the way you want it, you will store it in a Word document that we call an "Accomplishments Data Bank."
4. When you are ready to customize your Professional Profile™ you will copy-and-paste from your Data Bank *only* those accomplishment statements that most closely match the requirements for that specific opportunity, tweaking them as much as you can.
5. You will leave the other accomplishment statements in your Data Bank for another opportunity.

Helpful Clarifications, Explanations, Guidelines, Suggestions and an Example:

- You'll definitely use some of your accomplishments statements more frequently than others.

- But *you will never again create and submit the **same résumé** for a variety of **different positions***.

- Using the SAME résumé for DIFFERENT positions is senseless, and lazy, and it helps keep you unemployed or without clients.

- Because so many of your competitors have difficulty doing so, it is to your benefit that you are able to speak compellingly and articulately about your accomplishments.

- If your career or business has been based on PROJECTS more than accomplishments, you will be creating a PROJECTS DATA BANK.

- Here's something that will help you later: while writing your essays, be alert to little flashes of insight regarding the skills you used to achieve your accomplishments and jot them down in the margin. Trust these messages and capture them for later (Deb).

  Don't lose your focus by going into details – just a quick note and then back to your essay. Don't trust your memory. *Immediately* write them down. You'll be glad you did when we get to **Special Skills and Abilities.**

- Commit to giving yourself and your career the benefit of some valuable solitude. Not to go all New Age on you or anything, but you are about to take the first step to meeting your new "you."

- When you take the time to thoughtfully write each essay, you are preparing yourself to interview effectively because you will have already thought about and answered at least 95% of what the interviewer or potential new customer will likely ask you.

- All we are going to do now is write your accomplishment *essays*.
- *We are NOT going to write the actual accomplishment statements that will end up in your Accomplishments Data Bank and ultimately in your Professional Profile™. FIRST THINGS FIRST.*
- We will take care of that shortly. For now, capture the story.
- To organize your thoughts, you may find it helpful to think in terms of RESULTS AREAS. Here are some for your consideration. The list could be endless.

• Customer Comments	• Time	• Rework	• Cost	• Headcount Reduction
• Quality	• Market Share	• Productivity	• Profitability	• Personal Development

What others come to mind? Please write them here.

- To get you off on the right foot, with the permission of our client, we wanted to give you an example of an effective accomplishments essay. You'll see the accomplishments statement later.

> I had a friend of mine refer his plumber to me as a possible client. From the first time we met said he wasn't trying to do anything fancy for his business. He was a no frills type of guy. As a matter of fact he even refused to talk to me because he wasn't sure he needed anything. He had been a plumber for over 25 years and knew his trade inside and out. Then the company he worked for let him go after working for them for over 15 years. He called me wanting to know what he should do to start his own plumbing business. After getting his business license and corporate entity in place we set out create a web page for him and develop a basic social media strategy. This was no small feat for a plumber. Usually when someone says they want a website they bring you all sorts of pages and ideas but working with contractors and plumbers is a different language and style all its own. Luckily I had a little experience with contractors from my days in commercial insurance. So I used that knowledge to create a starting point for his website and social media plan. We put together Facebook fan page and added his business listing to Yelp. Not long after he called and was pretty excited to let me know he got his first Yelp referral after being listed for a few weeks. This was music to my ears. He was on his way. Now he is so busy we can hardly meet to update his pages. But I guess that is a good thing. **Word Count: 276**

So please, don't cut corners. Take your time. Do this well and you'll reap the benefits.

Exercise: Writing Your Accomplishments Essays:

Shall we begin, finally?

Please refer to your list of accomplishments and give each accomplishment a title. Later you will be asked to assign each a different color, so you could do that now if you wanted to.

Find a quiet place where you will not be interrupted by family, phone or e-mail. Center yourself and compose your thoughts.

Please write one 250-word essay per accomplishment, answering these four questions each time:

1. WHAT I did?
2. HOW I did it?
3. WHY I did it?
4. QUANTIFIED RESULTS of what I did?

- Don't get so hung up on Question Four that you skip the entire exercise. We don't know why, but some people do, but not you – right? With some thought / research into your old files or calling current or former colleagues, you can generally back into the numbers and answer Question Four.

- As you write your essays, the word "approximately" is a good one to use. Our only guidance is that you keep the quantified results reasonable, credible and easily explainable.

- Your target is 250 words per essay. Significantly less than 250 words and you'll short-change yourself from really thinking deeply about your accomplishments. Significantly more than 250 words and you will have difficulty getting to the essence of each accomplishment.

We have left the following pages blank if you want to brainstorm with yourself, take notes or write your essays here.

Please take as much time as you need to complete this exercise.

PLEASE DO NOT PROCEED ANY FURTHER UNTIL YOU HAVE WRITTEN A MINIMUM OF BETWEEN 7 AND 10 OF YOUR ESSAYS.

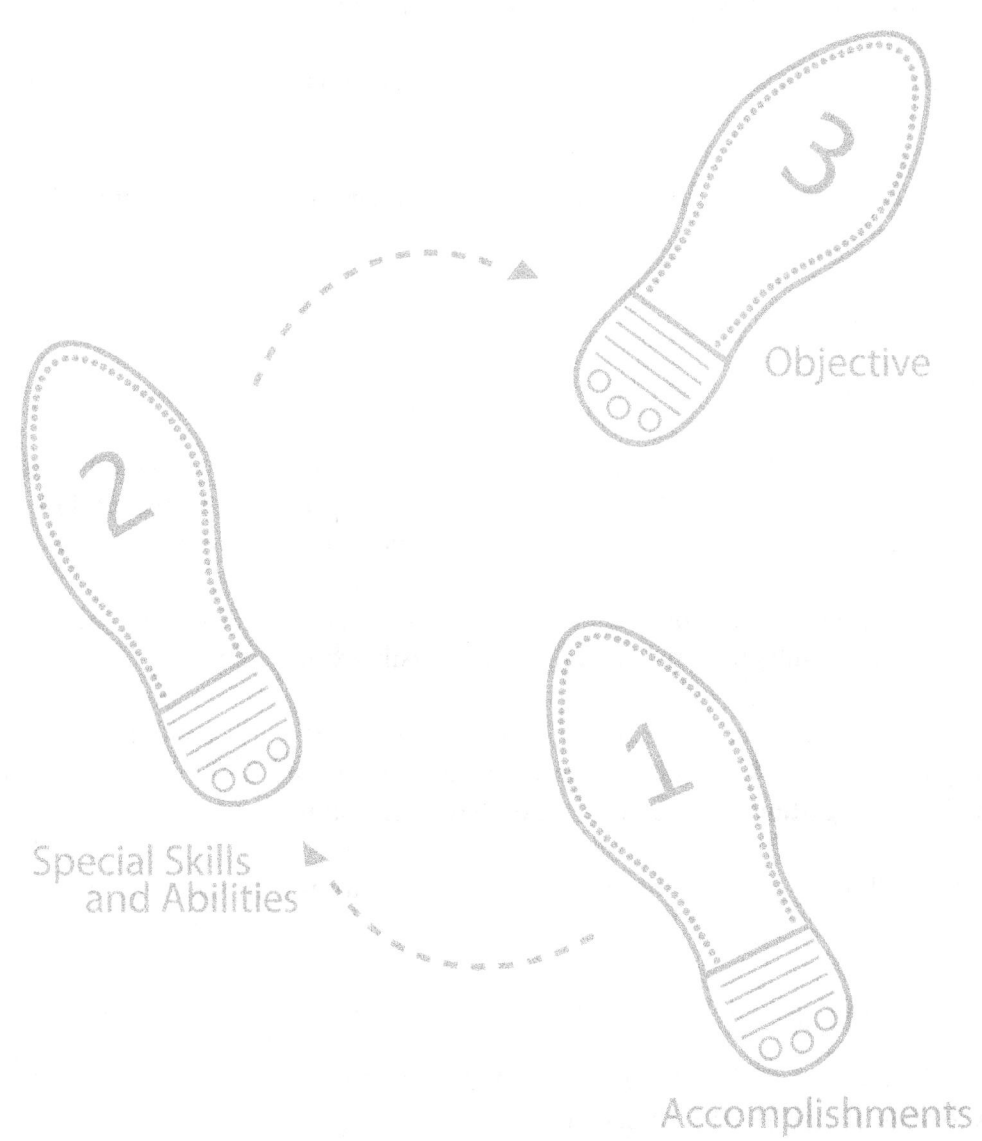

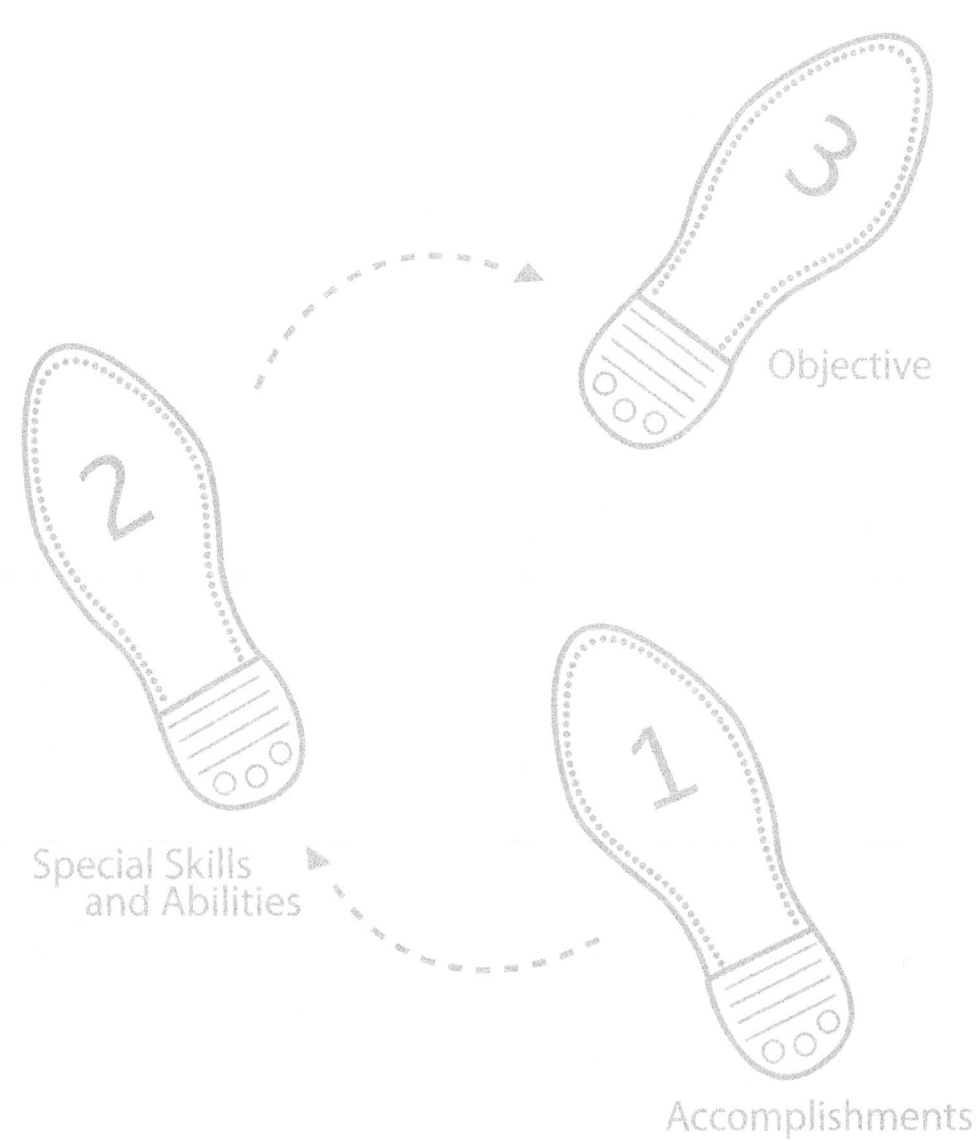

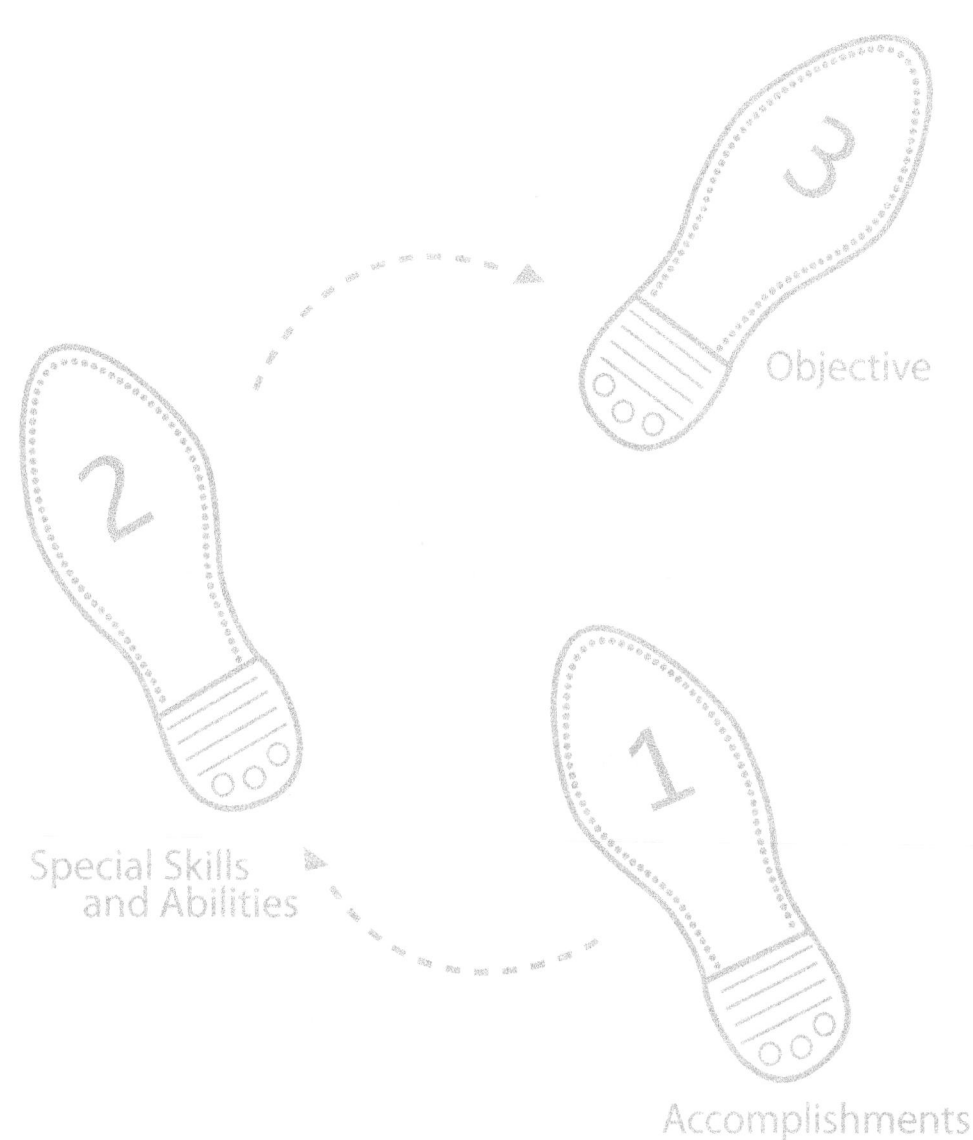

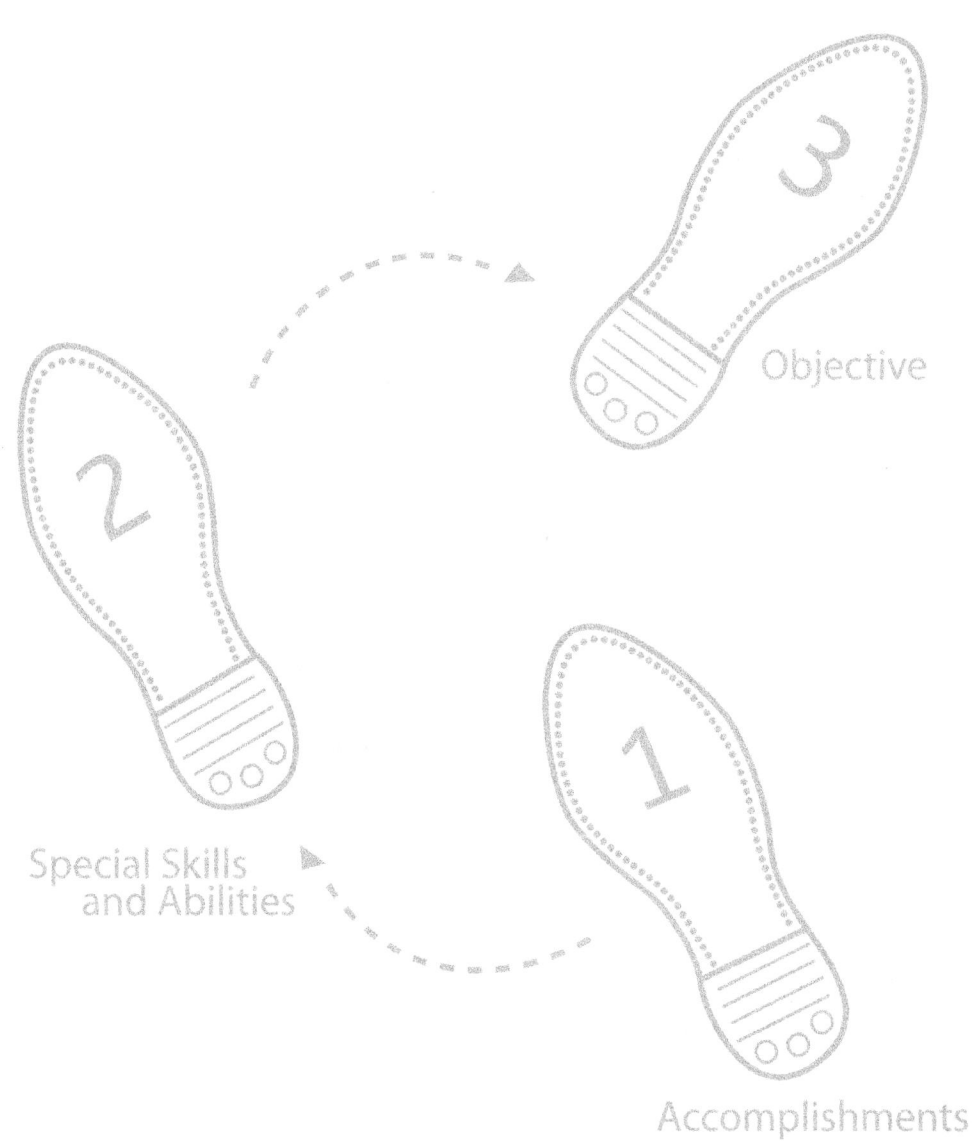

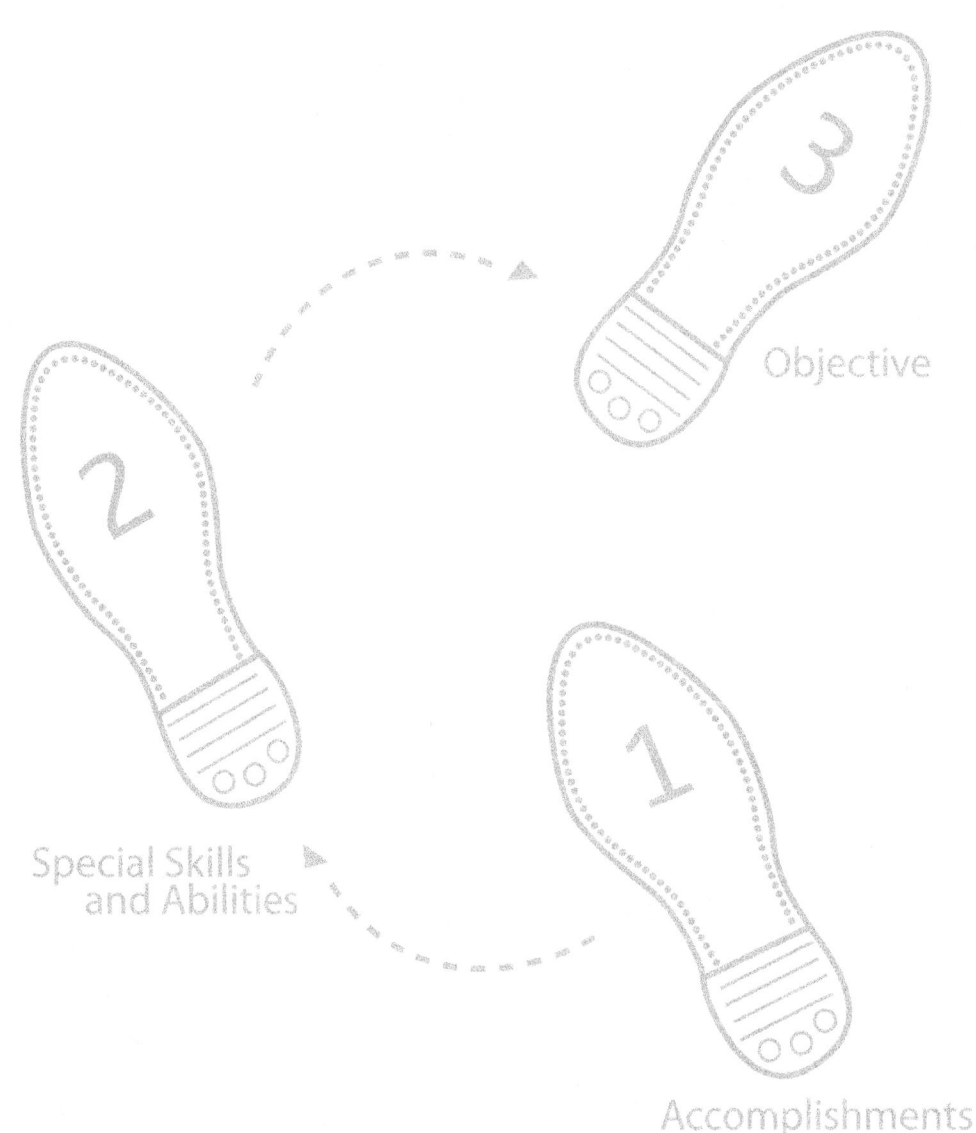

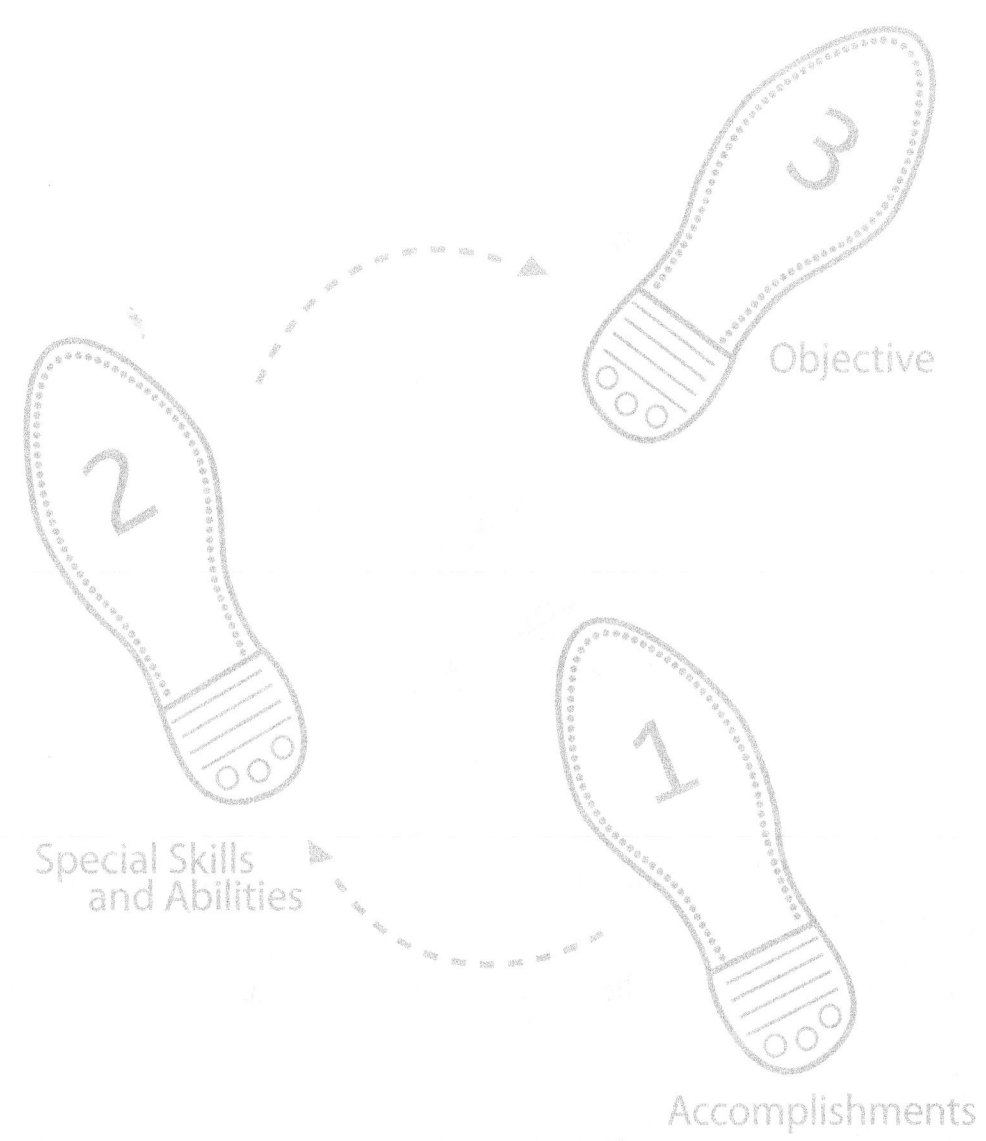

Welcome Back!

Excellent! Excellent! If you have not patted yourself on the back for having completed all of your essays, please stand up and do so now!

And give yourself a round of applause while you're at it. YOU deserve it.

You DO deserve it, don't you?

If you have not completed all of your essays, you should not be reading this. (Or perhaps you are beginning to think you'd like some support in this process? That is available too.)

Please tweak the tip of your nose, then go back and complete your assignment.

We mean it.

GO!

Welcome Back, *Again.*

All right. Let's move on.

Next, we turn to getting to the essence of each of your accomplishments – the writing of your **accomplishment statements.**

Exercise: Getting to the Essence of Your Accomplishments

For the moment, let us focus only on your first accomplishment essay.

Please reread your first essay, then stop and consider the essence of what you have written.

Buried within those 250 words is *the essence of your accomplishment.* What is it?

Your purpose now is to create a short paragraph, a little story – ideally six sentences at most – that summarizes the essence of your accomplishment.

Aim for one sentence each to answer each of the four questions (WHAT, WHY, HOW, and RESULTS), and two additional sentences to use as needed. If it goes over six sentences, it is not the end of the world, but aim for six. For our purposes, less is more.

One six-sentence paragraph can tell the story of each of your accomplishments.

Identifying the essence of your accomplishments can be daunting, particularly if you have unnecessarily complicated your task by significantly exceeding your 250-word target.

If you have written your essays in Microsoft Word, you may find this helpful:

- While in your essay, click on the "Review" feature and then "New Comment". Your right margin will change as Word readies itself for you to add comments.

- You were asked to answer four questions in each essay: WHAT, HOW, WHY and RESULTS. Reread your essay and find the four most relevant sentences that answer each of the four questions – one sentence per question. Highlight the sentence and click "New Comment." In the comment box that will open, type the appropriate word – (WHAT, HOW WHY, RESULT).

- If you have been thorough in your writing, you should easily be able to pick out those four sentences.

- When you have finished "Commenting" an essay you should have highlighted four sentence, each one answering one of the four questions, and have those four words in the margin.

- If you have not provided enough information in a category, you will immediately identify the gap and can make on-the-spot corrections, and add missing and pertinent details.

Here is our client's essay again. Rather than "Commenting" in the right margin, we have **bolded** up the sentences that we think best answer the four questions:

> I had a friend of mine refer his plumber to me as a possible client. From the first time we met he said he wasn't trying to do anything fancy for his business. He was a no frills type of guy. As a matter of fact he even refused to talk to me because he wasn't sure he needed anything. He had been a plumber for over 25 years and knew his trade inside and out. **Then the company he worked**

for let him go after working for them for over 15 years. He called me wanting to know what he should do to start his own plumbing business. After getting his business license and corporate entity in place we set out create a web page for him and develop a basic social media strategy. This was no small feat for a plumber. Usually when someone says they want a website they bring you all sorts of pages and ideas but working with contractors and plumbers is a different language and style all its own. **Luckily I had a little experience with contractors from my days in commercial insurance. So I used that knowledge to create a starting point for his website and social media plan. We put together Facebook fan page and added his business listing to Yelp. Not long after he called and was pretty excited to let me know he got his first Yelp referral after being listed for a few weeks.** This was music to my ears. He was on his way. **Now he is so busy we can hardly meet to update his pages.** But I guess that is a good thing.
Word Count: 276

Here are the sentences we would "Comment" that we think best answer the four questions:

What I did: *After getting his business license and corporate entity in place we set out create a web page for him and develop a basic social media strategy // create a starting point for his website and social media plan. We put together Facebook fan page and added his business listing to Yelp.*

Why I did it: *Then the company he worked for let him go after working for them for over 15 years. He called me wanting to know what he should do to start his own plumbing business*

How I did it: *Luckily I had a little experience with contractors from my days in commercial insurance. So I used that knowledge to create a starting point for his website and social media plan.*

Results of what I did: *Not long after he called with pretty excited to let me know he got his first Yelp referral after being listed for a few weeks. // Now he is so busy we can hardly meet to update his pages.*

And after playing the "SO WHAT?" game, here is his resulting accomplishment statement:

> *Self-employed tradesmen are sometimes hesitant to acknowledge and seek out small business consulting and coaching, even when the need is immediate. Such was the case with a plumber that a friend referred to me. He had 25 years experience and after 15 years with a company was laid off and decided he was ready to take responsibility for his own career. Having never had reason to develop business, marketing and social media plans, websites and related items, this was not an easy process for him to embrace. Yet we persevered, and within a few weeks of getting things set up, he got his first referral from YELP. Now he is so busy we can hardly meet to update his web pages. Another business up and running.* **Word Count: 126**

So – there you have one actual client accomplishment essay and resulting accomplishment statement, ready for inclusion in his Accomplishments Data Bank. See how it takes writing all of it down to then boil it down to the essential? Trust the process. You will get masterful at it if you will and like all things practiced, it gets easier each time.

Turning now to your little story of six or so sentences, please follow the same process, making edits as needed, playing the "SO WHAT?" game and filling your Accomplishments Data Bank. Don't worry about its organization right now. We'll get to that next.

Please move on and finish writing the rest of your accomplishment statements. We have left the next few pages blank for that purpose.

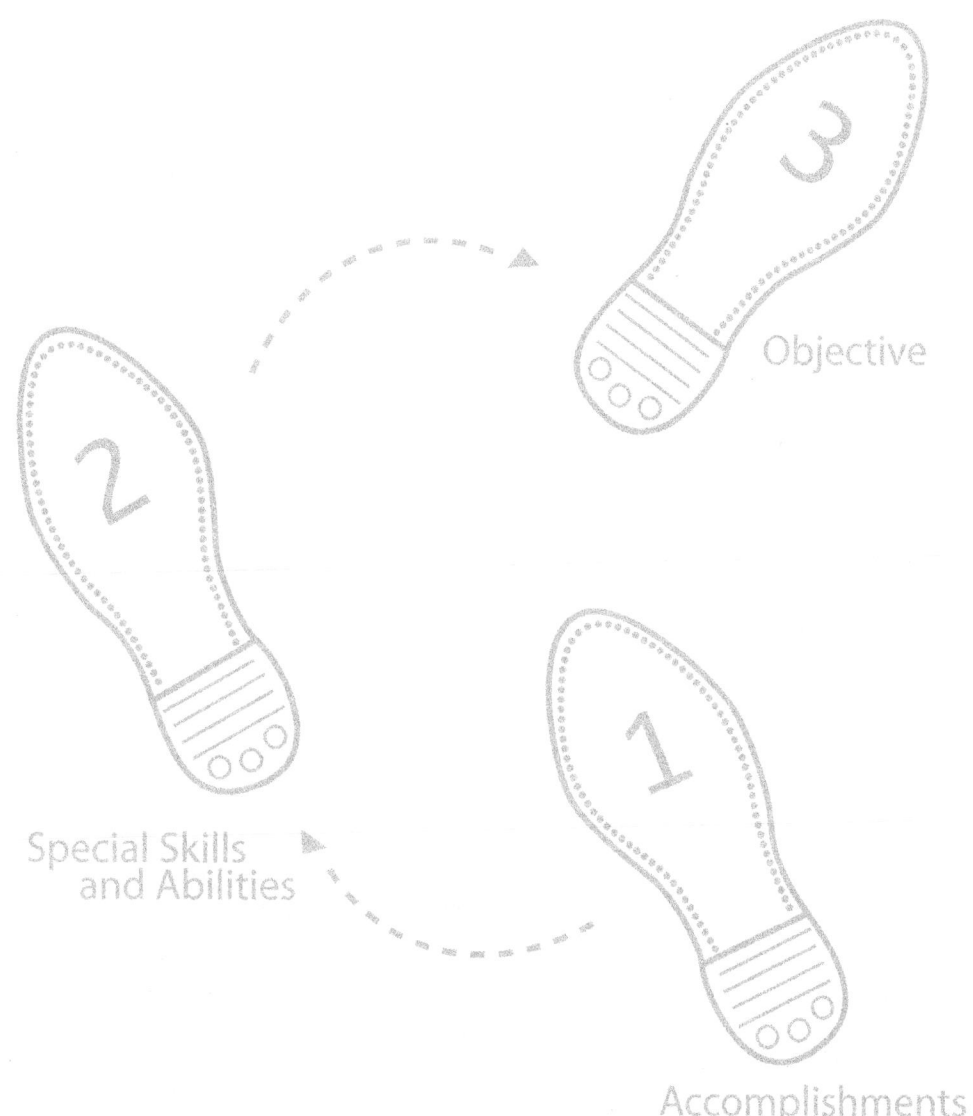

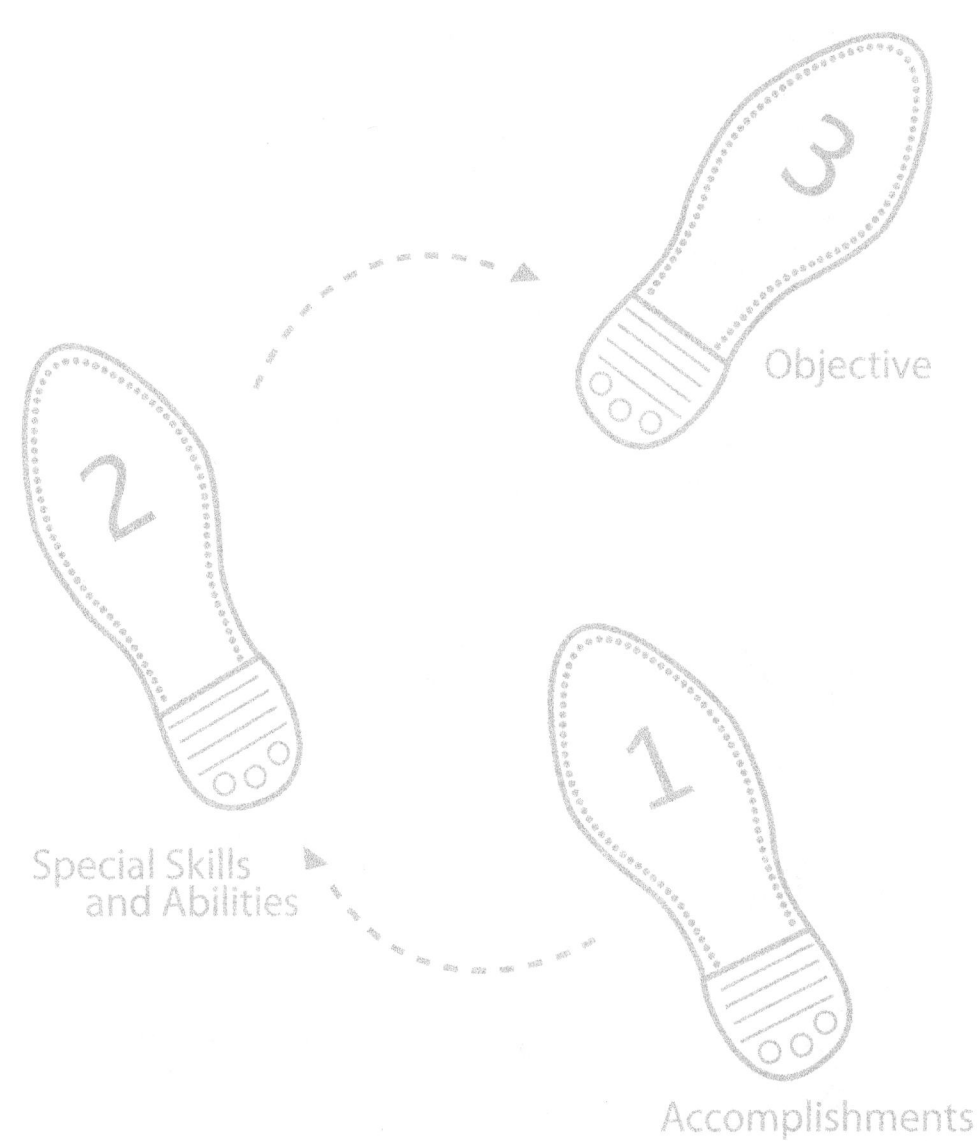

….. Time passes while you think and write, until at last we can say to you…

Congratulations! You have definitely completed the major challenge of the book!

There's still a good ways to go before you are done, but compared to what you've just .... accomplished ... the rest is a piece of cake.

Now let's take a look at your ACCOMPLISHMENTS DATA BANK.

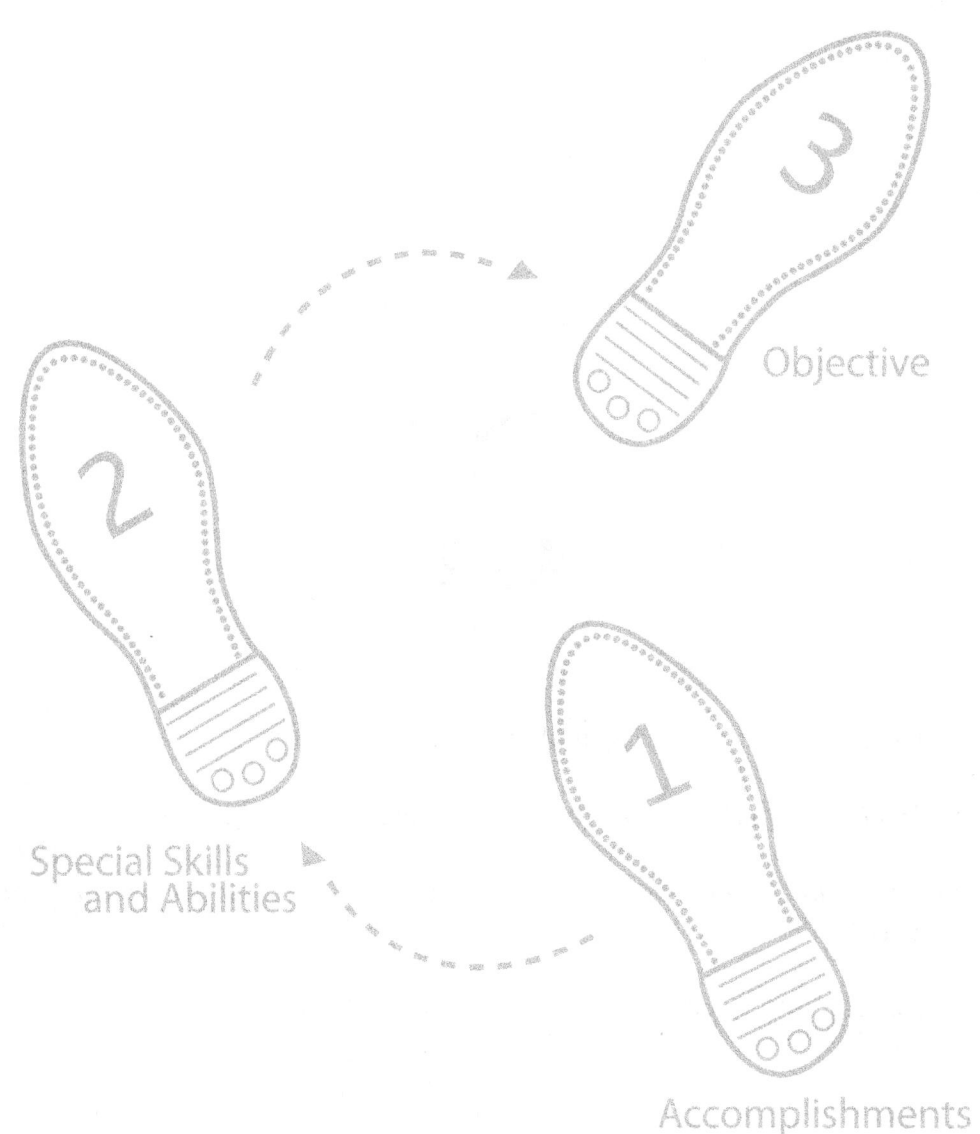

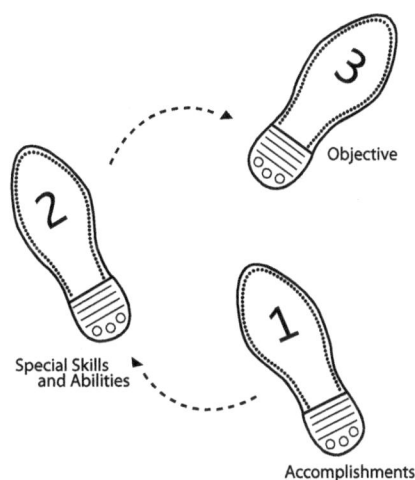

CHAPTER 3

Your Accomplishments Data Bank

REMEMBER: Everything we are doing is intended to make your Professional Profile™ a customized and unique document that stands out like a meatball on a plate of spaghetti and catches the eye of a potential new customer or employer.

Creating a custom profile is easy when you hold your accomplishments in your ACCOMPLISHMENTS DATA BANK, and *copy-and-paste only those that are relevant to the opportunity you are pursuing.*

You'll be creating a unique and original document for each job or client opportunity you pursue.

By now you may be groaning either *"All right already. I get it"* or maybe you are saying, *"NO WAY! Too much work!"*

If you're feeling some resistance, please take a deep breath and keep the faith. Once you understand the process and the benefits you will derive from it, using your Accomplishments Data Bank will be a pleasure.

Meanwhile, if you need a little something to boost your spirit and energy, let us give you a little taste of things to come for you.

Here is the completed **Accomplishments Data Bank** we created for another client, a corporate financial trainer. To maintain client confidentiality, certain elements have been removed. We will present a more complete Professional Profile™ at the end of the course.

Recall the guideline of six sentences per accomplishment statement? It is a guideline, not a commandment. What you'll see in a moment worked for this client.

DEVELOPMENT OF TRAINING MATERIALS

- Three of my colleagues from the Operations side of Company were scheduled to conduct Interest training in Bangalore. When one of them was suddenly taken ill, four days before scheduled to leave for Bangalore, I was asked to replace him. Having managed that function previously, I was quickly able to create an effective training program, and was happy to be of service. I had been in Bangalore the year before and looked forward to returning. I effectively represented my colleague and communicated the material in a manner that was entertaining, involving, interesting and effective.

- When the second of the three Operations managers who were going to Bangalore to conduct Name training learned that I was replacing their ill colleague and was developing training materials for the other person's sessions, he told me that he too had no training materials, and asked if I would develop his program for him as well. As I was already strapped for time to finish not only my own projects but my new Bangalore undertaking as well, I was tempted to say no. But having seen what can happen when Operations managers "wing it" when making both domestic and international presentations, I nonetheless agreed to help him as well. I met with him and his staff to learn what information they wanted to present. Then, using his guidelines, procedures and operations manuals, I quickly created a coherent, organized and effective training program for him. Knowing that he was not a trainer, I also coached him on how to present it effectively. He was astonished at the speed with which I put the program together, and was grateful for my willingness to help on such short notice. He expressed his gratitude by writing a letter to my manager and recommended me for an employee recognition award.

JUST-IN-TIME TRAINING:

- It is both critical and extremely difficult for banks to remain up-to-the-minute in the security aspects to prevent money laundering via US dollar funds transfers. As a Quality Assurance Technical Trainer at Company, on short notice, I chaired a joint team and developed and delivered specialized training for Compliance directors and senior managers and staffs for both classified programs (confidentiality agreement prohibits further discussion.) My training enabled various levels within the bank to close loopholes, expedite processing, meet more demanding deadlines and reduce payment volume by approximately 30% because there were less payments stopping for repair.

PRODUCTIVITY IMPROVEMENT:

- It is difficult for call center customer service representatives to maintain productivity standards and provide excellent service to customers when they themselves are angry and feel unappreciated by their management. I was assigned the responsibility to correct that problem at Company. By sitting with and observing a cross-section of the reps, I saw their competency and dedication to their customers, and the basis for their frustration with management. Based on my analysis, I documented my findings, developed and submitted solutions and facilitated joint meetings. The net of my work was an immediately visible mutual change in attitude, and an increase in productivity from a daily average of 16 cases up to 22, and a significant decrease in errors as management took corrective action.

PROACTIVE RELATIONSHIP BUILDING:

- One aspect of my job as negotiator was to track down and obtain overlooked or forgotten interest payments due us on bank remittances from other banks. This often involved large sums of money and banks are not required to voluntarily return the interest. Knowing that this would involve negotiations with a number of banks, I decided it would be more time-effective to establish business relationships with my counterparts in Bank, Bank, and other large banks at the outset, so that we could all save time and hassle in our future negotiations. My initiative resulted in improved business relationships among the banks, and spread to other types of payments. I never failed to regain the interest owed us, never totaling less than $5 million per month.

APPLYING GLOBAL BANKING SKILLS IN THE COMMUNITY

- Developed and conducted Financial Literacy Workshops within my community, some through churches and others through community centers. All have been very well received. In one case, a senior citizen retained my consulting services and after helping her complete her benchmark financial analysis, was able to help her to consolidate her debt, reduce it with a special debt consolidation loan, pay her credit cards to zero and have a $600 monthly surplus, which she will apply to her new loan balance and pay the loan off early. She is thrilled.

- For three years, as part of my duties with Company, I was a loaned executive to Non-Profit. As a Banker-Teacher, I taught a pilot program called "Name of Program." Aimed at young people in the Tri-State area, the program nurtured self-esteem while teaching these four modules: *The Basics of Banking, What are Checking and Savings Accounts? The Power of Credit, and Investment.* My participation was an additional duty, did not relieve me from any of my normal job duties and did add an additional 10 hours per week to my work load. The sacrifice was never too great because of the satisfaction I gained knowing that I may have helped at least one of my students escape the trap of debt or of living above their means

PERSONALIZED CUSTOMER SERVICE:

- As a Customer Service representative for Company, one of my clients was the United Nations. The bulk of their retirees lived outside of the United States and many of the more elderly retirees would call or write each month with questions regarding their retirement deposits. While they should have directed their questions to their own bank and resolving their problems was not part of my job requirements, it cost me very little effort and time to be of service. Over that six year period, rendering the level of service that I would like someone to give to my elderly parents brought the bank and me a continual stream of favorable customer comments, and a number of new accounts whose total worth I estimate to have been $10 Million dollars.

PRODUCTIVITY PROBLEMS SOLVED WITH PERSONAL INITIATIVE:

- As a Supervisor at Company, it soon became clear that throughout the company our internal clients were making the same processing errors and asking the same questions month-in and month-out. I decided to resolve the issue by creating and conducting a series of Brown Bag Lunch sessions throughout the company. After "selling" my fearful manager, I wrote the training material and case studies, conducted the programs, resolved absolutely all the problems, and in the process made my manager look like a hero in the eyes of his boss.

So what did you think of that **Accomplishments Data Bank**?

How beneficial would it be to you if you had a similar data bank?

Believe it or not, you are not that far away.

> **JOB SEEKERS AND SOLOPRENEURS**
>
> SITUATION: You just learned about the PERFECT job for you.
>
> Only applicants whose accomplishments prove they have the necessary experience will be considered.
>
> They will stop accepting résumés three hours from now
>
> Can you meet the deadline, or are you dead meat?
>
> If your ACCOMPLISHMENTS DATA BANK is current, you're golden.

A Recommendation:

- For the Accomplishments Data Bank to work effectively for you, you'll need to commit to keeping it current, adding new accomplishments as you achieve them.

  When you need them, it is much easier to refer to something you have written down when it was fresh, rather than try to remember and recreate from memory. Be proactive and maintain it for it will save you time later.

We have shown you how to convert an activity into an accomplishment. Now, let me (Don) tell you a brief story showing you how to recognize an accomplishment.

Someone I've known for years was hired shortly before the 2008 recession. When her company announced that upcoming department layoffs would be based on *last-in / first-out* and they would be offering packages to those who volunteered, she raised her hand because she was last-in and just wanted to get on with it.

Imagine her surprise when the company rejected her, saying that even though she was last-in, she was too valuable for lay-off. They wanted to keep her and had a job for her when the company completed its reorganization.

Without question, that's an accomplishment and it belongs in her Accomplishments Data Bank.

Can you imagine the powerful impact that accomplishment will have on a recruiter or a potential customer when they read her Professional Profile™?

"Wow! She's really a 'keeper!. Get her in here – NOW!!"

Whether you are looking for new work or new business, that's how it is when you think in terms of accomplishments, not activities. Your accomplishments resonate with the reader; you jump to the top of the pile as the competition melts away. You are the meatball, not the spaghetti.

You have accomplishments everywhere. Be alert and pay attention to find them.

Organizing Your Accomplishments: Subcategories and Key Words

Another of the primary differences between our Professional Profiles™ and the many generic reverse-chronological résumés is the flexible use of **Subcategories.** Subcategories are a key element in the REPRESENTATIVE PROFESSIONAL ACCOMPLISHMENTS section in a Professional Profile™, and generally are not used in reverse-chronological résumés.

After writing your essays and distilling them into your accomplishments statements, you will find it helpful to organize your accomplishments statements by subcategory in your Accomplishments Data Bank. This will make creating a custom Professional Profile™ that much easier.

Given that many résumés are screened in or out of contention by computer programs that search for "Key Words" related to the position, you will want to precisely tailor your Professional Profile™ to the key words of the position for which you are applying.

You do that by including in your cover letter and Professional Profile™ "key words" taken from the *requirements listed in the position description or elsewhere within the position announcement.*

In no particular order, here are some of the more frequently-used subcategories we have seen used:

• Cost Control	• Personal Flexibility
• Process Improvement	• Personal Initiative
• Time Management	• Personal Commitment
• Customer Relations	• Community Relations
• Attention to Detail	• Mentoring
• Manual Dexterity	• Management Development
• Planning	• Market Growth

For organizing your accomplishments statements in your Accomplishments Data Bank, we urge you to use the subcategories that make the most sense to you.

That said, when submitting your custom Professional Profile™ for a specific opportunity, **make certain to organize your accomplishments statements according to the key words and subcategories used by your potential new customer or employer--in the best order to showcase YOU as a CANDIDATE.**

For example, you may have a number of accomplishments statements stored under the subcategory of "Management Development" which the potential employer or customer may call "Supervisory and Management Training." When you create your Professional Profile™, use their subcategory, not yours.

Of course, if the position you are applying for has no written qualifications, select your Accomplishments and Subcategories based on what you know from experience about the requirements of the job.

The list of possible **SUBCATEGORIES** is endless. The ones you select will be determined by the position or business opportunity you are seeking.

Summarizing ACCOMPLISHMENTS

This is by far the most difficult step in creating a Professional Profile ™ Do the work. Trust the process. GREAT by-products await you! Trust us.

Here are the main points we have covered:

- Thinking about your accomplishments
- Converting activities into accomplishments by playing the "So What?" game
- Identifying your Power Words
- Identifying powerful words that describe you
- Writing your accomplishments essays
- Writing your accomplishment statements
- Creating Accomplishments data banks
- Using subcategories and key words to organize your accomplishments

Before going to the next chapter, please step back and take a moment to take stock of what you just read. Are you clear on the concept, or what questions do you have? How do you feel about what you have read? Any "Ah-Ha's?" Please make your notes here.

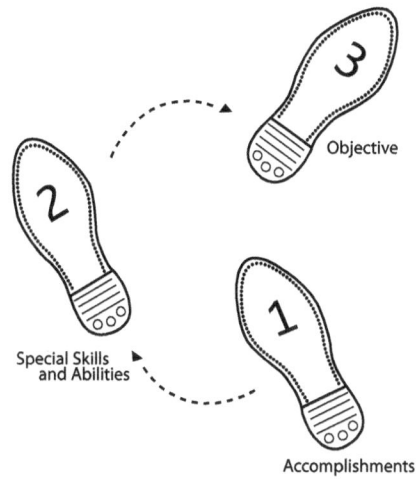

CHAPTER 4

Your Special Skills and Abilities

JOB SEEKERS AND SOLOPRENEURS:

Where do they belong? On your résumé. On your social media profile. On your business website:

The second element of your Professional Profile™ you will customize to present yourself as an ideal candidate for each opportunity you seek is the section for your Special Skills and Abilities.

WHY?

By now, you already know the answer. You want to be the meatball, not the spaghetti.

You don't want to lose a **SPECIFIC opportunity** by casually tossing a **GENERIC résumé** at it. Rather, you want to tailor your skills to the skills required for a new position or client engagement.

We imagine you *think* you know who you are and what your skills are. With complete respect for your opinion, our experience leads us to differ with you. When was the last time you took a complete and honest personal inventory of your accomplishments and the skills you used to achieve them? You may not currently know all of the real "you" if it has been sometime or never.

Please don't gloss over this section in some misguided attempt to hurry through the process. If you are going to do a hurry-up job of this, you will short-change yourself.

Why would you spend money and then not get your money's worth?

Special Skills and Abilities

All too often we impose our own very artificial and unwarranted limits on the positions or business projects we think we can do.

We think that since we have always done one particular kind of job or project, that's all we're qualified to do.

Wrong. Absolutely wrong.

As we identify your Special Skills and Abilities, you will see that many of your essential skills are applicable in a wide variety of work and business situations.

These skills are called **"transferrable skills."**

As the name suggests, these are skills that are transferrable from one situation, position or industry to another, totally different situation, position or industry.

Please don't go all *"yeah, sure"* **on me and close down. Who knows? What we are about to cover may be the most important "Ah-HA!" of all. It also ties in with improving your own Inner Game – an important game to win FIRST.**

A potential client or recruiter could very well ask you this relevant question: *"What are some of your Special Skills and Abilities?"*

If you were asked that very fair question, how would you answer? Could you answer quickly with steady confidence?

- If your immediate response would be to tell them about your high school or college courses, what you did in the military, or about your work with a current client or job duties and responsibilities, where you were born or your formative years, you would be shooting yourself in the foot.

- You would be missing a tremendous opportunity to instantaneously distance yourself from the competition.

On the other hand, if you have done your homework by relating your qualifications to those of the position for which you are applying, you have prepared yourself to knock the question, *"What are some of your special skills or abilities?"* right out of the park. This can be a game changer!

- *Your education, military experience and job duties, all of that, while important,* **is not what the recruiter or potential client is looking for**.

- *All of those are the* <u>activities</u> *in which you have been involved over the years.*

- *As you learned earlier, your* <u>activities</u> *are not your* <u>accomplishments</u>. *They are how you have spent your time during the course of the day.*

- *And as you no doubt know, your activities are not your SPECIAL SKILLS AND ABILITIES.*

Consider it from this perspective:

You Are Much More Than the Sum of Your Work History and Job Duties.

William Bridges, change management expert and author of several books including my (Don's) personal favorite, ***Creating You & Co***. (an extremely valuable book for you as you go about your search for work), affirms that "jobs" as the best way to get work done are going away. For proof, he cites down-sizing, outsourcing, right-sizing and working virtually.

According to Bridges, the trick is to learn not just to survive but to THRIVE in what he calls today's "dejobbed" world.

Creating You & Co. is a must-read book for you. When we accept a client for our top-of-the-line **Done FOR You** Professional Profile™ service, we ask them to get a copy of **Creating You & Co.,** read it and actually do the exercises. We want them to move beyond the superficial "activities" and become aware of the SPECIAL SKILLS AND ABILITIES that they *really* bring to what Bridges termed *"the World of Work."*

One client had been self-employed for forty years, and suddenly hit a wall. He stopped getting contracts. His reverse-chronological résumé was a disaster, and before we got to work on it, he read and completed the exercises in ***Creating You & Co***.

He dedicated a long weekend to the task, and when he finished, he said he had learned more about himself in that three-day period than he had in the past forty years. He thought that was a plus for the book and a pretty sad commentary on his life.

The book is out of print, but is available on-line. We urge you to get it and read it as a companion piece to your Professional Profile™. You will not regret it.

And in case you are wondering, we got his career back on track.

Determining In Detail What You Bring to the "World of Work"

Bridges earned his Ph.D. in the Humanities, and then began to teach American Literature. After a few short years, he found himself in a repetitive loop.

Taking stock of himself, he asked himself what he could do? Teach literature. Who made up his circle of friends? Other professors.

Trapped but really smart, he began researching and put together a local workshop to help people who were stuck get from where they were in life (Point A) to where they wanted to be (Point B).

He focused on helping people *thrive*, not just survive, in the transition, the gap between points A and B. In the process, he built himself a decades-long noteworthy international consulting career as an expert in change management, helping individuals and companies manage their transitions across the gap from Point A to Point B.

Creating You & Co. is his blueprint for thriving in today's "dejobbed" world.

One of the primary exercises in that book is determining what special skills and abilities you bring to the *"world of work."*

Using himself as a guinea pig, Bridges analyzed himself as far back as high school. Summarizing, he realized he possessed these <u>*special skills and abilities*</u>:

- He learned quickly
- He could apply what he learned in new and different circumstances
- He had effective written and oral influencing and communication skills
- He could persuade others to his way of thinking
- He got on well with all the guys - the ones on the chess team as well as the jocks, and all the guys in between
- He got on well with the girls too, and they did not scare him.

Here's the point. Bridges said that none of those items appear on his résumé, *but they are responsible for almost everything that does.* Get it?

- Did you get the importance of that last sentence? If you skipped over it, please reread it and think seriously about its relevance to you as you seek work or new business.

Those were some of his Special Skills and Abilities.

They set him apart. They are what he realized he brought to *"the world of work."*

What do YOU bring to the "World of Work?" What has been following you forward since high school and college that you may be forgetting about?

That is a difficult question to thoroughly answer.

Now that you have completed your accomplishments essays and also your accomplishments statements, you have only one more significant challenge: to complete two different **SKILLS EXERCISES.**

- Once you have completed them, you'll be able to answer that question, maybe not perfectly, but certainly with great clarity and more confidence than now.

Inner Game Fact: This is where the importance of the Inner Game comes into play. Without a strong sense of our best self, we will occur as an uncertain candidate and it is in those moments of doubting ourselves that others will doubt us too. People size up people quickly. Remember this. To be confident when meeting new prospects or recruiters REQUIRES we do what we must on the inside to believe first in our own selves and abilities. We will "broadcast" ourselves as we are in most instances.

For now, let's go back to our earlier Accomplishment example from the previous chapter.

Remember this one?

"The faster I worked and more focused I was, the more attention I paid and the more money I made. My number of No Charge (NC) calls to come back and redo my work dropped to zero. I have not been called back for a redo in eleven months."

If that were *your* accomplishment, what *skills* would you say you used? Please write your answers here.

Here are some we think you might have used:

- Attention to detail   *what* you were doing
- Manual dexterity   *how you were* doing it
- Planning   *when* - sequence of steps followed
- Time management   *how* you spent your time
- Flexible approach   *what* was and was not working; paid attention; made adjustments

How to Identify Your Special Skills and Abilities

To thoroughly identify your **SPECIAL SKILLS AND ABILITIES**, you'll first need to have written your Accomplishments essays.

However, if while you were writing them you honored our request that you make note of the skills you used and insights and flashes of brilliance you had, you'll already have a head-start on identifying your Special Skills and Abilities.

Those little thoughts we asked you to jot down in the margins were flashes of inspiration and your "intuitive" notes will now be helpful as you identify which skills and abilities you used to achieve each accomplishment.

For example, let's say *"Good with people"* popped into your head and you jotted it down while you were writing an accomplishment essay.

"Good with people" sounds like you would want to use it, doesn't it? But when you stop and ask, "What does that mean," you'll realize it is very vague, and therefore of little value for us.

Immediately after writing down *"good with people,"* you might have asked yourself what that really meant and how you could make it more specific?

Maybe *"Put new-hires rapidly at ease"* came to mind. This is more specific, and for our purposes, the more specific things are, the more useful they are.

Can you make *"Put new-hires rapidly at ease"* even more specific? Of course you can.

One example could be *"See quicker return on training dollars by helping new-hires fit in and become productive faster."*

With some research and thought, you could also "concretely" quantify that faster return, and that would be very impressive.

Play the "SO WHAT?" game until you can go no further. If nothing else comes to you, go with whatever you have because it is more useful than *"good with people."*

Here's an idea: Perhaps the skill of *"putting new-hires rapidly at ease"* could also be a topic for an accomplishments essay – yes?

If that had been your idea, to determine if it is worth an essay you would apply the "SO WHAT?" test and see where it leads you.

If what you came up with made sense, you would write another essay. If what you came up with is not that important, keep it for your Special Skills and Abilities Data Bank.

Either way, you win!

The point is to be alert and capture the quick flashing thoughts that will come to you. Keep that pad handy.

Are you ready to identify your Special Skills and Abilities? We are ready to help, but. . .

If you have not finished writing your accomplishments essays and your accomplishment statements, **please make this a priority first and then return to this point in the book.**

You must have completed both of those exercises in order to effectively complete this next one.

So, assuming we are all on the same page, let's go identify some Special Skills and Abilities.

Exercise: Identifying Your Transferrable Skills (Adapted from *What Color Is Your Parachute?* **by Richard Bolles/2001 edition.)**

In the last chapter, we asked you to give each of your accomplishments essays a title and also assign it a different color.

If you have not already done so, please give each accomplishment a title. Assign each title a number and color and write the titles in the spaces provided. .

Now, working on only one title at a time, go down the list reading each skill in turn. If you used it in the achievement of that accomplishment, put a ✔ in the corresponding box and column. After you have completed the first essay, follow the same process for your remaining essays.

You will have a whole bunch of check marks on these pages, so to make it easier to read, and to brighten up the pages, feel free to use corresponding colored pencils or markers.

When you have finished analyzing all of your essays, you will see a profile of the transferrable skills and abilities you have used to achieve your most significant accomplishments.

You may be surprised to see twenty or thirty of the skills have a lot of checks.

Give yourself time, and have fun learning about yourself!

With all the colors, the charts will be pretty, and you will see that you are "pretty amazing."

Do you prefer to complete this exploratory exercise on a Excel spreadsheet or more than once? Visit www.YourProfessionalProfile.com and find this form available for download under "FREE Stuff "(Excel or pdf formats)

Accomplishments (1-10)	1	2	3	4	5	6	7	8	9	10	Totals
Using Your Body											
Manual dexterity											
Precise eye-hand coordination											
Physical stamina											
High tolerance for discomfort/pain in warm or cold environment											
Excellent hearing, vision, sense of smell, touch, taste.											
Working with tools											
Hammering, sawing											
Sewing, knitting											
Cutting											
Sculpting											
Painting, finishing											
Objects											
Washing, cleaning											
Expedite/fill orders											
Preparing food											
Repair, restoration											
Lifting, pulling, hauling, carrying											
Heavy equipment											
Readying, putting together											
Driving (manual/remote control)											
Maintenance											
Taking apart/putting together											
Construction											
Building											
Remodeling											
Caring for											
Plants											
Animals											
Children/seniors											

Accomplishments (1-10)	1	2	3	4	5	6	7	8	9	10	Totals
Using your mind:											
Researching data											
Researching											
Interviewing, observing											
Exceptional math or verbal skills											
Exceptional memory											
Conceptualizing new ideas, creating or designing											
Managing											
Analyzing, comparing											
Using computers											
Developing computer hardware											
Developing computer software											
Accounting											
Higher math											
Planning, laying out step by step process											
Creative thoughts, solutions											
Organizing, data storage											
Developing strategies											
Executing strategies											
Providing counsel on strategies											
Influencing decision-makers											
Give and take, negotiating											
Authorizing actions, taking final responsibility											
Following through, tracking results											
Creating media presentations											
Design, conduct, evaluate training results											
Data management											
Cataloguing, recordkeeping											
Information clearing House, data retrieval											

Accomplishments (1-10)	1	2	3	4	5	6	7	8	9	10	Totals
Interpersonal skills:											
With individuals											
Carrying out orders, repetitive procedures											
Communicating effectively in person											
Communicating effectively in writing											
Communicating effectively electronically											
Tutoring, mentoring, coaching											
Diagnosing performance problems											
Networking, connecting people with others, resources											
Recruiting, assessment, selection											
Selling services, products for money											
Foreign-language skills-speak, read, write, understand, translate, interpret											
With large/small groups											
Clarity of expression											
Effective presentations											
Holds listeners attention											
Entertaining manner											
Performing											
Leading exercises and games											
Technical consulting											
Project management/coordination											
Convincing a group to accept your ideas											
Effective facilitator of group to draw out ideas											

Congratulations! That was a long exercise, and was it not worth the effort?

We hope you are feeling pretty darn good about yourself, now that you have identified so many Transferrable Skills you bring to the world of work, skills you can take from one job to another.

> ***INNER GAME INSIGHT:*** *As we discover more about ourselves in doing a comprehensive evaluation, we cannot help but re-encounter parts of ourselves we may have forgotten, minimized or marginalized. To re-acquaint our personal self with our professional talents boosts confidence in my experiences (Deb). Have a good time immersing yourself with your own great past and present! You are laying a solid foundation for your future.*

Exercise: Identifying Your MOTIVATED SKILLS

Your MOTIVATED SKILLS are a subset of your transferrable skills. They are the skills you love to use, and when you use them, you get your best results. As you initiate your search for new employers or customers, it will be important to look for opportunities to use your *"Motivated Skills."*

Please go back through your transferrable skills and identify your nine to twelve more important MOTIVATED SKILLS. Remember, these add to your value as an employee or a vendor and quite frankly, may be what you are really remembered for.

Record them in the chart below.

MY MOTIVATED SKILLS, THE ONES I REALLY LOVE TO USE, ARE:

With an open mind and creative thought, you will be able to identify other companies / industries where those skills will be relevant and valued.

Special Skills and Abilities Data Bank

As you complete the rest of the program and your profile, you will find it handy to have all of your Skills and Abilities, both Transferrable and Motivated, in one place where you can add to them, easily and quickly. Before we proceed, please take a moment and copy all of your Transferrable Skills to a fresh master list.

When your lists of Motivated and Transferrable Skills are up-to-the-minute complete, please create your **Special Skills and Abilities Data Banks** in a Word document or Excel spreadsheet.

Points to keep in mind

- Please make the commitment to yourself to keep this data bank current. You will thank yourself later!

- Please remember that, as with your ACCOMPLISHMENTS, you will never use all of your **SPECIAL SKILLS AND ABILITIES** at once in any one Professional Profile™.

- Based on the requirements of each opportunity you are pursuing, you will copy-and-paste into that Professional Profile™ only the most relevant special skills and abilities for that unique opportunity.

    *(Deb). A final thought about your **MOTIVATED SKILLS:** They are the essence of what you bring to the "World of Work" and if you have identified them beforehand, you will find many opportunities to present and discuss them in your correspondence, collateral material and during interviews.*

    Identifying MOTIVATED SKILLS not only benefits your image "on paper," it also boosts your inner awareness of what distinguishes you and that self acknowledgment is KEY to winning the Inner Game of getting work you truly want. People experience confidence when they meet it!

Speaking from personal experience, it was always more impressive when a job candidate could smoothly discuss their most significant skills, and give me (Don) examples to support their claims, rather than say, "uh, gee," and then look at the wall for an answer.

Before closing this chapter, we want to share with you the **Special Skills and Abilities Data Bank** that another client created. Because this has been refined over time, you will see it contains more detailed skills and abilities than were in the grid you just completed.

That's what we mean when we ask you to commit to keeping your **Special Skills and Abilities Data Bank** current. We evolve in ways we can forget if we don't update our professional experiences.

You'll see her completed Professional Profile™ later.

Sample: Client Special Skills and Abilities Data Bank

1. Marketing creativity

2. Event creativity

3. Written creativity

4. Committed to achieving and maintaining consistently high levels of client satisfaction

5. Hold high expectations for my own performance; strive for high levels of personal achievement

6. Maintain point and self-confident composure in free-flowing situations; adjust and thrive in new environments

7. Quick study; able to apply what I have learned and work effectively without supervision

8. Routinely achieve profit objectives while working within established budgets

9. Confident when faced with learning new software and computer applications

10. Consensus builder; strong personal influencing skills; rapidly put people at ease and build trust

11. Enjoy interaction with people of diverse cultures, social and economic backgrounds

12. Take initiative to create pragmatic, effective solutions to business problems

13. Have been told repeatedly that I am mature and competent beyond my age

14. Committed to continuous learning and personal growth

15. Happy person, committed to both my colleagues and my company

16. Effective at balancing multiple projects and seeing them through to completion

17. Unafraid to ask difficult questions or speak my mind, directly and politely

18. Willing to make a decision and see it through

19. Take personal responsibility for my actions

20. Build and maintain lasting friendships

Summarizing Special Skills and Abilities

Each time you submit your Professional Profile™ for a new position or client opportunity, **Special Skills and Abilities** is one of the three critical elements of your Profile that you must customize in order to present yourself as an "ideal candidate."

Here are the main points we have covered in this chapter:

- What are your **Special Skills and Abilities**?
- You are more than your work history and job duties
- The "World of Work"
- Identifying your Transferrable Skills
- Identifying your Motivated Skills
- Creating your Special Skills and Abilities Data Bank

> **SOLOPRENEURS AND JOB SEEKERS**
>
> Delve more deeply into meeting the "authentic YOU"
>
> Read ***Creating You & Co***. by William Bridges and
> ***What Color Is Your Parachute?*** by Richard Nelson Bolles

WATCH A VIDEO: You'll find more information on identifying and using your transferrable skills at www.YourProfessionalProfile.com/DonsVideos *("Identify and Use Your Most Important Skills to Get a Better Job")*

Before going to the next chapter, please step back and take a moment to take stock of what you just read. Are you clear on the concept, or what questions do you have? How do you feel about what you read? Any "Ah-Ha's?" Please make your notes here.

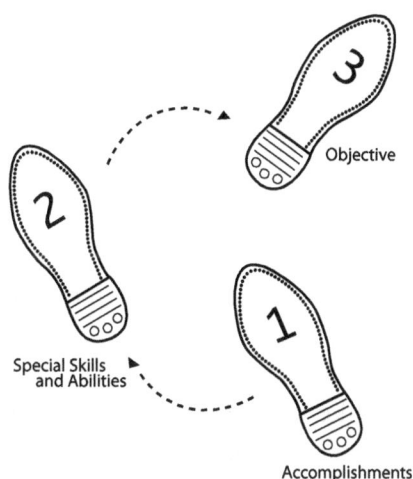

CHAPTER 5

Customize Your Objective

Some advisors say it is outdated to include an OBJECTIVE when you submit your résumé.

If you are using a bland, generic, commonplace reverse-chronological résumé, we agree. (Clearly, we feel strongly about this point!)

HOWEVER, since you are using a uniquely-crafted Professional Profile™, customized for the job or business opportunity you are seeking, we *definitely* want you to include a precisely-worded customized **OBJECTIVE.**

Before we show you how to tailor your **OBJECTIVE** for each position, we want to show you three examples of ineffective **Objectives,** and explain why each is so.

Ineffective Example 1: *"Experienced individual with proven ability in management, supervision, human resource management seeking position that will utilize my diverse background."*

This is a generic, shotgun objective. It lacks focus and requires the recruiter to be a mind reader. What industry? What level of management? Managing what and how many? What else besides Human Resources? It is about as compelling and meaningful as *"Have a nice day."*

Reading between the lines, it suggests desperation to me (Don). I never wanted to hire people who came across as desperate.

Ineffective Example 2: *"I am a people-oriented person and I'm seeking a position in which I can develop my supervisory skills while learning about the company."*

I couldn't help myself: The first time I read this, I found myself trying to remember the words to *"Cumbaya."*

Please don't ever forget: companies and clients are not in business to satisfy your wants and needs. YOU are the product, and before they will "buy" YOU, they want to know that YOU are the solution to their needs. They want to know what YOU have accomplished elsewhere and what you'll do for THEM.

Ineffective Example 3: *"Any position for which I am qualified."*

For so many reasons, it always saddened me to receive a résumé with this as its Objective.

Early on in my HR career, when I was still taking baby steps to learn my profession, I felt sorry for people who submitted résumés with objectives like that. Because my first employer cared about its employees, I thought we could help lost and floundering job applicants and called a few for interviews. My staff recruiter told me I was wasting my time, and theirs, because she had learned the hard way that people who presented themselves in that manner had nothing *specific* to offer our employer.

A side story: Some years back, I (Don) attended a very inspirational presentation called *"Homeboy Goes to Harvard."* Aimed at at-risk Latino kids, it was given by motivational speaker Richard Santana, (AKA "Mr. Chocolate.")

Among other profoundly insightful observations, Mr. Santana said, *"Stupid people learn from their own mistakes. Smart people learn from the mistakes of others,"* and he proved his point with tragic examples from his childhood in the *barrios* of Los Angeles. He told us he was not expected to live into his twenties. Please note the title of his presentation and check him out on YouTube. You'll be impressed.

Returning to **Ineffective Example 3**, I did not listen to my recruiter because I was young and thought I knew it all. Over a few months, I interviewed a number of applicants whose résumés had similar *"Any position for which I am qualified"* objectives. Each of those interviews was an exercise in futility.

When I told my recruiter I should have learned from her experience, she just smiled.

Please see **Prediction 5** in **Chapter 1.** Be sure your **OBJECTIVE** is specific.

We consider writing your OBJECTIVE to be a three-part process. Let's build some OBJECTIVES, shall we?

As we said earlier, Professional Profiles™ are not just for managers. The color of your collar is immaterial. As you'll see in the Appendix, the process works for job seekers and solopreneurs.

As we build custom **OBJECTIVES**, let's assume that in real life you are an Accounting Manager, or Electrical Engineer, or an Administrative Assistant, or a Grass Cutter, or a self-employed Human Resources Trainer.

PART ONE: <u>**The Position Title**</u>:

So now let's further assume you have seen position announcements or an RFP (Request for Proposal), have the necessary qualifications, and want to apply for one of these opportunities:

1. **Finance Manager** with Seattle Viaduct Hospital
2. **Process Engineer** with Seattle Viaduct Hospital
3. **Admitting Office Department Secretary** with Seattle Viaduct Hospital
4. **Grounds Keeper** with Seattle Viaduct Hospital
5. **Contract Human Resources Supervisory Development Trainer** with Seattle Viaduct

When the recruiter first looks at your Professional Profile™, the first thing they will see is an OBJECTIVE customized to match *the precise title of the job they are seeking to fill.*

Pretty straight-forward concept. But so many people ignore it.

Perhaps they think it is hokey or not necessary. **Wrong.**

Or maybe they ignore it because they think a résumé with a generic OBJECTIVE will be just as effective as one with a specific objective. Wrong. Please don't be lazy; customize your objective every time!

Or perhaps they want to keep their options open and so leave it to the recruiter or the computer software to figure it out. Wrong again. Not a wise move!

If you want to be the meatball and not the spaghetti, if you want to present yourself as an "ideal candidate" and thereby side-step the competition, a targeted **OBJECTIVE** is smart, not hokey! It is essential, and we hope by now there is no need to comment on "lazy" or "generic" or "keeping options open."

- Remember, your Professional Profile™ is not about what <u>you</u> want or need.

- It is about positioning you as the solution to the <u>specific needs of the customer or the company.</u>

So for this exercise, if in real life your position title is **Accounting Manager**, or **Quality Engineer**, or **Administrative Assistant**, or **Gardener,** or **HR Technical Skills Trainer**, please put aside your prior/current position or title and make your **OBJECTIVE** whatever the title is in the position announcement.

You have **Data Banks** bulging with relevant **Professional Accomplishments** and **Motivated** and **Transferrable Skills.**

You are seeking a new opportunity, not trying to hang on to the past. Unless you are flexible and prepared to redefine yourself, it will be tough going.

PART TWO: <u>The Required Skills</u>: As you read the position requirements, we want you to identify the two or three *most important* position requirements *that you meet very well*. You will use them when you write your actual OBJECTIVE.

PART THREE: <u>What Is YOUR Unique Contribution?</u>: Here is where you'll have your first opportunity to distinguish yourself from your competition.

- Companies frequently have needs they are not aware of, but as an alert employee or customer, we are certain you have recognized some.

- Having identified such a need, you can be certain it is one that is currently going unmet. This is great news for you as a job seeker!

- You now have the opportunity to make the company aware of their need AND present yourself as the solution to it.

- To complete **Part Three of the OBJECTIVE**, *identify a critical need the company has in that job <u>that you can satisfy.</u>*

Voila! The three parts of a custom **OBJECTIVE**. In the example that follows, see if you can identify the three parts.

OBJECTIVE: *"Full-time permanent Admitting Office Department Secretary position with Seattle Viaduct Hospital, a business that values expert office computer skills, sound knowledge of standard business correspondence, and a gentle, welcoming personal style that puts nervous patients at ease."*

After the recruiter reads that **OBJECTIVE**, particularly the last 12 words, can't you just see him or her pause to think for a moment, and then hear them say, *"Humm. That's right. It <u>would</u> be good if the person we hire could put nervous patients at ease. Yeah!"*

And just like that, your Professional Profile™ moves out of the pile of spaghetti and rises to become the stand-alone meatball.

Broken down, **here are the three elements of that OBJECTIVE**:

PART ONE: The Position Title: *Full-time permanent Admitting Office Department Secretary position with Seattle Viaduct Hospital,*

PART TWO: **The Required Skills:** *a business that values expert office computer skills, sound knowledge of standard business correspondence,*

PART THREE: **Your Unique Contribution:** *and a gentle, welcoming personal style that puts nervous patients at ease.*

Here are some other examples of an **OBJECTIVE** that would immediately catch a reader's interest.

Example 2:

OBJECTIVE: *"Full-time permanent lawn care position with Smith Property Management, Inc, a company that requires personal commitment, attention to detail, perfect attendance and immaculate grounds for tenants."*

Example 3:

OBJECTIVE: *"Third-shift warehousing position with Drake Shipping and Hauling, a company that needs a bondable, drug-free individual with 20 years of accident-free forklift driving, no Worker's Compensation injuries, and a can-do-let's-get-it-done attitude."*

While we'd prefer you didn't, we know there will be times when you will do a blanket mailing to companies or executive search firms. For those situations, this example may help.

Example 4:

OBJECTIVE: *"Full-time permanent Human Resources Director in a Philadelphia insurance company requiring Spanish fluency, extensive Latin American experience and that wants their human resources department to measurably cut costs and improve profitability."*

Example 5 (For Solopreneurs):

OBJECTIVE: *"Contract Human Resources Supervisory Development Trainer with Seattle Viaduct Hospital, a business requiring expert facilitation and platform skills and the ability to create an inviting and safe learning environment where students feel encouraged to practice new skills.*

Before continuing, please review the preceding samples and make certain you can identify the three components in each OBJECTIVE.

All right. Pretend you are reviewing a bunch of paper or on-line résumés.

Which **OBJECTIVE** would catch your attention and make you want to read more: Examples One through Five, or a generic **OBJECTIVE** that simply stated a position title, or was filled with air words focused on what the applicant wants?

We thought so, too.

Before we get into writing objectives, let me (Don) share an interesting hidden potential benefit you may get from using a clear and specific **OBJECTIVE**.

When I was a recruiter, I sorted résumés into three stacks: *Interested, Maybe,* and *Thanks-But-No-Thanks (TBNT)*.

The ones that simply were not a good "fit," were vague, poorly-written or were clearly shot-gunned ended up in the *TBNT* file. I kept the *Maybe* ones in reserve. And of course I jumped on the *Interested* ones like you would not believe. My primary criterion to get into the *Interested* pile was lots of information regarding problems faced and fixed, accomplishments, and skills relevant to positions I needed to fill.

Here's the point: In addition to the positions I was actively trying to fill, I *always* had one to two job requisitions that were hard to fill and for which my managers were not urgently pressing me to fill.

- Many times, after I had screened résumés into the *Interested* pile for the position an applicant had applied for, I identified other data points in their résumés that enabled me to interview and often hire them for one of the harder-to-fill requisitions.

- They made more money and I closed out more requisitions. It happened all the time, and it all started with an effective **OBJECTIVE**, followed by relevant skills, abilities and accomplishments. More about this later.

Exercise: Writing Objectives

While the three elements of an effective **OBJECTIVE** are fresh in your mind, let's take a few minutes and practice what you have learned.

Following the three-part process, in the following space, practice writing an **OBJECTIVE** for a position in which you are interested. If you don't have anything specific in mind at the moment, make one up.

Dedicate the most time to identifying **PART THREE** and wording it at tightly as possible.

OBJECTIVES Writing Practice:

When you've completed this exercise, please put it aside as a benchmark of your first try.

Before we close this chapter, we wanted to share several actual **OBJECTIVES** from real Professional Profiles™. We want you to know that in all cases, when the applicants submitted their targeted cover letters and custom Professional Profiles™, they were contacted in short order and interviewed. You'll find their actual cover letters and Profiles in the Appendix.

HR contacted this first person within 48 hours of receiving his credentials:

OBJECTIVE: *Director of Engineering for* Company's Division **product line**, *a position requiring significant project management, hardware and software research and development experience, metrics-based people management skills, and a deft touch to mentor and develop staff.*

The hiring manager contacted this person within one week:

OBJECTIVE: *Full-time Reservations Agent position with* Company, *a company that requires excellent communication skills, customer service skills and an outgoing individual who will go the extra mile.*

The hiring manager contacted this Baby Boomer about seven days after he submitted his credentials, only because it took that long for it to make it through the screening process.

OBJECTIVE: *Associate Organization Development Director in* Company, *an integrated* industry *provider requiring significant OD expertise in organizational needs assessment, business performance improvement, change management, and an extreme ability to coach senior management to excel.*

When the recruiter contacted this person several months after she submitted her packet, he apologized for the bureaucratic delay and their huge backlog of résumés.

OBJECTIVE: *Full-time, permanent Technical Trainer position for a Financial Service institution that requires in-depth knowledge of banking practices, multicultural training expertise, professional platform skills, a love of travel and a welcoming training style that sets high expectations while putting nervous learners at ease.*

This last one was different in that the sender was not applying for a specific position. Rather, as she explained in her cover letter, she was tapping into her network to request referrals.

OBJECTIVE: *A marketing role in which I am expected to analyze problems and needs, develop and implement creative and profitable solutions, and be accountable and rewarded for the results; willing to travel as necessary.*

So that covers how to write a targeted OBJECTIVE.

SOLOPRENEURS AND JOB SEEKERS

Presenting yourself as an "Ideal Candidate" begins with **customizing your OBJECTIVE** to the specific requirements of the position.

Trust the process.

We invite you to visit www.YourProfessionalProfile.com/DonsVideos and watch *"You Can Do What You Love.* It is a perfect example of a client with a laser-focused OBJECTIVE and achieving it. Remember, attitude and focus will help you through the "peaks and valleys" of searching for work you really want.

Before going to the next chapter, please step back and take stock of what you just read. Are you clear on the concept, or what questions do you have? How do you feel about what you read? Any "Ah-Ha's?" Please make your notes here.

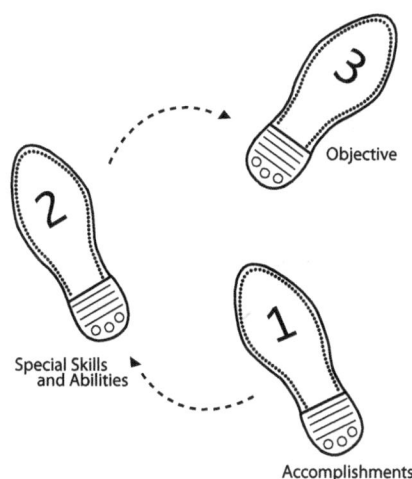

CHAPTER 6

"Part B" – The unchanging second half of your Professional Profile™

We have now covered the three critical parts of your Professional Profile™ that you must customize for each opportunity you pursue: your ACCOMPLISHMENTS, your SPECIAL SKILLS AND ABILITIES and your OBJECTIVE.

We are at the point where we want you to know that our Professional Profiles™ are . . . wait for it . . . functional résumés on steroids.

And we also want you to know that somewhere along the way functional résumés have gotten an unwarranted bad rap.

For some reason, many career counselors, HR specialists and recruiters have arbitrarily decided that when an applicant uses a functional résumé, he or she obviously has something to hide, frequently problems in work history.

Wrong. Absolutely wrong. That's what "Part B" is for.

As you will see when you study the real examples in the Appendix, whether short or long, each Profile contains its own "Part B" - *all* employment history time is accounted for.

When you assemble your credentials, this is the last section of your custom Professional Profile™. Whether your work history is wonderful or horrible, we want the screeners to fall in love with your skills and accomplishments, not with the chronology of your job history.

We wish that those whose job it is to screen résumés, social media sites and websites would do so having had a glimpse of the world through the eyes of the applicants or solopreneurs. They'd see a very different mindset.

In today's market, you - solopreneur and job seeker - need to stand out. And the most effective way for you to do that is to present yourself in the very best light possible - as effectively as possible - right from the very first words of your cover letters and résumés.

It's like dating. You are trying to make a positive first impression on someone – you are not going to immediately begin talking about that series of failed relationships; you are going to lead with your strengths.

Many exceptionally well-qualified people have been caught up in circumstances not of their making, and thus have a less-than-stellar job history – a condition that should not immediately lead to being discarded as a candidate.

There is no reason why you, a well-qualified solopreneur or employee, should be penalized and not considered because you choose to present yourself – and your accomplishments – by leading with your strengths.

To us it makes no sense that one be penalized for using a format that presents them at their best.

"Part B" is your generic and unchanging information that deserves to be presented in the best way.

Let's see how the Professional Profile™ process handles your boilerplate information - your work history, education, military, certifications and licenses, outside interests - and like that. We do it in a way that reaffirms that you are an ideal candidate. Other categories might include continuing education, special certifications, and internships.

Begin this second half of your Profile by presenting your next-most-relevant category Most often, that will be either your **WORK EXPERIENCE** or **EDUCATION**.

Once you have organized this information in an effective format, save it in a Word document (I think of it as "Part B" of the Profile) and leave it alone. You'll update it only when there is a good reason to.

Here's the thing: After customizing your **OBJECTIVE, SPECIAL SKILLS AND ABILITIES** and **ACCOMPLISHMENTS**, from here on in, the sequence in which you present your information is up to you because by the time the reader gets this part, you have hooked their interest, or you haven't. If you've followed our recommendations, it's very likely you will get a call.

When you need it, you'll just copy-and-paste Part B each time you submit a new Professional Profile™.

How to Present This Information

What to include and how you lay out this information is important.

Age discrimination, while illegal, is an on-going fact of life. If you have had a career that spans more than two decades, you have some decisions to make.

Boomers - You will be offered a lot of advice. Here are two of the most common gems:

- Omit anything that is over 20 years in the past

- Do not to include dates.

I (Don) am shaking my head in disbelief. While no doubt well-intended, those are superficial, transparent ploys suggesting that by omitting information one would normally expect to find in a résumé, a recruiter or potential client will be too dim to realize that the applicant is no longer young.

For the sake of discussion, assume the deception worked and the applicant is invited in for an interview: What happens when they show up and it is immediately obvious that they are O-L-D?

Oops! Give me a break.

Or Boomers, you can choose to be authentic and capitalize on your experience by completing the Professional Profile™ process in its entirely, including this section, getting clear on what you bring to the "world of work," and present yourself as the solution to needs going unmet.

> *Inner Game Insights: A person with a strong sense of self personally and professionally would in my opinion take on being authentic. Trust that your full, vivid and real world presentation of your accomplishments and skills will be appreciated. Is this not the caliber of company or client you want to work for? Shine bright by being true in your representation of YOU. ~ Deborah Drake*

How Do You Handle the "Age" Thing?

Straightforwardly. Honestly. Directly.

If you are at an age where age is an issue, put the new-found knowledge of this book to use and refocus your approach to capitalize on the wisdom and experience you have gained over your career.

And please – don't embarrass yourself by coloring your hair to try and look younger.

Do you recall these words in the previous chapter?

~~~

The hiring manager himself contacted this person about seven days after he submitted his credentials, only because it took that long for it to make it through the screening process.

OBJECTIVE: *Associate Organization Development Director in Company, an integrated industry provider requiring significant OD expertise in organizational needs assessment, business performance improvement, change management, and an extreme ability to coach senior management to excel.*

~~~

Here is the generic second half of his Professional Profile™. He was in his early 60s and we made the strategic decision not to hide anything. In the interest of full disclosure, after two rounds of interviews, he came in second. Lots of others never came in at all.

Repurposing the information in his Data Banks, he modified his Professional Profile™ and now teaches at his local university.

Like the waitress you read about earlier, the one with decades of guest service conflict management accomplishments who now works at the most elegant casino in our area, my client chose to treat his age and life experiences as a plus, not diminish them, and himself.

You'll see his complete Professional Profile™ in the Appendix.

PROFESSIONAL HISTORY:

Company, City, State. 6/05 – 6/10
My efforts impacted on $800M in gross revenue
Note: Company acquired Company in October, 2009
Senior Organization Development/Human Resources Consultant. 9/08 – 6/10
- **Scope of responsibilities:** Internal consultant, coach and program manager providing Organizational Development and Human Resources support for individuals and groups throughout the City Facility, with emphasis on the development and implementation of High Performance Work Systems (HPWS) in an approximately 900-employee manufacturing/packaging environment. Primary products include Product, Product, Product, and Product
- **Volume of annual business supported:** $800 million. This plant led all of Company's plants (five in North America and two in Puerto Rico) in all profit indicators over the last four years
- **Reason for leaving:** As a result of company merger I spent my final four months providing OD and HR support to senior management, staff and employees in preparation for acquiring company to shut the plant
Senior Organization Development Consultant. 6/05 – 9/08
- **Scope of responsibilities:** Internal consultant, coach and program manager providing Human Resources business partner support for client group of 350+ in this facility of 600+ hourly and 260+ salaried associates
- Firmly aligned with Operations and willingly made myself accountable with managers with P&L responsibilities to identify business problems that threatened the bottom line, then developed and implemented OD solutions to resolve those problems and achieve business objectives
  - Volume of annual business supported: $800 million
  - Reason for leaving: promoted to current position

Company. City, State 2/03 – 6/05
Lead Consultant: - Offered clients an array of strategic and tactical organizational and human resource development options, including access to a network of HR professionals with wide-ranging expertise.
- **Industry focuses:** pharmaceutical, manufacturing and technology
- **Consulting specialties:** Strategic Human Resource Development, Organization Management, Team Development, Effectiveness and Tuning, Internal Consulting Competence and Leadership/ Management Development.
- **Consulting assignments included:** Design and facilitation of a four day world-wide Marketing and Sales meeting for an RTP-based technology firm; design and facilitation of off-site meetings for a product development team, a pharmaceutical support function, teambuilding for a corporate media buying team. Coached executives in mid-sized and small firms on a variety of leadership issues and initiatives.
- **Representative assignment included:** Team building sessions for a major manufacturer of power transmission and distribution products; creation and facilitation of a sales strategy simulation during the global management meeting of a company creating data management solutions for service providers of mobile data traffic and multimedia applications; individual coaching to managers, executives and team leaders in the pharmaceutical industry.

Company. City, State 1/01 – 2/03
Senior Manager Organization Development
My efforts impacted on $5B in gross revenue
- **Scope of Responsibilities:** OD lead for the Office of Change Management in US Pharma that included: Organization Development, Project Management, Financial Management and Resource Management mandated to comprehensively assess and then manage the organization's capacity and ability to address change issues company-wide.

- Company. 7/97 – 1/01
  Manager Organization Development Consultant –
  My efforts impacted on $1.2 B in gross revenues
  - **Scope of responsibilities**: Primary OD support for several business, product and service units in US Pharma including: Marketing Analysis and Commercial Support, NeuroHealth and the Customer Response Center (CRC)
    Reason for Leaving: Position elimination with the Company/Company merger.

Company. City, State. 2/96 – 7/97
Manager Employee Development and Organizational Effectiveness (Consulting Assignment)
My efforts impacted $135M in gross revenues
- **Scope of responsibilities**: Creation and implementation of employee development strategy, including management/supervisory development, performance management, technical and customer service skills, 360° assessments and feedback, organization development.
- Reason for Leaving: End of consulting assignment

Company, Division. City, State. 2/93 – 3/95
Director/AVP - Executive Development & Succession Planning. 2/94 – 3/95
My efforts impacted $750M in gross revenues
- **Scope of Responsibilities:** Creation/implementation of development strategy linking sector, division, and firm-wide strategic objectives. Critical components included: 360° assessment / individual feedback; personal strategic development action plans; in-place professional developmental assignments.

  Manager, Executive Training & Development (Division Name) 2/93 -2/94
- Reason for Leaving: New COO took control over a major portion of my development and succession planning responsibilities; I requested and received a severance package.

Company / Division. City, State. 9/88 – 2/93
My efforts impacted $750M in gross revenues
Management Development Consultant – Division 9/88 – 8/91
Senior Management Education Consultant -- Division Corporate. 8/91 – 2/93
- **Scope of Responsibilities:** Managed / facilitated various corporate management, technical and performance skills development programs. Created and implemented development process linking individual performance goals and strategies to those of their Division business units; utilized process in various divisional business units with a total population of over 6000. Introduced 360° feedback instrumentation in Division
- Reason for Leaving: Company offered an opportunity to expand my skills in strategic organization development.

Company. City, State. 9/83 – 9/88
My efforts impacted on $75B in gross revenue
- ***Communication & Training Consultant.*** (Company). 11/85 – 6/88
- **Scope of Responsibilities**: Partnered with executive management in an intensive company-wide culture change initiative.
- ***Management Development Consultant***. Employee Development Office/Corporate Headquarters. 11/83 – 8/85
  - Reason for leaving: Chose not to relocate to City, State.

COMMUNITY RELATIONSHIPS AND TEACHING EXPERIENCES

I continue to acquire additional skills and knowledge in order to put them to practical use, both for my own benefit and that of others because I am committed to sharing my talents and knowledge with others. Some of my current and past projects are noted below. You are free to contact each person listed to discuss real-life applications, methodologies and successes.

- FM Radio Station. City, State. - From 1997 until 2005 I was a volunteer at this Public Radio station located on the campus of University. In 1998 I began hosting a weekly jazz program that focused on educating listeners and primarily playing traditional jazz of the big band and Be-bop genres. In addition, I created weekly three-minute educational spots for the *Jazz Artist of the Month* segment.

- **STATE MUSEUM OF LIFE AND SCIENCE.** City, State – from 1998 - 2005 I became a member of the Board of Directors of this nationally-known institution and held various committee assignments including Chair of the Strategic Issues Committee and member of the Search Committee. In addition, I provided – pro bono - ongoing leadership and management development training workshops to the museum's management team

- **EXECUTIVE SERVICE CORPS.** Emeritus Board Member
- **NATIONAL BLACK MBA ASSOCIATION.** Lifetime Member
- **CITY BLUES FESTIVAL.** Volunteer/Emcee
- **UNIVERSITY GRADUATE SCHOOL OF EDUCATION.** Adjunct professor in program for educators serving at-risk high school students
- **COLLEGE OF CITY.** Designed and delivered a course on intervention strategies for elementary school educators

EDUCATION

University	University
City, State	City, State
M.Sci. /Adult Education HRD *1982*	BA Communication Arts *1970*
GPA: 3.8/4.0	

CERTIFICATIONS
- MBTI Myers-Briggs Type Inventory
- SkillScope ® and Profilor ® *360°* Feedback Instruments
- LIFO ® Life Orientations Model
- IMA/Accelerating Change ®

OUTSIDE INTERESTS
- Jazz
- Community service
- Voice-over recordings
- Reading
- Exercise

Your Job History Can Do You In

Remember this OBJECTIVE from the previous chapter?

~~~

OBJECTIVE: *Full-time Reservations Agent position with* Company, *a company that requires excellent communication skills, customer service skills and an outgoing individual who will go the extra mile.*

~~~

As you'll see, this young man's work history had some obvious problems. And by now we are certain you know that hiring managers and potential customers often use job history to eliminate an applicant.

Looking at the employment dates here, had this client offered up this information right at the start of the first page of his reverse-chronological résumé, if I were the recruiter, I would have routed it to the TBNT file. In a New York minute.

RELEVANT PROFESSIONAL EXPERIENCE

Company, City, State **September 2010- March 2011**
Customer Service/ Sales Temporary Jobs.
- Answered a high volume of calls in inter-national retailer call center.
- Recruited people to come to taste test for fast food restaurant.
- Organized customer information in order to conduct focus group study.
- Helped conduct study in focus group with prototype products.

Company, City, State **January 2009- March 2010**
Customer Service Professional/ Sales Professional.
Scope of responsibilities:
- Business development with customers about building credit for their business
- Organizing customers information for effective follow-up
- Explaining the benefits of building business credit instead of using personal credit for their business
- Customer follow-up

Company, City, State **February 2008- January 2009.**
Customer Service/ Sales Associate.
Scope of responsibilities:
- Gather patients medical information
- Suggest and figuring out which machine and breathing mask would be best for the patient to get a good night's sleep.
- Send out machine and mask; follow up with customers to make sure they were getting proper results.
- Follow up with customers about progress made in helping them receive their equipment.
- Organize patient information to track progress.

Company, City, State **April 2007-December 2007**
Dealer Relations Representative - Call Center.
Scope of responsibilities:
- Work with 30 sales professionals in call center covering 50 states providing sales advertising and customer leads to dealerships nationwide.
- Support dealers in opening new accounts and upgrading existing service
- Quickly and effectively solve customer challenges
- Maintain quality control/satisfaction records, constantly striving to improve customer service
- Provide follow-up service to respond to customer concerns and to alleviate potentially difficult situations with professionalism and sensitivity.

EDUCATION
- **Continuing Education**: College, City, State.
- **Graduated** Name **High School**, City, State. June 2006

OUTSIDE INTERESTS (In addition to motivational speaking)
- Reading
- Art
- Exercise
- Basketball
- Public Speaking
- Dogs

However this information was "Part B" of his Professional Profile™

He followed the process and led with his strength (Skills and Accomplishments.) By the time his now-boss got to his job history, she was already captivated by his accomplishments, skills and the style of his résumé. Already favorably predisposed toward him, by the time she got to his inconsistent job history, it was no longer a huge red flag and an immediate disqualifier that it would have been had she seen it first.

He was so happy with the results, he sent an unsolicited video testimonial. Please visit www.YourProfessionalProfile.com./DonsVideos and click on *Eric Castaneda Testimonial for Résumés That Resume Careers.*

Closing Out This Discussion . . .

I (Don) like to include **OUTSIDE INTERESTS** as the final category in the Professional Profiles™.

I learned a long time ago that an effective résumé will present as many interesting and relevant facets of the person as possible, until the person can speak personally on their own behalf.

A quick story. When I finished graduate school and began looking for a job, my father put my résumé together for me. He told me to include **OUTSIDE INTERESTS** as the final component. I asked him why I would want to do that, because I thought outside interests were personal and therefore not part of a business résumé. (Even I once upon a time was inclined to follow "conventional" wisdom. Thank goodness for my father's insight!)

Dad told me that what people included there was the last thing the reader read and the applicant could sometimes establish a kind of personal link with the recruiter. He called it "remote control." That made sense to me and since I was seriously into photography, I included it.

Even though I had no experience in hotel management, a family friend thought I'd be a good fit for Marriott Hotels and opened a door for me. They liked what they saw in my résumé because they called me for an interview. It lasted twelve hours, and when I left, I walked out with a job offer to become a human resources director (back then it was called a personnel director) in one of their hotels.

As we were wrapping up, I noticed the interviewer had circled "photography" A LOT in red ink and I asked him why. He told me he was into photography and it caught his eye. *Hmmmm.* He also told me that, while not a job requirement, given all the employee activities in the hotel, it was a plus for the property's HR director to know how to use a camera.

Positive connection. Remote control. COULD make a world of difference. Convinced? Hope so.

Dad knew what he was about.

After I had been on board for a while, I asked the interviewer (now my boss) why they hired me, since my HR and hotel management experience were nonexistent? He said they hired me based on their assessment of the *transferrable skills* they saw in me, skills they could develop. The photography was just icing on the cake.

Feel free to organize Part B of your Professional Profile™ as you see fit; this layout worked well for others.

With your **ACCOMPLISHMENTS** and **SKILLS Data Banks** complete, and knowing how to customize your **OBJECTIVE,** you are just about set to step out and present yourself the ideal candidate, the solution to needs going unmet.

CONGRATULATIONS! You now understand the nuts-and-bolts of how to write a Professional Profile™.

Next up – **Sample Professional Profiles™.**

Before going to the next chapter, please step back and take another moment to take stock of what you just read. Are you clear on the concept, or what questions do you have? How do you feel about what you read? Any "Ah-Ha's?" Please make your notes here.

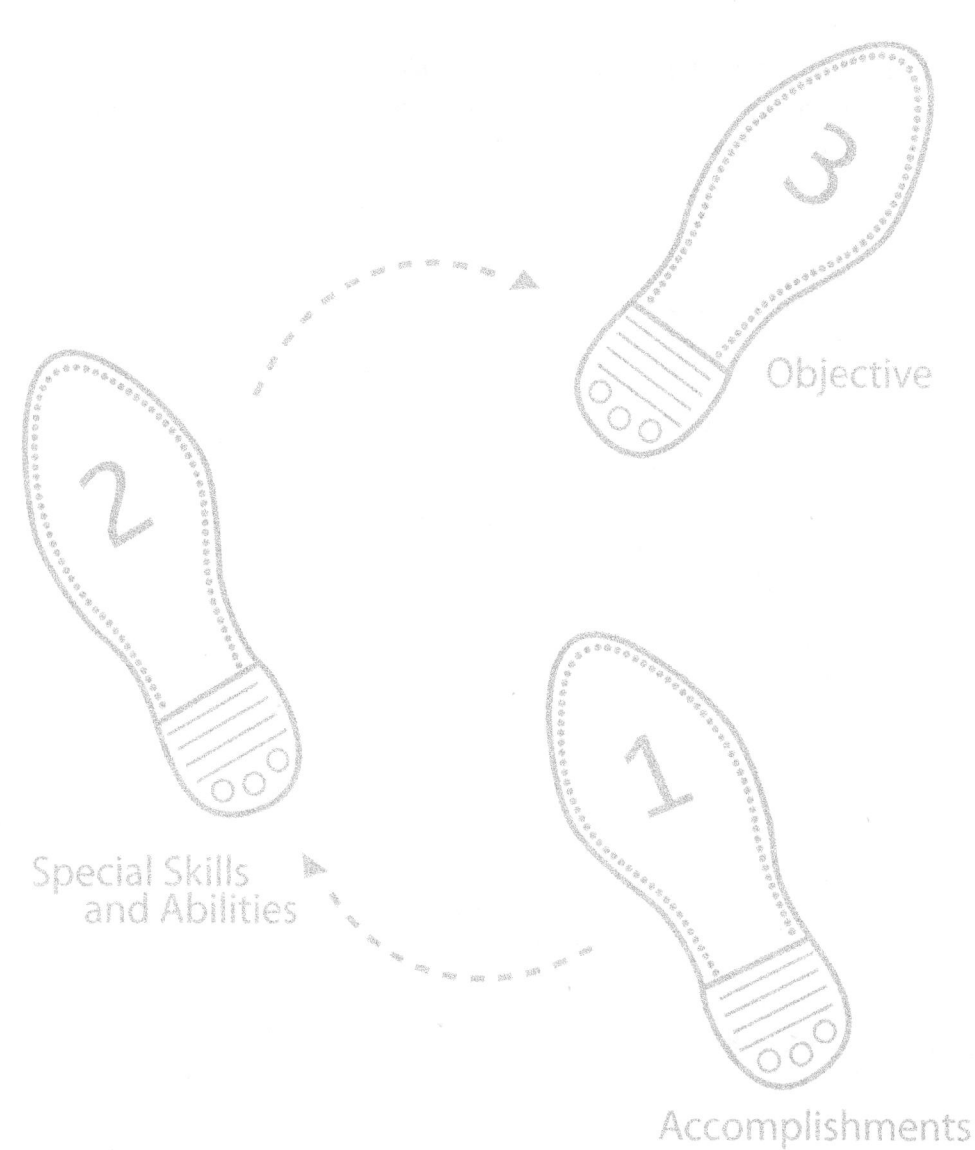

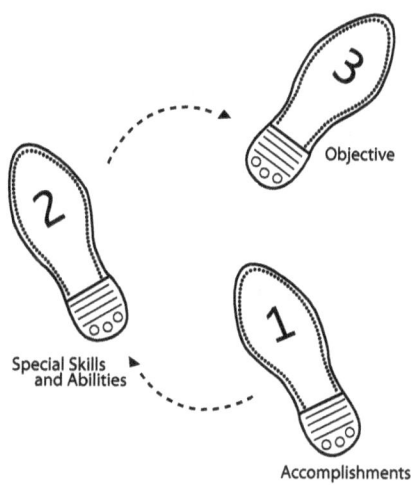

CHAPTER 7

Working with Your Special Skills and Accomplishments Data Banks

THE NARRATIVE STYLE OF Professional Profile™

To introduce the basic **Narrative style** of Professional Profiles™, we wanted to give you an opportunity to work with fully-stocked **Accomplishments** and **Skills / Abilities Data Banks.**

Introduction to Selectivity Exercise: Using Your Data Banks

For purposes of this exercise, *"Selectivity"* refers to which accomplishments and which special skills and abilities to leave in the Data Banks for future use, and which to select, tweak and copy-and-paste into a new Professional Profile™.

You'll be practicing with the basic format - the *NARRATIVE.*

With her permission, you'll be working with the actual ACCOMPLISHMENTS and SPECIAL SKILLS AND ABILITIES DATA BANKS that a colleague and I developed for her own successful job search.

When you have completed the exercise, we'll share her actual Professional Profile™ with you and you'll be able to see how your selections compared with what she used for her search.

- As a reminder: with so many people in the job market, in order for YOUR phone to ring with someone calling YOU for an interview, you will stand out more effectively with a custom Professional Profile™ than you will with a generic reverse-chronological résumé.

What is noteworthy? Even with all the layoffs during the recession of 2008 - 2009, even though she has accepted a new position within her company, her Professional Profile™ is still making her memorable and generating calls from referrals, recruiters, and those who knew she had been looking.

- Remember, in order to package yourself as the best candidate *for each position* you will apply for, you will never submit a one-size-fits-all generic Professional Profile™ for multiple positions.

- Rather, based on the requirements for each position, you will select from your Data Banks your most relevant ACCOMPLISHMENTS and SPECIAL SKILLS AND ABILITIES for each position for which you apply.

So, regarding ACCOMPLISHMENTS and SPECIAL SKILLS AND ABILITIES DATA BANKS, the question becomes *"what to leave in and what to leave out?"*

This person was not applying for a specific position; rather, after selecting her primary motivated skills and her most significant professional accomplishments, she sent her Professional Profile™ to her network and asked for referrals. More about that strategy in the Bonus Section.

Here is her actual Objective.

OBJECTIVE: *A full-time, permanent Marketing management position where I will be expected to analyze marketing problems, identify needs, develop and implement creative and profitable solutions, be held accountable for the results, and rewarded accordingly*

Exercise: Selectivity / Using Your Data Banks

As you commence the exercise, imagine you are a recruiter and you have just read her *OBJECTIVE*. Think for a moment about what *Special Skills and Abilities* and what *Representative Professional Accomplishments* you might expect to see in her Professional Profile™.

Remember, as you read through her Data Banks, some of her *Accomplishments* and *Special Skills* will be more relevant to her *Objective* than others. She will only include the ones that are relevant to her current **OBJECTIVE**.

The purpose of this exercise is to analyze the contents of both Data Banks, then select and include only those *Special Skills* and *Accomplishments* that relate most directly to the needs and responsibilities of a marketing management position.

- *Before starting, we suggest you photocopy both of her Skills and Accomplishments Data Banks so you can cut-and-paste your selections on the following blank pages.*

Her **SKILLS DATA BANK** contains twenty skills. Please select between nine and twelve you feel would complement her *OBJECTIVE*. Note the ones you would copy-and-paste into each of the boxes of the table. Give thought to how you would organize them for maximum impact.

Her **ACCOMPLISHMENTS DATA BANK** contains twenty-three accomplishment statements.

- To effectively present your *ACCOMPLISHMENTS*, you will need to organize them into subcategories. If you were applying for a specific position, your subcategories would be the primary areas of responsibility listed in the position description and you would slot the accomplishments you selected into those categories.

- However, since in this exercise you are not applying for a specific position but rather are *seeking referrals* from a number of people, you'll have to create your own *subcategories* and decide which REPRESENTATIVE PROFESSIONAL ACCOMPLISHMENTS will most effectively support your Marketing *OBJECTIVE*.

The best way to accomplish that is to do this:

As you read through her accomplishments, jot down two or three words that describe the essence of the accomplishment. Two possible ones could be ***"Profitability through Planning"*** and ***"Marketing Creativity."*** I'm sure you will think of many others.

- After you have read all of her accomplishments and made your topic notations, group them into similar categories. Then give each separate category a descriptive name, one that you believe would be picked up if someone put the Professional Profile™ through a Key Word Search.

Remember:

- Your Professional Profile™ could be in a seventeen-inch high stack of résumés or one of hundreds on a computer. To be read, it has be found. To be found, it has to **stand out.**

- *You only have the first ¾ of the first page (maybe seven to ten seconds) to capture the reader's interest so that they want to read on.*

- That means you want to have communicated your *OBJECTIVE* and *SPECIAL SKILLS AND ABILITIES* and begin telling the reader about your *ACCOMPLISHMENTS* by half-way down the first page.

- To grab and hold their interest, you must be certain to open the *Accomplishments* section with your most impressive, powerful and relevant accomplishments that compliment your OBJECTIVE.

OBJECTIVE: *A full-time, permanent Marketing management position where I will be expected to analyze marketing problems, identify needs, develop and implement creative and profitable solutions, be held accountable for the results, and rewarded accordingly*

All right! Let's go identify some ***SPECIAL SKILLS AND ABILITIES*** and ***REPRESENTATIVE PROFESSIONAL ACCOMPLISHMENTS.***

Data Bank: Special Skills and Abilities

1. Marketing creativity

2. Event creativity

3. Written creativity

4. Committed to achieving and maintaining consistently high levels of client satisfaction

5. Hold high expectations for my own performance; strive for high levels of personal achievement

6. Maintain poise and self-confident composure in free-flowing situations; adjust and thrive in new environments

7. Quick study; able to apply what I have learned and work effectively without supervision

8. Routinely achieve profit objectives while working within established budgets

9. Confident when faced with learning new software and computer applications

10. Consensus builder; strong personal influencing skills; rapidly put people at ease and build trust

11. Enjoy interaction with people of diverse cultures, social and economic backgrounds

12. Take initiative to create pragmatic, effective solutions to business problems

13. Have been told repeatedly that I am mature and competent beyond my age

14. Committed to continuous learning and personal growth

15. Happy person, committed to both my colleagues and my company

16. Effective at balancing multiple projects and seeing them through to completion

17. Unafraid to speak my mind, directly and politely

18. Willing to make a decision and see it through

19. Take personal responsibility for my actions

20. Build and maintain lasting friendships

Data Bank: Representative Professional Accomplishments

Reminder: *There are no subcategories in this Accomplishments Data Base. Using the unique qualifications of each position for which you are applying,* **you will create relevant subcategories for each Professional Profile™ you submit, then** *select the most relevant accomplishments and copy-and-paste them into the appropriate subcategories.*

1. During my first New Home Open House program, I wondered: *"Why do we devote two whole pages to an ineffective map when each home listing is equipped with directions?"* No one could answer that question for me since they'd been doing it that way for a while, so I created an alternative, which the newspaper adopted and still uses to this day. My solution was to group homes located in the same region together to make it easier for the reader to find homes in areas they are interested in; it encouraged the listing agent to offer a web address for more information and it returned the back two pages of the map to the advertising sales staff as additional space they could sell for revenue generation. (Newspaper)

2. As Member Relations Director, I managed a number of member committees. The *"Women on the Move"* committee was one of my most committed and dynamic. Within the company, I know of at least five sister Clubs that have copied my design. It has been a very successful forum for building political and community relations. The relationship of which I am most proud is the one we have established with Borders Books. On my initiative, I contacted their regional marketing director and we have formed an ongoing relationship bringing visiting authors to speak at dinner events at the Club. It has been a popular win/win for Borders, the authors, my members, and the Club. (Business Club)

3. Clay Aiken's Foundation approached the Club to partner with them in a fundraiser for charity. We accepted their offer, and I was responsible for marketing the event. Within one month, we had sold out the event to the maximum capacity of our facility. Working with his Foundation, I developed marketing pieces, helped design and write ad copy for our newsletter and members' website (both of which I wrote and maintained), developed and implemented an e-mail and poster campaign for the Club, and facilitated an introduction to the local newspaper's Features Editor. This was the first event of this kind we had done and it was a stellar success; over 50 members participated and we raised over $300,000 for his foundation, which funds summer camps for kids with special needs. (Business Club)

4. New to my job, I analyzed my accounts and requested a current run of spending reports. I noticed that several accounts had been spending well over their contracted amount as they advertised with the newspaper. I approached these accounts about signing a new contract at a level equal with their spending. Every one of the six accounts I approached with this option thanked me for my diligence and signed their new and higher contract levels. This resulted in an additional $40K in revenues for my newspaper win-win for the newspaper as well as the client.

    By signing a higher contract level, the newspaper could count on the client achieving this higher level of spending for the next year and the client could count on the newspaper to supply them with lower rates than they had been receiving before. They could advertise more often and still spend the same. One of these accounts had previously been my manager's when she had been a sales person. I encouraged this account to sign at a level which was double what they had done before. They did and both my manager and her manager congratulated me for doing what my manager had been unable to do. (Newspaper)

5. Harry Potter. Timed with the release of one of the movies, we put on a themed adult/child dinner that included tickets to the movie at the IMAX across the street. We decorated and organized the dining room to look like the Hogwarts dining hall with four long tables based on the four houses in the Harry Potter books. When members came with a child, the child was placed under the Sorting Hat and I had someone with a great voice backstage calling out the names of the Houses, according to where we had seated them for their reservation. The dinner, the room decorations, everything worked to perfection and the members and their children loved it. One member loved it so much that he asked to speak personally with the person who created it – me! When we meet now, he calls me "Harry Potter." He asked me how long I will remain with the Club because Disney needs to pick me up sometime soon! (Business Club)

6. Members consistently praise the Club for the innovative activities I developed: the Harry Potter themed dinner, other themed dinners relating to IMAX movies, a private after-hours tour of the Titanic exhibit at the Museum of History ending in a black tie dinner at the Club featuring the menu of the final dinner served aboard the Titanic (members still talk about it three years later). Limousine scavenger hunts through Raleigh, stopping in several different restaurants to get clues for the hunt. Trips to the Art Museum for our Art Committee complete with lunch and a docent-led private tour. The list is extensive and member satisfaction ratings significant. It is gratifying to know how well received my work has been and the positive image it has created for us in the community. (Business Club)

7. I like to design/create marketing solutions that are cost-effective, simple, and aesthetically pleasing. For the last five years, I have been responsible for all aspects of the publication of the Club's bi-monthly newsletter. I taught myself Quark and performed all layout, design, writing and photography. After several issues, I realized that the process was taking too much of my time, and I decided to see if the Corporate graphics designers could do the work, thereby expediting the process while saving me time and money. They were delighted to help, and by using their services and more advanced software, my design time went from two weeks to two days, and the cost (excluding postage) went from $1,800 per month to $756 – an annual savings of $12,528 for the Club and approximately 300 hours a year for the Club and for me. (Business Club)

8. As a result of a corporate acquisition and reorganization in January 2007, some of my original Director of Member Relations job duties shifted and I assumed half the responsibilities of a laid-off Private Events director. My new title was Food and Beverage Director of Sales, and I had a $1.5 million sales plan to meet, one that was based on aggressive increases in both food and beverage prices as well as revenue targets. Since there was no marketing plan for this position, the first thing I did upon acquiring this new responsibility was to create and implement a comprehensive one, because up to this point, Private Events had simply relied on word-of-mouth. Four months into the year, we are on track to make plan. (Business Club)

9. For all of 2006, I was personally responsible for the Club's retention of members. January began with a 72% retention level, and by year-end, we had improved it to 78%. That 6% increase was a hard-fought victory in a small and already-saturated market and it placed us in the top 20% of all of the Clubs. I was recognized for this achievement. To achieve this accomplishment, I developed and implemented a variety of creative and well-received activities and events that were successful in (1) getting honest feedback about why members were not renewing, and (2) educating and convincing a significant portion of members to maintain / renew their memberships. (Business Club)

10. Founding member of Club's Chapter Toastmasters International. In response to Member interest, researched the organization and managed all aspects of the creation and certification of the chapter. As of May 2007, the Chapter had 22 Members. The Chapter had attained the highest performance designation of President's Distinguished Club. Served in elected role as VP of Education May 2002 to June 2003 (Business Club)

11. With only three months experience and only minimal training in my new job, my colleague / peer who was supposed to train me left the club, leaving me as the sole Private Event Director. I met the challenge head-on with a positive attitude tackling it through 13 hour days and six day a week work schedule. One colleague commented that she wasn't sure how I managed to do it with a smile on my face every day. I surpassed budget for each month. Period 5 was the largest; The Private Event plan was $118,000; I exceed it by $29,000 with a final total of $149,000. I executed each event perfectly, without dropping a single ball. (Business Club)

12. The Member Relations Director position planned and sold events based on what the members were interested in. However, at times I created and hosted events that were off everyone's radar screens, i.e. Chocolate Brunches, dance classes paired with a big dance event, Chocolate and Wine tastings, Scotch tastings and Hurricane Voo-Doo parties to ward off bad hurricanes. Because I was never afraid of trying something new, I constantly sold not just events, but new ideas and change to Club members, my own staff and Club management. I'm proud to say I always received the support I needed to make each new idea a success. (Business Club)

13. Due to resignations, terminations, and transfers of managers and supervisors, as well as higher-than-normal turnover among staff, our Club was in a constant state of change and turmoil for over two years. While somewhat uncomfortable, I am flattered that because of the relationships I had made with many of my members, a number of them have come to me to personally to share their concerns, rather than gossiping and complaining among themselves. Their trust gave me a number of opportunities to conduct damage control, and I know of at least six members that I was able to retain as a result of having established strong personal as well as professional relationships. (Business Club)

14. Over the last five years, I have become good friends with many of our members, and when one of them, a man in his 60s, suddenly found himself in the job market, he asked a number of people for a letter attesting to his character, including me. I was honored and touched that this man, more than twice my age, thought enough of me to ask for a letter. He later reported to me with deep gratitude that the letter I wrote was instrumental in helping him secure a new and better position. (Business Club)

15. After years of business as usual the newspaper decided it was time to change their Real Estate Classified Sales department and hired four new Sales Executives. I was one of them. I was the only one hired from the outside – everyone else came through internal transfer. We were formed into teams of two. However, after three weeks, my partner, upset with the changes made to her position, left the company. She was to have trained me, and for the next two months I managed my accounts on my own. Having received very little training prior to her departure, and little assistance after she left, I did what I do best: I rolled with the punches and largely trained myself.

My accounts flourished while I taught myself how to place ads and found answers to my questions by developing close relationships with my co-workers. During that transitional time, my manager praised me for picking things up so quickly and for being such a great team player; when I asked her for constructive criticism, she didn't have anything to offer.

The newspaper replaced my former partner and I trained my new one in the manner in which I wish I had been trained. We developed a strong relationship that was the envy of the department, precisely what our manager wanted to achieve when she initially implemented the new changes. Other co-workers could see the strength and respect in our partnership and expressed a disappointment that they didn't have that kind of relationship with their partner as well. Eight months later my partner was recognized as being a key player; she received a promotion and credits me for it. (Newspaper)

16. One lesson I learned the hard way was that the climate set by the person in charge has a direct impact on the morale, commitment and productivity the entire organization. Tension among the staff and members in the light of a new General Manager was both high and continuous. His managerial style and manner of communication was not that to which we had been accustomed. He had come to us from another property within the company. Even though I was one of the youngest of his department heads, I took it upon myself to speak privately with him on more than one occasion.

    I felt uncomfortable walking the line between our boss and my colleagues, and developed a plan for how I wanted to conduct the conversation. My Manager and I agreed that I would share the feelings of the department heads while not attributing comments to any particular individual. My approach worked perfectly, and the results were dramatic. Within two months, everyone in the Club, including members, noticed and commented on the visible and sustained improvement in the climate and morale in the Club. I am proud of my initiative, and my willingness to face my fear and proceed. (Business Club)

17. During a university internship, I worked in Alaska for a cruise ship company. Over that nine- month period I worked my way up from cleaning toilets and waiting tables to a supervisory position. Toward the end of my internship, my ship struck a rock in Tracey Arm and began to sink. I kept my calm and did my part to help evacuate the 93 elderly passengers in just 21 minutes. Our entire crew was commended in the national press for having "responded professionally and according to protocol." (Juneau Empire, July 29, 1999) (Cruise Ship Company)

18. Private Events was a separate career track within my company, and was completely separate from my area of Member Relations. Our Club had two Private Events directors, and they did a phenomenal job. However, on one occasion, staffing and coverage between the two of them did not happen and both were off at the same time. When this happened, a scheduled event, worth about $1,000 net, was on the verge of failure. Since many in the Club looked to me for help in times of special need, they brought this situation to me.

    Private Events used their own proprietary software, and Member Relations directors are not cross-trained in its use. However, since I believe in being cross-trained in other areas, and because I was interested and had taken the initiative to learn it, I not only knew their software, I had it installed on my computer. Faced with an immediate need to pull the event together ON-THE-SPOT, I did exactly that. As a result, the Club member had a flawless event, and I saved the Club, the Private Events function, and the individual whose event it was a great deal of embarrassment. (Business Club)

19. Having come from the hourly ranks, I am very aware of the importance of managers paying attention to high-potential employees, and being willing to go to bat for them when necessary. I have been fortunate to have hired employees with aptitudes for greater responsibility, and am committed to facilitating their personal development. One young woman stands out for me. She came in as a front desk clerk and rapidly mastered all aspects of that position. Based on her demonstrated performance, positive member feedback and engaging personality, I followed our procedures to get her onto a fast track to becoming a department head. In less than one year, while working full-time for me, she completed our in-house training program and passed all of her exams with flying colors and is now a Membership Director. One of the very first people she enrolled as a member was Clay Aiken, and no, they were not friends. (Business Club)

20. Our corporate headquarters had a formal mentoring program that involved all tenured Member Relations Directors. The company hired a young woman right out of college and into the position of Member Relations Director in a Club about 80 miles away from me. I was assigned to mentor her. I knew from first-hand experience that the Company's self-directed training program for certification as a Member Relations Director did not adequately and quickly train a new-hire to pass the exams.

Because I also knew that her Club manager had given her only a six-month window to become certified, I decided to create a custom mentoring program designed to fill the voids I knew from personal experience existed because while working full-time, it took me over a year to pass the exams. While still maintaining my workload, I worked with her diligently on the phone, on both my time and company time, and spent one full weekend working with her at her Club. She passed her exams with flying colors and credits me with her success. Corporate and property general management recognized me for my willingness to go beyond expectations. (Business Club)

21. Based on prior performance, I was selected to update and improve not only our Club's new-hire training program but the accompanying handbook as well. I conducted a gap analysis as I analyzed all aspects of what I went through in the program, and what I read in the handbook, comparing the ideal with what actually took place. Upon completing that process, I recommended updates to the Handbook and the service-training program. Club Management accepted all of my recommendations and I received both a performance bonus as well as commendations from Club manager. My work enabled future new-hires to receive a more in-depth orientation to the Club, and for the Club to achieve a more rapid return on their training dollars. (Business Club)

22. I completed my university Senior Internship during my Junior year aboard a small cruise ship in Alaska. While working full-time on my ship duties, I completed my senior project, which was the creation from scratch of a comprehensive New-Hire Employee Handbook for use aboard ship, which to the best of my knowledge is still in use. Company management was so impressed with my work and my work ethic that they offered me a management position at the end of my internship. Flattered, I nonetheless declined and returned to complete my degree. (Cruise Ship Company / University)

23. After planning everything to the nth degree, I experienced the BEST THREE DAYS OF MY LIFE – my wedding. From the tiara to the train of my dress to the table arrangements – I planned everything, and had hands-on involvement in most of it as well. Everything within my control went just as I had envisioned it. Why is my wedding an accomplishment for my résumé? Because by utilizing my contacts

with the industry and the area, and by doing many things myself, I created an elegant $15,500 wedding for only $8,371, a savings of $6,629. *I promise you that I am just as detail-oriented, cost-conscious and frugal when it comes to spending my employer's money as I am with my own.*

End of SPECIAL SKILLS and ACCOMPLISHMENTS DATA BANKS

When you cut-and paste on the following blank pages, follow this template to organize your solution:

YOUR NAME
Your Street Address
Your City, State, Zip
Your Cell, Your Email and Website Address

OBJECTIVE: A full-time, permanent Marketing management position where I will be expected to analyze marketing problems, identify needs, develop and implement creative and profitable solutions, be held accountable for the results, and rewarded accordingly

SPECIAL SKILLS AND ABILITIES

REPRESENTATIVE PROFESSIONAL ACCOMPLISHMENTS

[Subcategory]

[Subcategory]

[Subcategory]

[Subcategory]

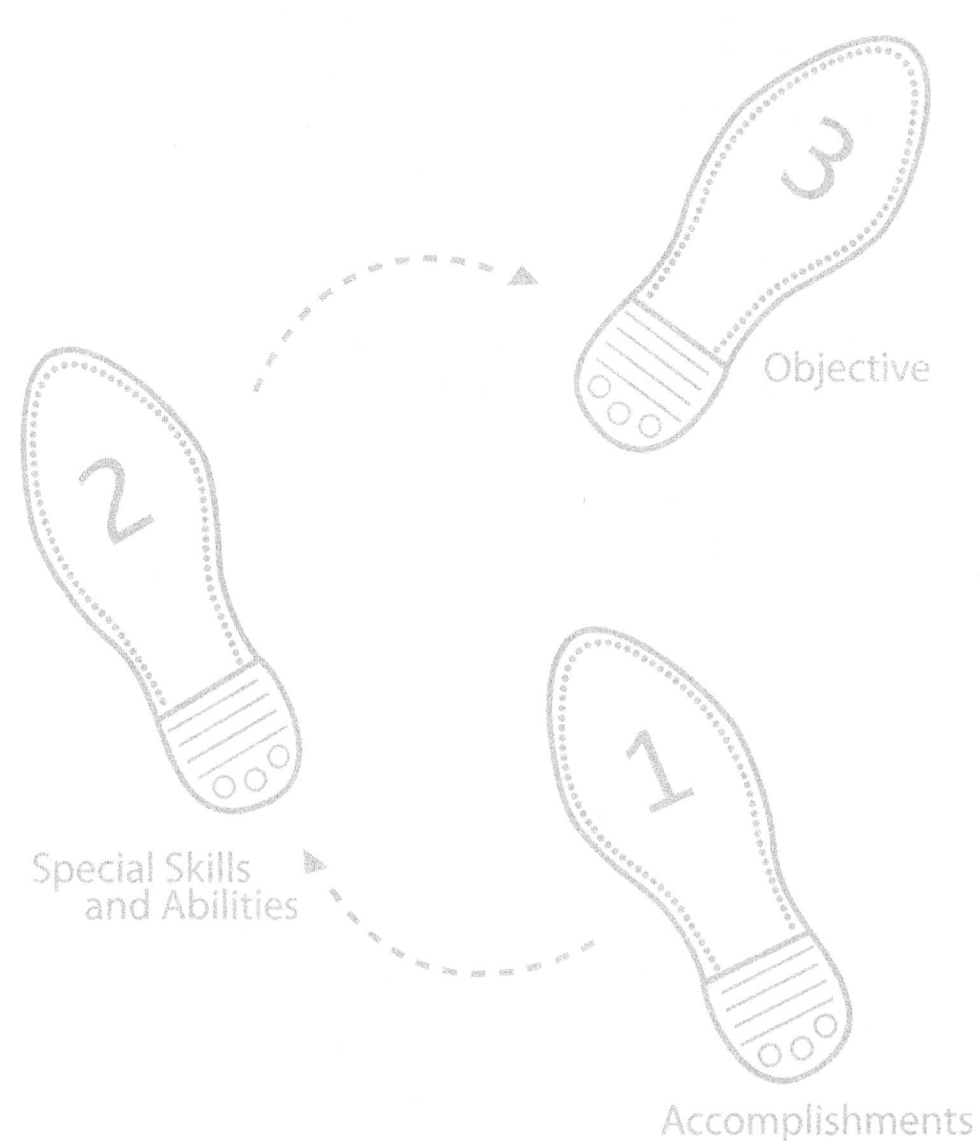

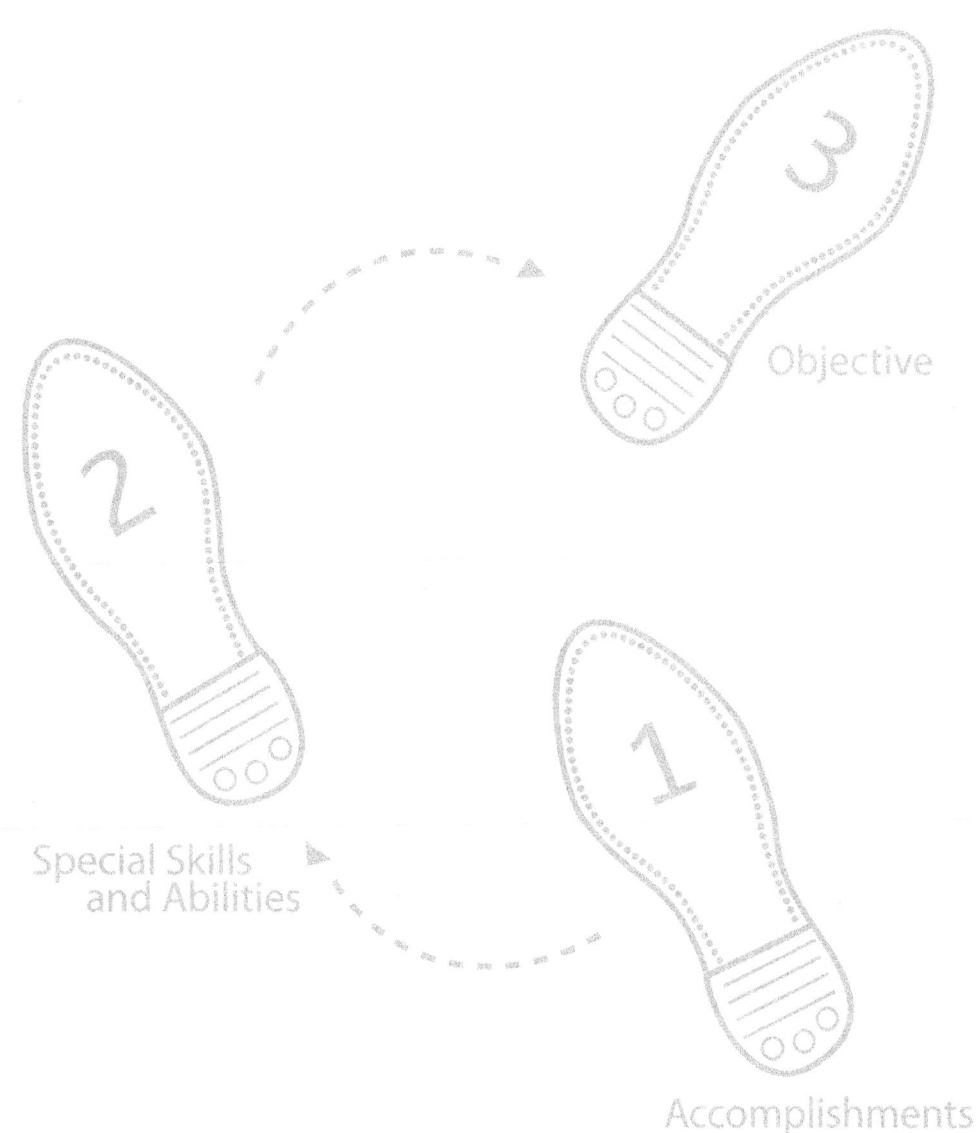

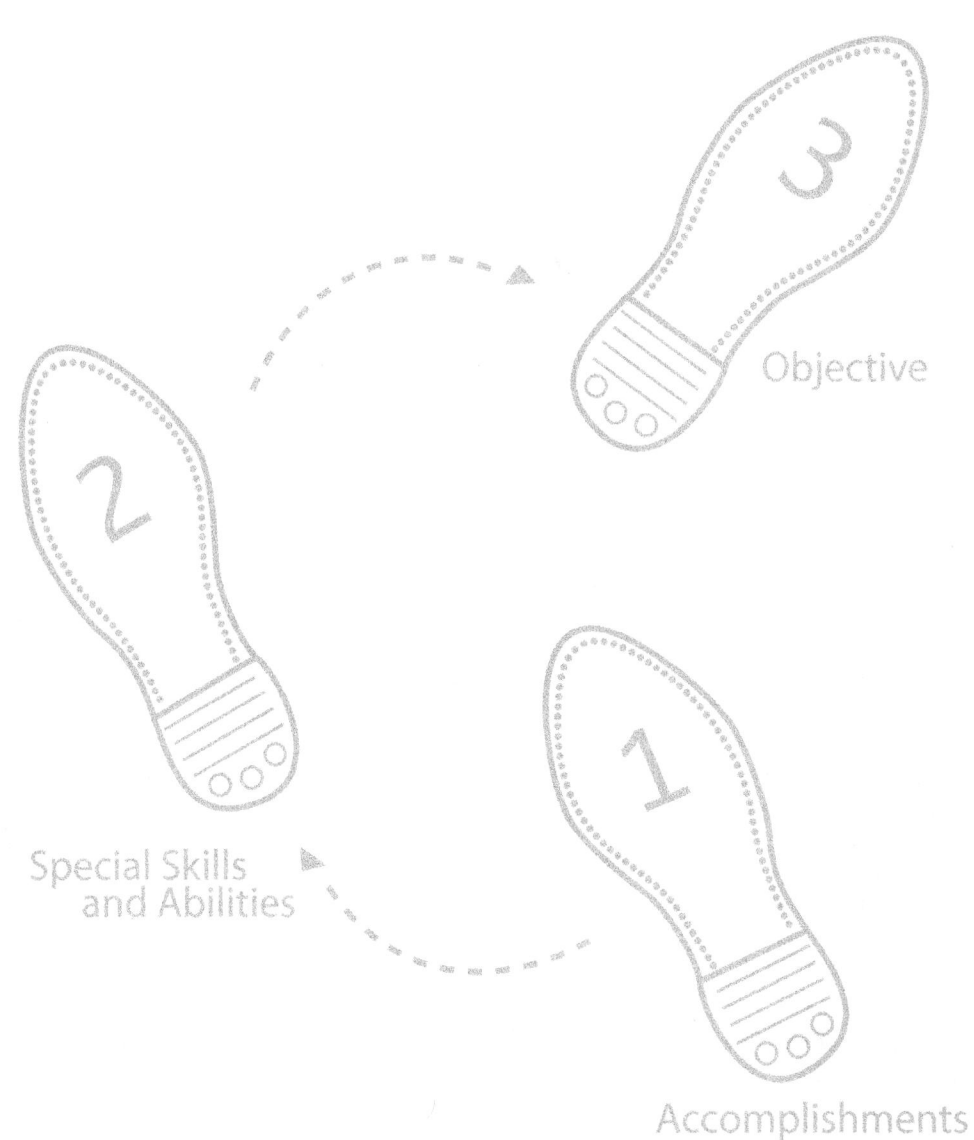

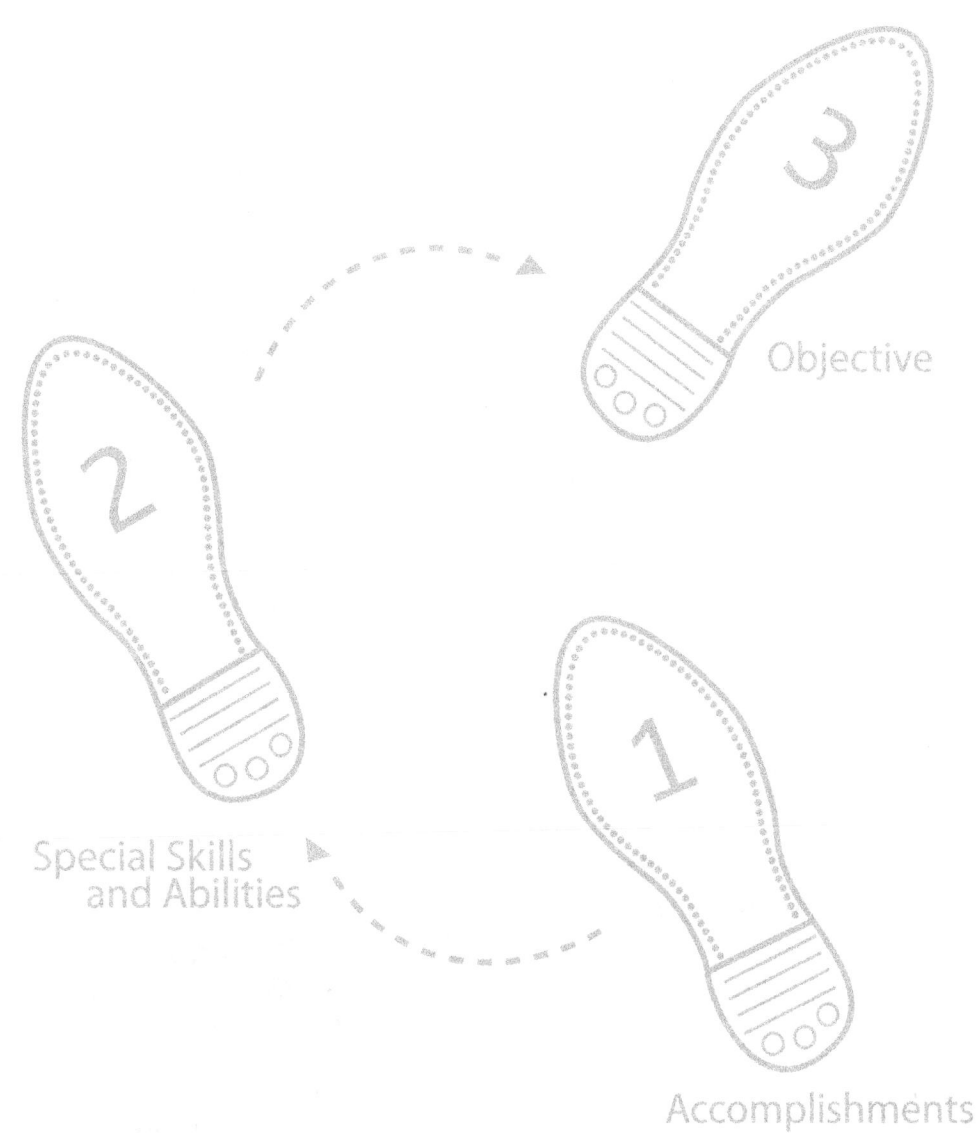

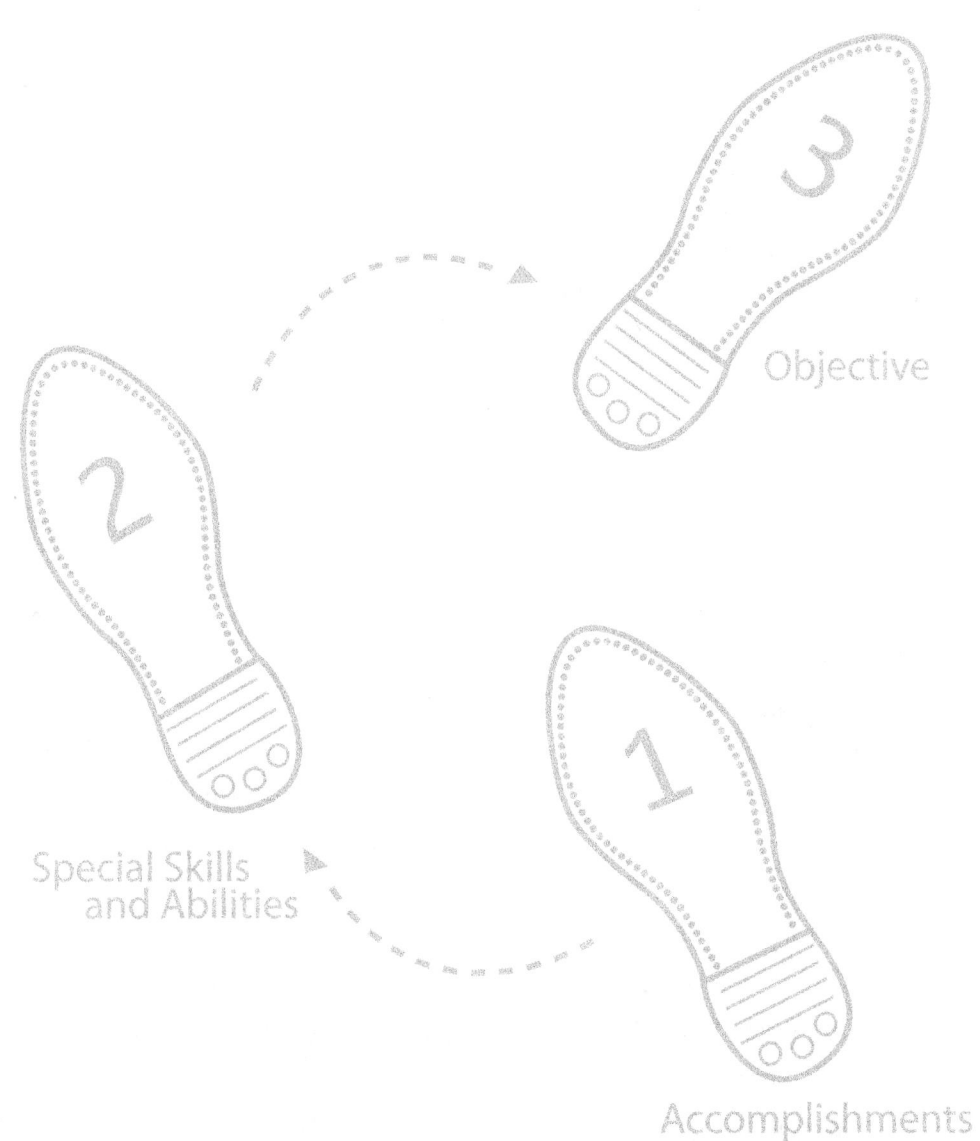

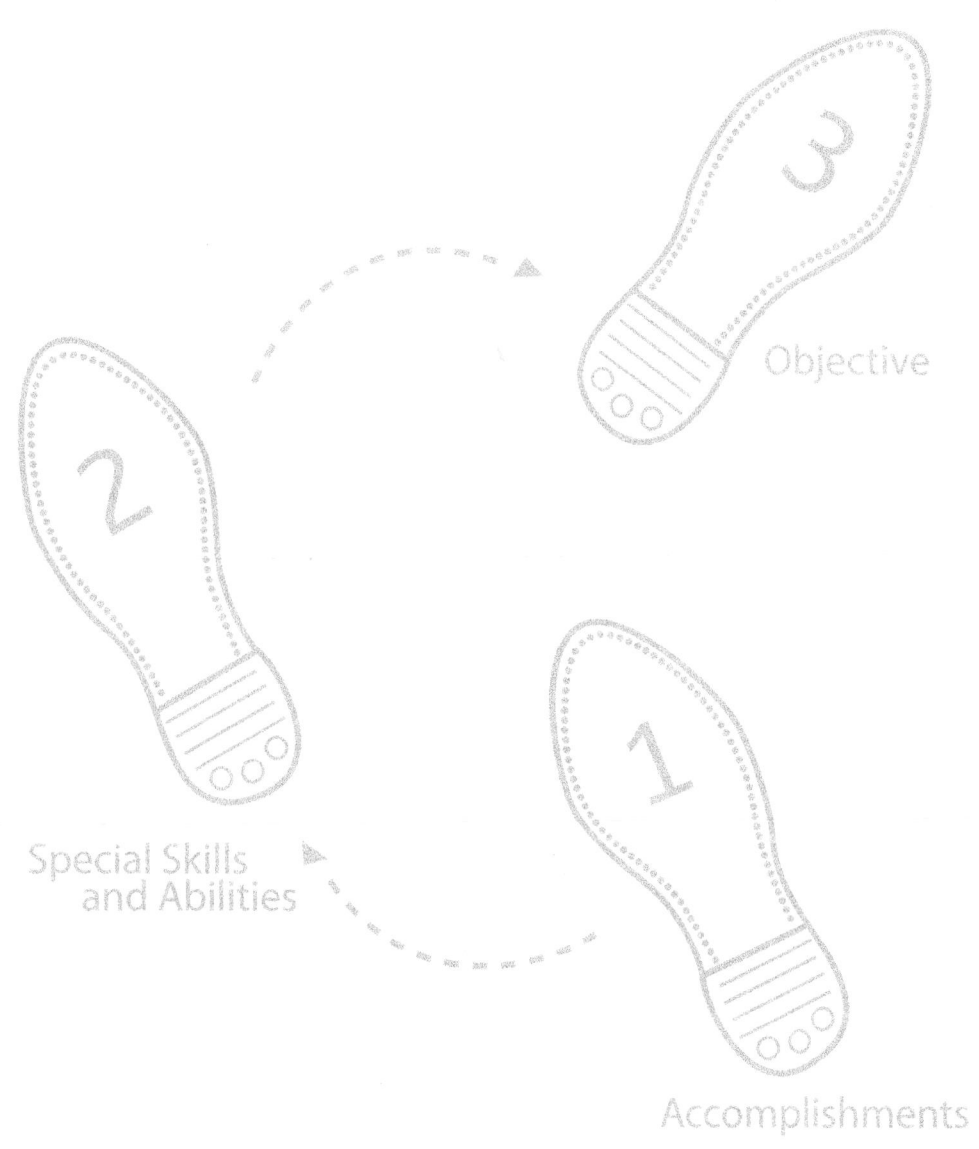

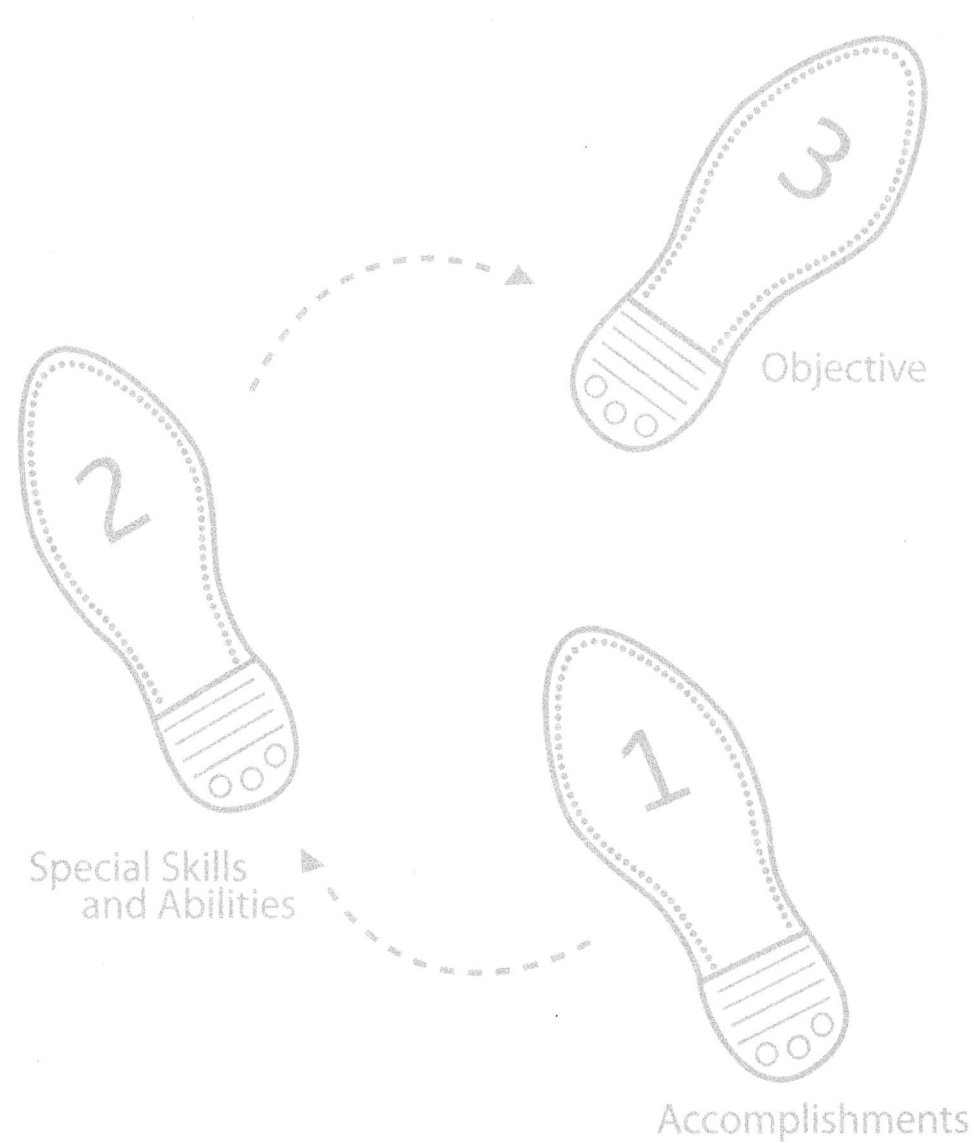

So. How was that?

We hope you had to give a good deal of thought before making decisions about what to leave in and what to leave out.

If you stuck with it, give yourself a pat on the back. You earned it, and you may have a little headache as a result of sorting things out. That's good because it shows you were engaged in the process.

By that very action of putting yourself in her shoes, then thinking and deciding how best to present yourself, you are separating yourself from the mass of your competitors, the ones who put together one single **generic résumé**, then shotgun it to all sorts of **specific** positions, and then wonder why their phone does not ring.

Her complete Professional Profile™ follows. You'll notice that she added "**Personal Traits**" to **SPECIAL SKILLS AND ABILITIES**. If you want to do that as well, or prefer to use other words to tell the reader what you bring to the *"world of work,"* please do so.

We encourage you to tailor this process to your needs and your personality, just as we want you to tailor your Professional Profile™ to each opportunity.

Here is her complete **NARRATIVE** Professional Profile™. Using an 11 point font, her accomplishments begin half way down the page.

Before you begin reading, we would like to make a prediction, and we hope we are wrong.

We predict that when you see her Professional Profile™, alarm bells will likely go off inside your head when you see that it is more than two pages.

If that is the case, take a couple of deep breaths. Those are your old tapes kicking in, the ones that say you cannot have a résumé more than two pages in length, or that if your résumé looks different, it will be rejected, or… or… or…

Remember: you WANT to stand out, and you cannot do that when your credentials look just like everyone else's.

Remember too that using the Professional Profile™ you are about to see, she is *still* memorable two years later.

Deep breath. Turn the page. **Client's Professional Profile™ for Comparison:**

CLIENT'S NAME
Street Address
City, State, and Zip
Telephone Numbers
E-Mail Address

OBJECTIVE: A full-time, permanent Marketing management position where I will be expected to analyze marketing problems, identify needs, develop and implement creative and profitable solutions, be held accountable for the results, and rewarded accordingly

PERSONAL TRAITS, SPECIAL SKILLS AND ABILITIES

Hold high expectations for my performance, strive for high levels of personal achievement	Maintain poise, self-confidence in free-flowing situations; adjust and thrive in new environments	Quick study; able to apply what I have learned and work effectively without supervision
Routinely achieve profit objectives while working within established budgets	Committed to achieving and maintaining consistently high levels of client satisfaction	Confident when faced with learning new software / computer applications
Consensus builder; strong personal influencing skills; rapidly put people at ease, build trust	Take initiative to create pragmatic, effective solutions to business problems	Happy person, committed to both my colleagues and my company

REPRESENTATIVE PROFESSIONAL ACCOMPLISHMENTS

MARKETING CREATIVITY FOR PROFITABILITY, FUNDRAISING AND GOOD WILL

- During my first New Home Open House program, I wondered: *Why do we devote two whole pages to an ineffective map when each home listing is equipped with directions?"* No one could answer that question for me since they'd been doing it that way for a while, so I created an alternative, which the newspaper adopted and still uses to this day. My solution was to group homes located in the same region together to make it easier for the reader to find homes in areas they are interested in; it encouraged the listing agent to offer a web address for more information and it returned the back two pages of the map to the advertising sales staff as additional space they could sell for revenue generation. (Newspaper)

- As Member Relations Director, I managed a number of member committees. The "Women on the Move" committee was one of my most committed and dynamic. Within the company, I know of at least five sister Clubs that have copied my design. It has been a very successful forum for building political and community relations. The relationship of which I am most proud is the one we have established with NATIONAL BOOK STORE. On my initiative, I contacted their regional marketing director and we have formed an ongoing relationship bringing visiting authors to speak at dinner events at the Club. It has been a popular win/win for BOOK STORE, the authors, my members, and the Club. (Business Club)

- Clay Aiken's Foundation approached the Club to partner with them in a fundraiser for charity. We accepted their offer, and I was responsible for marketing the event. Within one month, we had sold out the event to the maximum capacity of our facility. Working with his Foundation, I developed marketing pieces, helped design and write ad copy for our newsletter and members' website (both of which I wrote and maintained), developed and implemented an e-mail and poster campaign for the Club, and facilitated an introduction to the local newspaper's Features Editor. This was the first event of this kind we have done and it was a stellar success; over 50 members participated and we raised over $300,000 for his foundation, which enables summer camps for special needs kids (Business Club)

- Harry Potter. Timed with the release of one of the movies, we put on a themed adult/child dinner that included tickets to the movie at the IMAX across the street. We decorated and organized the dining room to look like the Hogwarts dining hall with four long tables based on the four houses in the Harry Potter books. When members came with a child, the child was placed under the Sorting Hat and I had someone with a great voice backstage calling out the names of the Houses, according to where we had seated them for their reservation. The dinner, the room decorations, everything worked to perfection and the members and their children loved it. One member loved it so much that he asked to speak personally with the person who created it – me! When we meet now, he calls me "Harry Potter." He asked me how long I will remain with the Club because Disney needs to pick me up sometime soon! (Business Club)

ACHIEVING PROFITABILITY THROUGH PLANNING

- New to my job, I analyzed my accounts and requested a current run of spending reports. I noticed that several accounts had been spending well over their contracted amount as they advertised with the newspaper. I approached these accounts about signing a new contract at a level equal with their spending. Every one of the six accounts I approached with this option thanked me for my diligence and signed their new and higher contract levels. This resulted in a $40K increase in revenues for my newspaper, and a win-win for the newspaper as well as the client.

  By signing a higher contract level, the newspaper could count on the client achieving this higher level of spending for the next year and the client could count on the newspaper to supply them with lower rates than they had been receiving before. They could advertise more often and still spend the same. One of these accounts had previously been my manager's when she had been a sales person. I encouraged this account to sign at a level which was double what they had done before. They did and both my manager and her manager congratulated me for doing what my manager had been unable to do. (Newspaper)

- As a result of a corporate acquisition and reorganization in January 2007, some of my original Director of Member Relations job duties shifted and I assumed half the responsibilities of a laid-off Private Events director. My new title was Food and Beverage Director of Sales, and I had a $1.5 million sales plan to meet, one that is based on aggressive increases in both food and beverage prices as well as revenue targets. Since there was no marketing plan for this position, the first thing I did upon acquiring this new responsibility was to create and implement a comprehensive one, because up to this point, Private Events had simply relied on word-of-mouth. Four months into the year, we are on track to make plan. (Business Club)

- With only three months experience and only minimal training in my new job, my colleague / peer who was supposed to train me left the club, leaving me as the sole Private Event Director. I met the challenge head-on with a positive attitude tackling it through 13-hour days and six-day work weeks. One colleague commented that she wasn't sure how I managed to do it with a smile on my face every day. I surpassed budget for each month. Period 5 was the largest; The Private Event plan was $118,000; I exceed it by $29,000 with a final total of $149,000. I executed each event perfectly, without dropping a single ball. (Business Club)

- The Member Relations Director position planned and sold events based on what the members were interested in. However, at times I created and hosted events that were off everyone's radar screens, i.e. Chocolate Brunches, dance classes paired with a big dance event, Chocolate and Wine tastings, Scotch tastings and Hurricane Voo-Doo parties to ward off bad hurricanes. Because I was never afraid of trying something new, I constantly sold not just events, but new ideas and change to Club members, my own staff and Club management. I'm proud to say I always received the support I needed to make each new idea a success. (Business Club)

- When my company announced that there would be layoffs in my department, they said they would be making the cuts on the last-in / first-out basis. They called for volunteers and offered a fair package. Since I was the last in, I raised my hand because I just wanted to get on with it. I was astonished and then exceptionally gratified when my managers refused my offer, telling me I was too valuable to be let go and that they had a position for me in the new organization. I believe that says a lot about my productivity and work ethic. (Newspaper)

COURAGE / PERSONAL INITIATIVE

- One lesson I learned the hard way was that the climate set by the person in charge has a direct impact on the morale, commitment and productivity the entire organization. Tension among the staff and members in the light of a new General Manager was both high and continuous. His managerial style and manner of communication was not that to which we had been accustomed.

    He had come to us from another property within the company. Even though I was one of the youngest of his department heads, I took it upon myself to speak privately with him on more than one occasion. I felt uncomfortable walking the line between our boss and my colleagues, and developed a plan for how I wanted to conduct the conversation.

    My Manager and I agreed that I would share the feelings of the department heads while not attributing comments to any particular individual. My approach worked perfectly, and the results were dramatic. Within two months, everyone in the Club, including members, noticed and commented on the visible and sustained improvement in the climate and morale in the Club. I am proud of my initiative, and my willingness to face my fear and proceed. (Business Club)

- During a university internship, I worked in Alaska for a cruise ship company. Over that nine month period I worked my way up from cleaning toilets and waiting tables to a supervisory position. Toward the end of my internship, my ship struck a rock in Tracey Arm and began to sink. I kept my calm and did my part to help evacuate the 93 elderly passengers in just 21 minutes. Our entire crew was commended in the national press for having "responded professionally and according to protocol." (<u>Name of newspaper</u>, July 29, 1999) (Cruise ship company)

MENTORING AND EMPLOYEE DEVELOPMENT

- Our corporate headquarters had a formal mentoring program that involved all tenured Member Relations Directors. The company hired a young woman right out of college and into the position of Member Relations Director in a Club about 80 miles away from me. I was assigned to mentor her. I knew from first-hand experience that the Company's self-directed training program for certification as a Member Relations Director did not adequately and quickly train a new-hire to pass the exams.

  Because I also knew that her Club manager had given her only a six-month window to become certified, I decided to create a custom mentoring program designed to fill the voids I knew from personal experience existed because while working full-time, it took me over a year to pass the exams. While still maintaining my workload, I worked with her diligently on the phone, on both my time and company time, and spent one full weekend working with her at her Club. She passed her exams with flying colors and credits me with her success. Corporate and property general management recognized me for my willingness to go beyond expectations. (Business Club)

- I completed my university Senior Internship during my Junior year aboard a small cruise ship in Alaska. While working full-time on my ship duties, I completed my senior project, which was the creation from scratch of a comprehensive New-Hire Employee Handbook for use aboard ship, which to the best of my knowledge is still in use. (Cruise ship company / University)

COST-CONSCIOUS, HANDS-ON CREATIVITY

- After planning everything to the nth degree, I experienced the ***BEST THREE DAYS OF MY LIFE*** – my wedding. From the tiara to the train of my dress to the table arrangements – I planned everything, and had hands-on involvement in most of it as well. Everything within my control went just as I had envisioned it. Why is my wedding an accomplishment for my résumé? Because by utilizing my contacts with the industry and the area, and by doing many things myself, I created an elegant $15,500 wedding for only $8,371, a savings of $6,629. *I promise you that I am just as detail-oriented and cost-conscious when it comes to spending my employer's money as I am with my own.*

PROFESSIONAL EXPERIENCE:

HER EMPLOYER, CITY, STATE - July 2007 – Present
Real Estate Classified Advertising Sales Executive
Scope of responsibilities:
$1 million sales plan
Direct liaison for over 20 accounts contract levels ranging from $2,500 to $500K
Responsible for account development, recruiting new business and cultivating current business
Responsible for selling print, online, insertions and magazine advertising to all accounts

HER EMPLOYER, PROPERTY LOCATION. CITY, STATE - May 2001 – July 2007
Member Relations Director - February, 2002 to Date
Manager-in-Training - May, 2001 – February, 2002
Professional Accomplishments: Star Certified: Member Relations Director and Front Desk Attendant
Scope of responsibilities: Manage plethora of activities that increase member retention and food service revenue. Supervise two direct reports.
HER EMPLOYER, CITY, STATE - May - November, 1999 *(University Internship)*

Promoted to **Relief Lead Customer Service Representative Supervisor -** July – November, 1999
Name, phone number and e-mail address
Customer Service Representative - May – July, 1999
Scope of responsibilities: Supervised eight customer service employees providing range of dining and housekeeping services to an average of 100 passengers per trip from Seattle to Alaska, California and British Columbia

HER HOTEL EMPLOYER, PROPERTY. CITY, STATE - December 1997 - May 1999
Front Desk Shift Leader - October 1998 - May 1999
Front Desk Clerk - December 1997 – October 1998
Professional Accomplishment: Certified **HOTEL** New Hire Trainer
Scope of responsibilities: P&L responsibility for this 302-room property; supervised six

EDUCATION:
UNIVERSITY, School of Hospitality Management (accredited institution) CITY, STATE
Bachelor of Science in Hospitality Management - May, 2001
Minor: Food and Beverage. GPA: 3.0 and Dean's List

COMMUNITY COLLEGE. CITY, STATE December, 1998
Associate of Arts in Hotel and Motel Management G.P.A: 3.0

OUTSIDE INTERESTS:
- Traveling
- Hiking
- Backpacking
- Boxers
- Horseback riding
- Coordination of themed events
- Cooking and gourmet experimentation

Exercise Comments

OK. You have now gone through the complete process of creating a Professional Profile™ in the NARRATIVE format.

You might disagree with some of the *Special Skills* and *Accomplishments* she included or left in the Data Banks.

You might disagree with the order of presentation.

Perhaps you think it is too long. Or not.

Perhaps you noticed that some of her accomplishments were longer than six sentences.

Perhaps you would have created different subcategories.

Perhaps you found yourself getting to know her and like her.

Whatever your opinions – it's all good because **the only right answer is the one that worked for her.**

There was, however, a thought process.

After thinking about the intended recipients of her letter and Professional Profile™, and the impact she wanted to create as they read the documents, she ***intentionally*** decided to present herself as she did.

The key word is "*intentionally*" and that flexibility is the difference between a tailored Professional Profile™ and the more rigidly-structured one-size-fits-all reverse-chronological résumé.

And as I said, her credentials made her memorable and kept generating calls, even after she exited the job market.

"Judge by results. Often harsh. Always fair."

Before going to the next chapter, please step back and take stock of what you just read. Are you clear on the concept, or what questions do you have? How do you feel about what you read? Any "Ah-Ha's?" Please make your notes here.

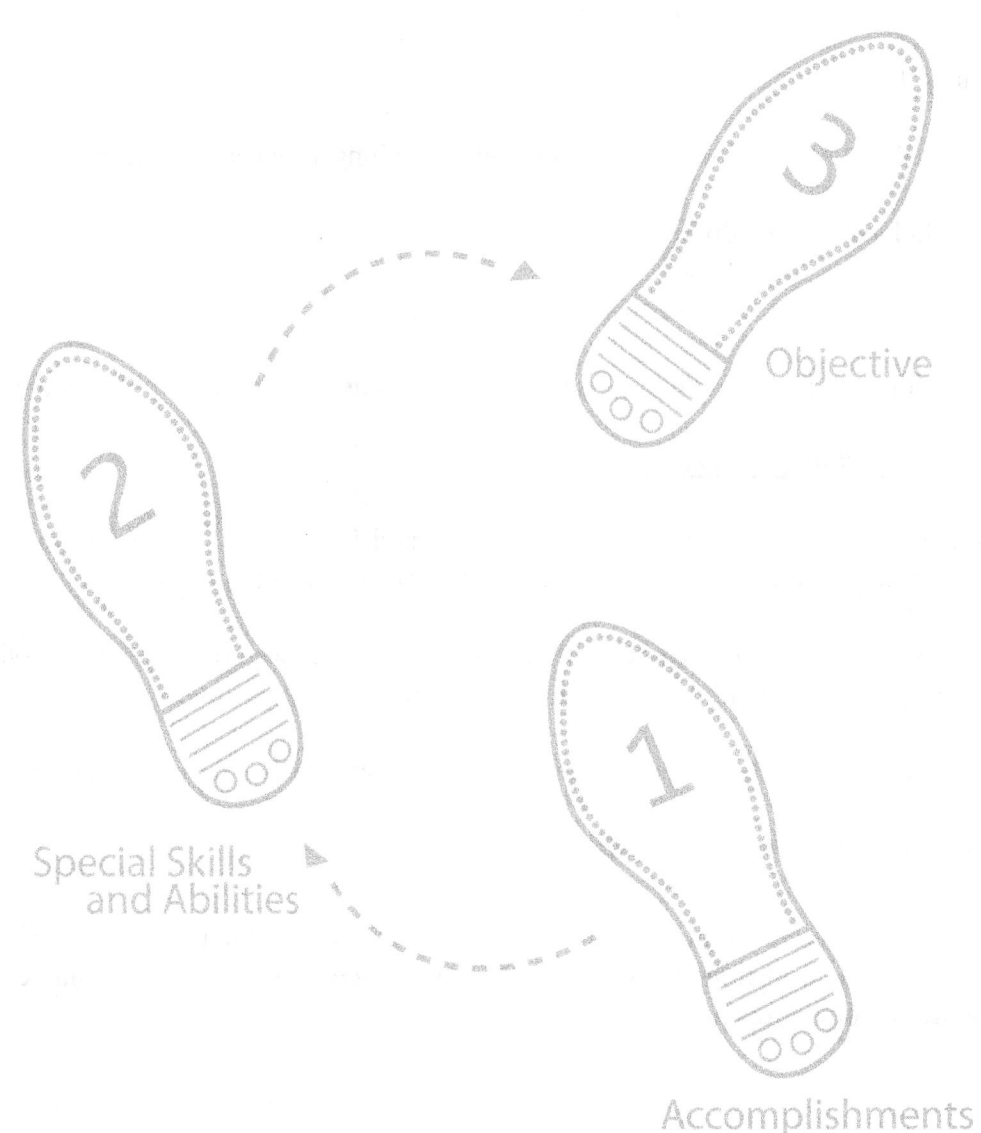

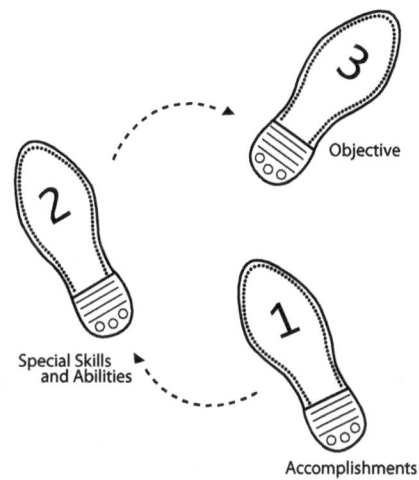

CHAPTER 8

The One-Page + Addendum Style

The **ONE-PAGE + ADDENDUM** style is what you can use when a company demands you submit a one-page résumé.

This format is prepared as a table and it fits on one page. Tightly, but it fits. On her document, she used the header for her contact information.

The intent of the Professional Profile™ is to enable you to be the meatball and stand out from the spaghetti.

When you combine the **One Page** with the **Addendum**, you comply with the company's one-page requirement AND memorably differentiate yourself from your competition.

Much as I would love to claim credit for the brilliance of the **One Page + Addendum** format, I can't. My daughter created it. She has taken what I taught her to a new level. She has given me permission to use her work. It was her Professional Profile™ you just read.

Here is her **One-Page.**

ALL CONTACT INFORMATION PRESENTED IN THE HEADER

Objective	A full-time permanent marketing management position where I am expected to analyze problems and needs, develop and implement creative, profitable solutions, and be accountable and rewarded for the results.
Experience	**Company / Position**

July 2007 to Date. City, State
- $1 million sales plan.
- Direct liaison for over 20 accounts ranging in dollar volume from $10k to $500k.
- Responsible for recruiting new business and selling vast array of products to current business.

Company. May, 2001 – June, 2007
Company/Position – (*Promotion*). January, 2007 to June, 2007. City, State
- $1.5 million sales plan
- Salesperson & planner for member & non-member events: weddings, anniversaries, legislative& business events
- Planned / Executed private event direct marketing campaign including creation of collateral materials for Club's Private Dining, Meeting & Wedding planning services

◆**Company/Position – (*Promotion.*) February, 2002 – January, 2007. City, State**
Planned, sold and marketed wide variety of business and social club events to Club's 1300 Members.
- Basing decisions on what membership asked for, increased Member Events from 40 events per year to 140 per year resulting in positive increase in revenue and increased member satisfaction.
- Responsibilities: Member to Club Liaison, Managed eight, member driven committees; Marketed all Club services via web site and newsletter; Supervised, hired, and trained two, full time front desk concierge agents. Primary responsibility – Member Satisfaction

◆ **Company/ Manager-in-Training. May, 2001 – February, 2002. City, State**
- First of six admitted to ClubCorp's first Manager-In-Training program - Only FIU student to be accepted
- Trained in: Membership, Food and Beverage, Member Relations, Catering and Kitchen
- Promoted into department head position prior to the end of the program

Internships	**University - Community Relations Intern** *(Second Internship - Senior Year)*

January, 2001 – May, 2001. University. City, State
- Active committee participant: created and executed events hosted by the University. Including Commencement Ceremonies, FIU Miami Film Festival, FIU Food & Wine Extravaganza (A..K.A The South Beach Food & Wine Festival hosted by Food & Wine Magazine)
- Asked by University to remain with the department in an Event Director capacity upon graduation

Company. Relief Customer Service Supervisor *(Promotion)* July – November, 1999
Company. Customer Service Representative - May – July, 1999
Company. May - November, 1999 *(University Internship)* City, State
 • Supervised eight customer service employees providing range of dining and housekeeping services to 100+ passengers per trip from Seattle to Alaska, California and British Columbia
5-Star Hotel. Front Desk Shift Leader. October, 1998 – May, 1999
5-Star Hotel. Front Desk Clerk. December, 1997 – October, 1998
5-Star Hotel (While a Full-time College Student) December, 1997 – May, 1999
- Certified **Hotel** New Hire Trainer, P&L responsibility for 302-room property; supervised six

University. May, 2001. Miami, FL

Education	- B.S., Hospitality Management - 3.0 GPA and Dean's List (accredited institution).

Community College. December, 1998. Miami, FL
- Associate of Arts in Hotel and Motel Management GPA: 3.0

Interests	- Traveling & hiking
	- Personal growth seminars: Rich Dad Poor Dad Goal Setting Seminar and Real Estate Investing Seminars (all self-financed)
	- Personal Interest in Real Estate – Own and Manage one Investment Property
	- Software: website content creation, proficient and self-taught in Microsoft Word, Excel, PowerPoint and On-Line Services

There you have the essentials, packed onto just one page. If that's all a company wants, they have it. She devoted a good deal of space to "Internships" because they were unique experiences for her and helped set her apart.

How would you use the space? Special certifications? Military experience? Professional affiliations? Volunteerism? Special licenses?

Remember, one of the purposes of an effective Professional Profile™ or résumé is to show as many relevant facets of you as there are, until such time as you can speak for yourself.

The **One-Page** contains a lot of information, but my daughter is an over-achiever and one page can only convey so much, most of it generic. She goes above-and-beyond in all that she does, and she created a brilliant twist – she calls it a **One Page +** *Addendum.*

With the **One-Page**, she is in compliance with the mandate for a one-page document.

With the *Addendum*, she is simply providing additional information; the company is free to consider it or discard it.

Clever. Inventive. Shows initiative. An astute reader will learn something important about her character.

The *Addendum* contains the same SPECIAL SKILLS AND ABILITIES as well as the same REPRESENTATIVE PROFESSIONAL ACCOMPLISHMENTS as presented in the **Narrative** format.

What makes the *Addendum* format additionally unique is the inclusion of the two paragraphs immediately preceding the SPECIAL SKILLS table.

- Please note the gentle phrasing of the first paragraph in which she acknowledges the one-page requirement and then politely explains why she went beyond it.

- The second paragraph is a free-form opportunity to tell the reader something important about herself, her values and work ethic. Not a lot. Just an interesting taste.

For your purposes, think about a critical piece of information you want the potential employer or customer to know about you – something unique that will make you the meatball and leave the spaghetti on the plate.

The approach is powerful and she has used it effectively.

If you are considering using the *One-Page + Addendum* format, we offer two points of caution:

1. For the first two paragraphs of the *Addendum*, use no more than one-and-a-half inches of space;

2. For the SPECIAL SKILLS AND ABILITIES table, use no more than three inches. Make certain you will have at least the last three inches of the printable space on that page to get into the REPRESENTATIVE PROFESSIONAL ACCOMPLISHMENTS.

Here is the complete **ONE-PAGE** + *ADDENDUM*
ADDENDUM: NAME, TELEPHONE, EMAIL ADDRESS

<u>***ALL CONTACT INFORMATION PRESENTED IN THE HEADER***</u>

Objective   A full-time permanent marketing management position where I am expected to analyze problems and needs, develop and implement creative, profitable solutions, and be accountable and rewarded for the results.

Experience   **<u>Company / Position</u>**
<u>July 2007 to Date. City, State</u>
- $1 million sales plan.
- Direct liaison for over 20 accounts ranging in dollar volume from $10k to $500k.
- Responsible for recruiting new business and selling vast array of products to current business.

<u>Company. May, 2001 – June, 2007</u>
<u>Company/Position – (Promotion). January, 2007 to June, 2007. City, State</u>
- $1.5 million sales plan
- Salesperson & planner for member & non-member events: weddings, anniversaries, legislative& business events
- Planned / Executed private event direct marketing campaign including creation of collateral materials for Club's Private Dining, Meeting & Wedding planning services

◆**<u>Company/Position – (*Promotion*.) February, 2002 – January, 2007. City, State</u>**
<u>Planned, sold and marketed wide variety of business and social club events to Club's 1300 Members.</u>
- Basing decisions on what membership asked for, increased Member Events from 40 events per year to 140 per year resulting in positive increase in revenue and increased member satisfaction.
- Responsibilities: Member to Club Liaison, Managed eight, member driven committees; Marketed all Club services via web site and newsletter; Supervised, hired, and trained two, full time front desk concierge agents. Primary responsibility – Member Satisfaction

◆ **<u>Company/ Manager-in-Training. May, 2001 – February, 2002. City, State</u>**
- First of six admitted to ClubCorp's first Manager-In-Training program - Only FIU student to be accepted
- Trained in: Membership, Food and Beverage, Member Relations, Catering and Kitchen
- Promoted into department head position prior to the end of the program

Internships   **<u>University - Community Relations Intern</u>** *(Second Internship - Senior Year)*
<u>January, 2001 – May, 2001. University. City, State</u>
- Active committee participant: created and executed events hosted by the University. Including Commencement Ceremonies, FIU Miami Film Festival, FIU Food & Wine Extravaganza (A..K.A The South Beach Food & Wine Festival hosted by Food & Wine Magazine)
- Asked by University to remain with the department in an Event Director capacity upon graduation

<u>Company. Relief Customer Service Supervisor</u> *(Promotion)* **<u>July – November, 1999</u>**
<u>Company. Customer Service Representative - May – July, 1999</u>
<u>Company. May - November, 1999</u> *(University Internship)* **<u>City, State</u>**
- Supervised eight customer service employees providing range of dining and housekeeping services to 100+ passengers per trip from Seattle to Alaska, California and British Columbia

<u>5-Star Hotel. Front Desk Shift Leader. October, 1998 – May, 1999</u>
<u>5-Star Hotel. Front Desk Clerk. December, 1997 – October, 1998</u>
<u>5-Star Hotel (While a Full-time College Student) December, 1997 – May, 1999</u>
- Certified **Hotel** New Hire Trainer, P&L responsibility for 302-room property; supervised six

<u>University. May, 2001. Miami, FL</u>
Education
- B.S., Hospitality Management - 3.0 GPA and Dean's List (accredited institution).

<u>Community College. December, 1998. Miami, FL</u>
- Associate of Arts in Hotel and Motel Management GPA: 3.0
- Traveling & hiking

Interests
- Personal growth seminars: Rich Dad Poor Dad Goal Setting Seminar and Real Estate Investing Seminars (all self-financed)
- Personal Interest in Real Estate – Own and Manage one Investment Property
- Software: website content creation, proficient and self-taught in Microsoft Word, Excel, PowerPoint and On-Line Services

This is an addendum to my résumé. A single page résumé shows the reader only a fraction of the candidate's skills and experience. For my job search, I have created data bases of my most relevant *Personal Traits, Special Skills and Abilities*, and my most significant *Representative Professional Accomplishments*. The ones that follow most closely coincide with your position requirements.

This is what I have learned: My post-college work with both the *NEWSPAPER* and the BUSINESS CLUB has taught me that I am here to make a difference by making improvements. I am not here to maintain the status quo. At first, coming out of an hourly job into my first salaried position, I did not realize I could improve upon current procedures if I saw a way to make work processes more effective or efficient. Once I realized I could, I took the initiative and I made changes, which resulted in a more effective use of time and money for co-workers and for the bottom line as well.

PERSONAL TRAITS, SPECIAL SKILLS AND ABILITIES

- Hold high expectations for my performance, strive for high levels of personal achievement
- Routinely achieve profit objectives while working within established budgets
- Consensus builder; strong personal influencing skills; rapidly put people at ease and rapidly build trust

- Maintain poise, self-confidence in free-flowing situations; adjust and thrive in new environments
- Committed to achieving and maintaining consistently high levels of client satisfaction
- Take initiative to create pragmatic, effective solutions to business problems

- Quick study; able to apply what I have learned and work effectively without supervision
- Confident when faced with learning new software / computer applications
- Happy person, committed to both my colleagues and my company

REPRESENTATIVE PROFESSIONAL ACCOMPLISHMENTS

MARKETING CREATIVITY FOR PROFITABILITY, FUNDRAISING AND GOOD WILL

- During my first New Home Open House program, I wondered: *Why do we devote two whole pages to an ineffective map when each home listing is equipped with directions?"* No one could answer that question for me since they'd been doing it that way for a while, so I created an alternative, which the newspaper adopted and still uses to this day. My solution was to group homes located in the same region together to make it easier for the reader to find homes in areas they are interested in; it encouraged the listing agent to offer a web address for more information and it returned the back two pages of the map to the advertising sales staff as additional space they could sell for revenue generation. (Newspaper)

- As Member Relations Director, I managed a number of member committees. The "Women on the Move" committee was one of my most committed and dynamic. Within the company, I know of at least five sister Clubs that have copied my design. It has been a very successful forum for building political and community relations. The relationship of which I am most proud is the one we have established with NATIONAL BOOK STORE. On my initiative, I contacted their regional marketing director and we have formed an ongoing relationship bringing visiting authors to speak at dinner events at the Club. It has been a popular win/win for BOOK STORE, the authors, my members, and the Club. (Business Club)

- Clay Aiken's Foundation approached the Club to partner with them in a fundraiser for charity. We accepted their offer, and I was responsible for marketing the event. Within one month, we had sold out the event to the maximum capacity of our facility. Working with his Foundation, I developed marketing pieces, helped design and write ad copy for our newsletter and members' website (both of which I wrote and maintained), developed and implemented an e-mail and poster campaign for the Club, and facilitated an introduction to the local newspaper's Features Editor. This was the first event of this kind we have done and it was a stellar success; over 50 members participated and we raised over $300,000 for his foundation, which enables summer camps for special needs kids (Business Club)

- Harry Potter. Timed with the release of one of the movies, we put on a themed adult/child dinner that included tickets to the movie at the IMAX across the street. We decorated and organized the dining room to look like the Hogwarts dining hall with four long tables based on the four houses in the Harry Potter books. When members came with a child, the child was placed under the Sorting Hat and I had someone with a great voice backstage calling out the names of the Houses, according to where we had seated them for their reservation. The dinner, the room decorations, everything worked to perfection and the members and their children loved it. One member loved it so much that he asked to speak personally with the person who created it – me! When we meet now, he calls me "Harry Potter." He asked me how long I will remain with the Club because Disney needs to pick me up sometime soon! (Business Club)

ACHIEVING PROFITABILITY THROUGH PLANNING

- New to my job, I analyzed my accounts and requested a current run of spending reports. I noticed that several accounts had been spending well over their contracted amount as they advertised with the newspaper. I approached these accounts about signing a new contract at a level equal with their spending. Every one of the six accounts I approached with this option thanked me for my diligence and signed their new and higher contract levels. This resulted in a $40K increase in revenues for my newspaper, and a win-win for the newspaper as well as the client.

  By signing a higher contract level, the newspaper could count on the client achieving this higher level of spending for the next year and the client could count on the newspaper to supply them with lower rates than they had been receiving before. They could advertise more often and still spend the same. One of these accounts had previously been my manager's when she had been a sales person. I encouraged this account to sign at a level which was double what they had done before. They did and both my manager and her manager congratulated me for doing what my manager had been unable to do. (Newspaper)

- As a result of a corporate acquisition and reorganization in January 2007, some of my original Director of Member Relations job duties shifted and I assumed half the responsibilities of a laid-off Private Events director. My new title was Food and Beverage Director of Sales, and I had a $1.5 million sales plan to meet, one that is based on aggressive increases in both food and beverage prices as well as revenue targets. Since there was no marketing plan for this position, the first thing I did upon acquiring this new responsibility was to create and implement a comprehensive one, because up to this point, Private Events had simply relied on word-of-mouth. Four months into the year, we are on track to make plan. (Business Club)

- With only three months experience and only minimal training in my new job, my colleague / peer who was supposed to train me left the club, leaving me as the sole Private Event Director. I met the challenge head-on with a positive attitude tackling it through 13-hour days and six-day work weeks. One colleague commented that she wasn't sure how I managed to do it with a smile on my face every day. I surpassed budget for each month. Period 5 was the largest; The Private Event plan was $118,000; I exceed it by $29,000 with a final total of $149,000. I executed each event perfectly, without dropping a single ball. (Business Club)

- The Member Relations Director position planned and sold events based on what the members were interested in. However, at times I created and hosted events that were off everyone's radar screens, i.e. Chocolate Brunches, dance classes paired with a big dance event, Chocolate and Wine tastings, Scotch tastings and Hurricane Voo-Doo parties to ward off bad hurricanes. Because I was never afraid of trying something new, I constantly sold not just events, but new ideas and change to Club members, my own staff and Club management. I'm proud to say I always received the support I needed to make each new idea a success. (Business Club)

- When my company announced that there would be layoffs in my department, they said they would be making the cuts on the last-in / first-out basis. They called for volunteers and offered a fair package. Since I was the last in, I raised my hand because I just wanted to get on with it. I was astonished and then exceptionally gratified when my managers refused my offer, telling me I was too valuable to be let go and that they had a position for me in the new organization. I believe that says a lot about my productivity and work ethic. (Newspaper)

COURAGE / PERSONAL INITIATIVE

- One lesson I learned the hard way was that the climate set by the person in charge has a direct impact on the morale, commitment and productivity the entire organization. Tension among the staff and members in the light of a new General Manager was both high and continuous. His managerial style and manner of communication was not that to which we had been accustomed.

  He had come to us from another property within the company. Even though I was one of the youngest of his department heads, I took it upon myself to speak privately with him on more than one occasion. I felt uncomfortable walking the line between our boss and my colleagues, and developed a plan for how I wanted to conduct the conversation. My Manager and I agreed that I would share the feelings of the department heads while not attributing comments to any particular individual.

  My approach worked perfectly, and the results were dramatic. Within two months, everyone in the Club, including members, noticed and commented on the visible and sustained improvement in the climate and morale in the Club. I am proud of my initiative, and my willingness to face my fear and proceed. (Business Club)

- During a university internship, I worked in Alaska for a cruise ship company. Over that nine month period I worked my way up from cleaning toilets and waiting tables to a supervisory position. Toward the end of my internship, my ship struck a rock in Tracey Arm and began to sink. I kept my calm and did my part to help evacuate the 93 elderly passengers in just 21 minutes. Our entire crew was commended in the national press for having "responded professionally and according to protocol." (Name of newspaper, July 29, 1999) (Cruise ship company)

MENTORING AND EMPLOYEE DEVELOPMENT

- Our corporate headquarters had a formal mentoring program that involved all tenured Member Relations Directors. The company hired a young woman right out of college and into the position of Member Relations Director in a Club about 80 miles away from me. I was assigned to mentor her. I knew from first-hand experience that the Company's self-directed training program for certification as a Member Relations Director did not adequately and quickly train a new-hire to pass the exams. Because I also knew that her Club manager had given her only a six-month window to become certified, I decided to create a custom mentoring program designed to fill the voids I knew from personal experience existed because while working full-time, it took me over a year to pass the exams.

  While still maintaining my workload, I worked with her diligently on the phone, on both my time and company time, and spent one full weekend working with her at her Club. She passed her exams with flying colors and credits me with her success. Corporate and property general management recognized me for my willingness to go beyond expectations. (Business Club)

- I completed my university Senior Internship during my Junior year aboard a small cruise ship in Alaska. While working full-time on my ship duties, I completed my senior project, which was the creation from scratch of a comprehensive New-Hire Employee Handbook for use aboard ship, which to the best of my knowledge is still in use. (Cruise ship company / University)

COST-CONSCIOUS, HANDS-ON CREATIVITY

- After planning everything to the nth degree, I experienced the ***BEST THREE DAYS OF MY LIFE*** – my wedding. From the tiara to the train of my dress to the table arrangements – I planned everything, and had hands-on involvement in most of it as well. Everything within my control went just as I had envisioned it. Why is my wedding an accomplishment for my résumé? Because by utilizing my contacts with the industry and the area, and by doing many things myself, I created an elegant $15,500 wedding for only $8,371, a savings of $6,629. *I promise you that I am just as detail-oriented and cost-conscious when it comes to spending my employer's money as I am with my own.*

End of *ONE-PAGE + ADDENDUM*

Reviewing the First Two Styles of Professional Profiles™

You have now seen the exact same information presented in two different formats – Narrative and One-Page + Addendum.

Before we move to the third and final format (Technical + Narrative) we invite you to pause a moment and clarify your thoughts regarding the first two formats.

Please take a moment and visualize the information you intend to present – your accomplishments statements, your special skills and abilities, and your "Part B" – and how it would look in each format.

Given the circumstances in which you will submit your Professional Profiles™ and targeted cover letters, which of these two formats do you feel will help you be memorable while representing you most effectively?

Keeping in mind that you want your Professional Profile™ to stand out in a unique and authentic manner, please jot down the pros and cons - your thoughts and impressions - of both formats.

Before going to the next chapter, please step back and take stock again of what has been presented THAT WORKED! Are you getting clear on the concept, or what questions do you have? How do you feel about what you read? Any "Ah-Ha's?" Like we've said before, please make your notes here.

We hope you are getting excited about your own future!

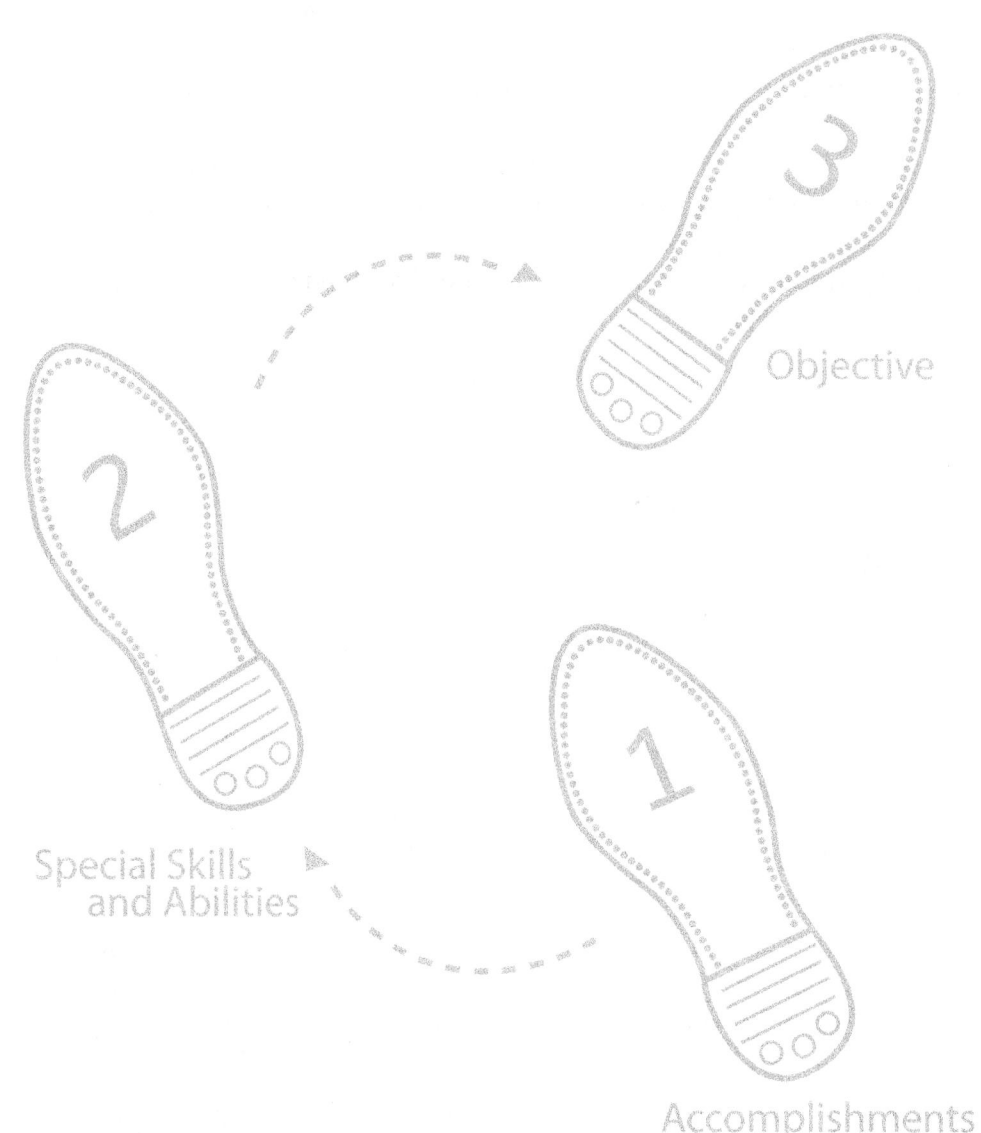

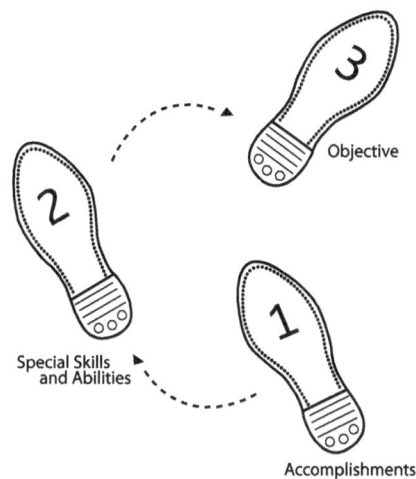

CHAPTER 9

The Technical + Narrative Style

Here is the third variation. Like the *Addendum* format, I (Don) cannot take credit for it. My son combined my *Narrative* format with one he learned from a colleague and modified it for his technology-based job search when he got out of the Navy.

This format makes it very easy to know at a glance what technical expertise the applicant has in terms of hardware, software, operating systems, database management, systems administration and the like. You'll find several examples of this format in the Appendix.

I (Don) like this format very much, and use it for my Profile. Don't let the word "Technical" intimidate you. If you are not a "technical" person (as I am not) but have specific things you want the reader to immediately see, (as I do), this is an effective and attention-getting format.

Out of a field of over 50 applicants, my son used this Professional Profile™ to secure the interview that resulted in a position as systems engineer at a prestigious engineering university.

It would have been much easier for him to have simply listed job duties and responsibilities, rather than wrestle with **accomplishments.** We spent a lot of time asking and answering the question, *"SO WHAT?"* until we transformed his "activities-based" reverse-chronological résumé into an accomplishments-based Professional Profile™.

As you read his credentials, you may notice that my son does not have a college degree. While I cannot prove it, I believe that it was his orientation to results and his willingness to present himself in terms of what he had *accomplished* in the Navy and civilian jobs that set him apart from the other applicants, (most of whom had degrees), and won him the position.

Perhaps you would like to give some thought to the implications of that last paragraph – yes?

Specialized Industry Knowledge:
Computer and Information Technology, Defense and Federal Systems

Operating Systems Expertise
Windows - XP Pro, 2000, NT, ME, 98, 95, Workgroups, DOS, UNIX(HP-UX 10.20)

Hardware Expertise
DELL, Compaq, Hewlett-Packard, Digital, IBM PCs, Laptops, and compatibles, PDAs, RAID, XYLAN/Alcatel, Cisco Switches, 3COM, SCSI, Scanners, Printers, CD/DVD RW Drives, Jaz, Zip, Tape Drives, Digital Cameras, Smart Phones, PKI

Software Expertise
Adobe PhotoShop, IE 7 and previous versions, Ghost, Microsoft Office Professional 2007 and previous versions, MS Exchange 5.5, WordPerfect, MS FrontPage, VISIO, Netscape, Norton (AntiVirus, CleanSweep, Ghost), McAffee, Norton Internet Security, SpyBot, AVG, WinZip, TeamViewer

Database Expertise
MS Access, Centuras SQLBase

Network Protocol Expertise:
DNS, DHCP, Ethernet, FastEthernet, Fiber, Token Ring, IIS, IP, WINS, TCP/IP, Wi-Fi

Network Management Expertise:
Network Administration, Network OS Installation and Upgrades, Network Security

Systems Administration Expertise:
2003/2000/NT 4.0 Server Administration – add/delete/modify accounts, user rights/limits/passwords, tape backups/restores. Exchange Server 5.5 Administration – add/delete/modify accounts, user rights/limits/passwords, tape backups/restores. Software and Server OS Installations and Upgrades. Systems Troubleshooting. Systems Storage Management. Security Risk Management Network Software Installations.

Network Support Expertise:
Support Desktop Systems Configurations and Troubleshooting, Expert Support Problem Resolution, Very Strong Positive Customer Support and Team Player

Web, Application & Messaging Servers Expertise: MS Exchange 5.5, FrontPage 2000, and 2002, 2003, LanChat, Game Server, MP3 Server

NAME/Address/Telephone/Email

Objective: UNIVERSITY Systems Engineer / Network Administrator

Overview of Professional Experience

Top-Secret and SCI clearance since 10/00 through US Navy and authorized access to Federal Bureau of Investigation (FBI) 01/02 – 07/06. Ten years experience in these areas: managing, configuring, upgrading, adds/moves/changes to LANs/WANs, servers, PCs, and laptops. Level I & Level II desk-side/phone/remote support, troubleshooting Network systems design, implementation, and administration. Effectively manage and maintain equipment worth millions of dollars

RELEVANT PROFESSIONAL EXPERIENCE:
Network Set-up:

Administrator on GOVERNMENT AGENCY'S Secret network operating on W2K and Unclassified network running XP Pro.

One of five techs to install 130+ Compaq workstations, HP printers and scanners and over 100 P.O.S. (Point Of Sales) Partech systems on the Windows 2000 platform in allotted one month time frame without errors

Member of team that set up over 20,000 FBI Dell workstations, 2,400 printers, 1,200 scanners (including multifunction printer/scanner/copier/fax), 1,300 Cisco Switches, and over 1,200 Cisco Routers. All accomplished on time, on budget and without error

Implemented relocation of eight servers on two networks using TCP/IP communications with an Ethernet backbone on a Windows NT 4.0 platform. 24/7 user support

Utilized Top Secret/SCI Clearance to provide desk-side & phone support to users running Windows NT 4.0 workstation. Completed NT administration functions; adds/moves/changes including assisting the replacement of well over 1500 Dell and HP workstations; installing NT4.0 and all civilian and government applications to Navy standards; documented PCs, printers, scanners; assisted in the offload of old PCs to DRMS (Defense Reutilization and Marketing Service)

Personally responsible for 2 networked medical and dental programs SNAP (System Non-tactical Allocated Program) Allocated Medical System (SAMS) and Dental Management Information System (DENMIS) consisting of 9 workstations and the main database on a Compaq Rack Mounted Server.

Accountable for: configuration/installation/maintenance of software, user management, global point-of-contact for customer support. Successfully upgraded program from DOS to Windows 32- bit in minimal down time

Page 2 – Name, Relevant Professional Experience – Continued

DATA MIGRATION:

Migrated GOVERNMENT AGENCY'S existing field offices and smaller remote sites from a token ring Novell network base infrastructure to a scalable fiber Ethernet infrastructure that supports their current capacity and beyond

SYSTEM UPGRADES:

Implementation team member for - replacement of over 5,000 3-Com 905 NICs with 990 NICs. Ran CAT5 and Fiber drops for the US Navy and GOVERNMENT AGENCY

Independently reloaded an entirely new ATIS Server (Networked TAG RAID Database and a 7-Bay CD-ROM) on a Digital Polaris ZX 6000 Series SCSI Server. Installed Windows NT Server 4.0, Centura's SQLBase Server 6.1.2-PTF4, MS Office 97 suite and Microsoft Service Pack 3

Independently installed and configured NETg training software on UNCLASS network, which consisted of over 30 CD's. Trained co-workers on the management of the software and user database

Disassembled a 9 slot XYLAN Switch with over 100 CAT 5 cables and 10 fiber connections for maintenance and reassembled in minimal downtime

Provided special project coordination and implementation of software and operating system upgrades, and assisted groups with migrating and testing new software to support their individual needs. Involved in the deployment of, and provided support for, the following applications: MS Office, Microsoft Outlook, Internet Explorer, Netscape, WinZip, which I have installed on end-user's workstations

STAFF TRAINING:

Trained over 150 appointed GOVERNMENT AGENCY employees in group and individual sessions to become proficient as PKI RAs (Registration Authority) in the allotted time

Trained over 40 GOVERNMENT AGENCY Computer Specialists on their startup and installation scripts and how to reclone their workstations, enabling all users to learn and apply uniform applications and procedures to effectively use new Dell systems. Completed all training within budgeted time frame

Developed and implemented training for over 30 Navy co-workers by group and individual sessions on installation of software, management of users, proper backups and restores, and fixes for common system configuration issues.

Developed and implemented training for over 50 Navy co-workers in the use and administration of the network to include NT4.0 server farm integration and basic network troubleshooting tips through the writing / presentation of lectures / briefs

DATA MANAGEMENT:

Managed Ship's supplies and parts database on an HP UX 10.20 OS (SNAP) used by the entire ship of 800+ clients

CUSTOMER INTERFACE:

Managed user rights, network and server access, and mail box limits on all three Classified and Unclassified networks, comprised of 25 servers and more than 1,000 workstations running various operation systems while serving on USS Blue Ridge (Communications Ship and personal vessel of the Pacific Fleet US Admiral)

Provided full-time, 24/7 support to users, including: network/server support Windows NT. 4.0 platform; on-site desktop support for PCs with Windows 95/98/NT4.0/2000 operating systems and continuous on-site support for Applications, Printers, Scanners, CD R/W drives, NICs

* As NT Administrator, stood day and night shifts on board ship and on shore in Japan. **Day duties:** consisted of taking trouble calls, entering them into an MS Access database trouble log, resolving user hardware, software or network problems, or escalating as necessary and providing Level I and II (telephone) support, or Level III on-site support. Provided excellent customer service: created/deleted/ modified user accounts and email accounts, resolved wide range of trouble calls including faulty hardware problems, missing or corrupt files, training users how to use their workstation, applications and connecting hardware. **Night duties**: ran system backups, weekly network reboots, maintained action log of actions/alarms/situations, answered trouble calls, handled any open trouble calls the day shift were unable to complete, downloaded up-to-date virus updates, uploaded them to the servers and pushed them out to every workstation

PROFESSIONAL HISTORY:

TECHNICAL CONTRACT COMPANY, Federal Group – Senior Systems Engineer – 9/2004 – 7/2006
GOVERNMENT AGENCY ITS Support Contractor: 9/2005 – 7/2006 (completion)
Solely responsible for the Denver Field Office and all eighteen surrounding Colorado and Wyoming offices as the support for the local ITS (Information Technology Specialist)

Administrators. Provide the ITSs with troubleshoot training techniques prior to and/or when problems arise. Voluntarily created batch scripts that simplified tasks which notably saved them time and money.

GOVERNMENT AGENCY *PKI Deployment*: Contract duration *9/2004 – 7/2005* (completion)
In a team of 4, traveled to 26 major US GOVERNMENT AGENCY field offices/cities in a 10 month span as a RM (Registration Manager) to register all personnel in each office, install card readers, volunteered to train appointed individuals to become RAs (Registration Authorities - PKI Administrator) in each office totaling over 150 Admins, and without being asked, created simple step-by-step procedures for the RAs to follow which the GOVERNMENT AGENCY uses as a modified standard GOVERNMENT AGENCY-wide.
Reason for Leaving: Contract completed 7/2006, no contracts followed

*TECHNICAL CONTRACT COMPANY –CRUISE SHIP CLIENT – **Contract duration: 6/2003 – 7/2003***
One of five chosen to travel to Monfalcone, Italy to install P.O.S. Systems, Compaq workstations, HP scanners, digital scanners, printers, network printers, multi-function printers and BOCA printers throughout CRUISE SHIP CLIENT'S newest ship, the Glory. All competed within the allotted one month time frame without errors.
Reason for Leaving: Contract and installation completed

*TECHNICAL CONTRACTS COMPANY. –GOVERNMENT AGENCY CLIENT – **Contract duration: 1/2002 – 3/2003 & 8/2003 – 6/2004***
Team member and batch scripts writer on GOVERNMENT AGENCY'S Project installation team traveling nationwide to upgrade GOVERNMENT AGENCY'S networks, servers, and desktop PCs. Direct- responsibility for creating install scripts for ITs to run on each site's workstations
Reason for Leaving 3/2003: Downsized when GOVERNMENT AGENCY was forced to make budget cuts
Reason for Leaving 6/2004: Contract completed 4/2004, no contracts followed
Network Systems Administrator / Technician

US Navy, 9/1998 – 9/2001. Rank: E-4. Honorable discharge.
Served our country as a Network / Systems Administrator / Technician (multi-purpose) on board the only Communications Ship in the Pacific Ocean, USS Blue Ridge (LCC 19), Yokosuka, Japan. Responsible for managing three networks, each with a different security classification: Unclassified, Secret, SCI/Top Secret.
Reason for Leaving: Completed enlistment commitment

CERTIFICATIONS AND EDUCATION:
DCSE (Dell Certified System Expert) 1999
Information Systems Technology (IT) "A" School. US Navy. Great Lakes, IL. 1997
Security Clearance: Top Secret/SCI currently in OPR. Initially awarded October, 2000 through Department of Defense

REFERENCES:
Provided as appropriate

~ **End of *TECHNICAL + NARRATIVE*** ~

Summarizing the Three Styles of Professional Profiles™

Well, we are pretty much as the end of our Professional Profile™ rope.

Over the last four chapters you have:

- Learned how to effectively present your generic and unchanging information **(Part B)**
- Had the opportunity to practice using Data Bases in the "Selectivity" exercise around Special Skills and Abilities and Representative Professional Accomplishments and then
- Compared your selections with a successful Professional Profile™
- Learned how to construct the three different Professional Profile™ formats:

  - Narrative
  - One-Page + *Addendum*
  - Technical + *Narrative*

You now have the tools to kick your search for new customers or new work up to the next level and make your phone ring with a recruiter or potential client on the other end of the line.

BUT before you head out, we'd be sorry to see you apply **the same old "spaghetti" cover letters** and **job search strategies** with your brand new, cool and unique **stand-out-like-a-*"MEATBALL"* Professional Profile™.**

So, please proceed to **Chapter 10 - the Bonus Section** for our parting gift to you.

And with the **Bonus Section** under your belt, feel free to browse the **Appendix** and read the real cover letters and real Professional Profiles™ that got real results for real people.

Did you make it this far determined to understand why we are so committed to people doing the work to establish a Professional Profile™ for themselves that they will also PROACTIVELY maintain?

Are you clear on the concept, or what questions do you have? How do you feel about what you read? Any "Ah-Ha's?" Please make your notes here.

And we'd love to hear from you. Many of the people we have worked with struggled at first, but then told us they were glad for the experience. Why?

They had a better picture of themselves professionally, they were excited to talk about! We'd love the same for you.

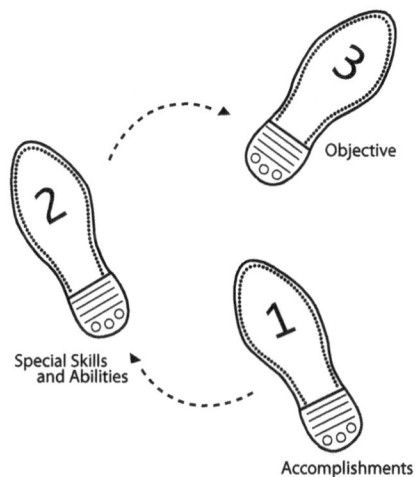

CHAPTER 10

The Bonus Section

The Bonus Section is all about being the meatball!

Stand Out!

We will help you with:

- **Targeted Cover Letters**
- **Exploratory Cover Letters**
- **Job Search Strategies**
- **Four Magic Sentences**

Using Your New Professional Profile™ in Ways that Make You Stand Out

When clients read their new Professional Profiles™ the first time, they are frequently stunned and amazed at all they have accomplished. Some even cry. Truly.

We absolutely love it when their eyes light up, or sometimes go misty, and they ask, *"Who **is** this person and **where** have you been all my life?"*

We hope you have that same experience. (We'd love to hear from you about your experience -- before you officially start the process, as you are going through it, and after you can call it done!)

You now have everything you need to create your own Professional Profile™. We've fulfilled our part of the deal, and the next steps, creating your own Skills and Accomplishments Data Banks, your Part B, your Professional Profiles™, and then using them effectively, is up to you.

As our parting gift to you, we'd like to offer some suggestions and strategies for using your new Professional Profile™. They've worked very effectively for others and we expect they will for you as well.

There's no sense to having gone to all this effort if you are going to use your new tool in the same old ways.

Introduction to Cover Letters

For years I (Don) kept a collection of the most ludicrous, ineffective, embarrassing and downright funny cover letters I received and kept them in a file called, *"WHAT? Are You Kidding Me?!"* But somewhere along the way, it went away.

Going back thirty years, I can still recall the best three of the bunch.

My favorite was a typed letter from a minister who sold a full range of insurance products on the side.

Right in the first paragraph, he told me his last name was Bishop and told me, and I quote, *"You can call me Bish."*

"Bish" had prepared a neatly-typed letter in which he provided a detailed list of everything he expected the company to do for him, once we hired him.

The list was extensive, and he amplified it with precisely-drawn lines going to empty spaces all over the page. In very meticulous printing, he added probably 15 additional expectations and explanations.

His letter made a lasting impression on me, but not a good one. I didn't call him.

The second letter was from an experienced sales representative. His résumé was complete and impressive. I did not mind that his cover letter slipped over onto a second page because it contained a good deal of relevant information.

As I turned the page, I was getting more and more interested in what he had to say. That is, until he ended the letter telling me in no uncertain terms that the only way he would consider accepting an offer would be if we agreed, in writing, to let him bring his wife on all trips, fly them both First Class, put them up only in premier hotels and pay them each a daily stipend of $1,000.

He was serious. So was I. Thank you, noooo.

The third letter came from a young woman just out of college. Evidentially someone had advised her that flattery was the absolute best way to get an interview.

She gushingly dedicated all but the short final paragraph to praising my employer up one wall and down the other. I would have been honored to work for the company she said we were.

According to her, we were a leading force of social change in the community (which we absolutely were not), that our customer service was legendary (which it absolutely was not), and that we were a significant global presence (which made me laugh as we were just starting to think two time zones beyond ours.) She closed with an impassioned plea to give her the honor of working with such a wonderful organization.

In due time, all three applicants received a TBNT letter.

I know that those three are extremes, and that you would never jeopardize a potential opportunity with such silliness on your part.

Nonetheless, silliness happens, as they say.

Elements of Targeted Cover Letters

This three-part format has worked well for me and for others. I urge you to consider using it yourself.

With such high levels of unemployment and so many résumés to process and maybe read, recruiters, interviewers and potential customers are busy people. Their eyes can only take so much, so forego using platitudes and air-words. Get to the point. Give them what they need.

Part One:

In a couple of short sentences, tell the recipient what you want, or the position for which you are applying, and if applicable how you learned about the opportunity.

Part Two:

Since you will already know the key requirements of the position and know you are a good match before you submit your Professional Profile™, create a two-column *"Parallel Assessment"* table.

Give the left column the heading **"YOU SEEK"** and using bullet points, summarize the three to five most critical requirements for the position.

Since you are applying for a position where your qualifications match their requirements, title the right column, **"I OFFER"**. Then provide a bullet-pointed parallel assessment of how you match their key requirements, thus showing yourself as the "ideal candidate," the solution to their needs.

A slight variation: when you review the real examples in the Appendix, please pay attention to the cover letter for the **New College Graduate**. The company was not looking for an entry-level engineer, so our client had no requirements upon which to create the **YOU SEEK / I OFFER** table. We suggested he research entry-level engineer postings in his field, compile a generic list of the main requirements, create a bullet-pointed YOU SEEK column, and then compare himself to it. It worked.

Part Three:

Don't just close with a limp spaghetti *"thank you very much for your time."* **Give them a "call to action."**

Even though your phone number is on your Professional Profile™ and letterhead, repeat it in the closing and tell them you will follow up with them in $\underline{X}$ number of days. Seven business days seems like an appropriate time frame. Make sure you honor your word. Invite them to call you sooner than that.

Please turn the page for a **sample cover letter**.

Your Name
Street Number and Name
City, State, Zip Code
Telephone and Email

Date

Name
Position
Company
Address
City, Sate, Zip

Dear Mr. or Ms. XMXMX,

I am responding to your March 29th posting on your website for a marketing manager to manage your Classified Ad Department.

Based on the requirements covered in the job posting, I believe I am about a 95% ideal match for the position.

You Seek:	*I Offer:*
1. Ten years experience profitably managing staff of seven classified ad specialists during this recession. Position requires deft hand in providing client-focused customer service while maintaining profitability	• Nine years of ever-more-complex managerial and sales experience. In NEWSPAPER, I increased classified ad revenues by 7% in this terrible economy. In BUSINESS CLUB, I exceeded both retention and membership targets by 8%
2. Ability to deal simultaneously with multiple accounts	• Sold ad space to over 20 accounts and increased Club membership by 16%
3. Professionally deal with customers in environment of pressure and tight deadlines	• Have earned reputation as being able to defuse conflict, keeping both my cool and the clients, and getting the job done
4. Track record of hitting or exceeding targets and managing within operating budget	• Based on my results and abilities, I have a history of asking my manager to increase my targets. Because of my results, when my company downsized, they adjusted their layoff policy to retain me

I'm looking forward to speaking with you and can be reached at 000.123.4567. If I do not hear from you in seven business days, I'll call you on *DATE* to be sure you received this letter.

Sincerely,

Your Name

So. There you have our cover letter for responding to a specific position.

Strategy for Exploratory Letters for Mass Mailing

While we would prefer you follow the process and apply for specific positions rather than doing an exploratory mailing campaign, we know there will be occasions when you will need to do a mass mailing, like to search firms or asking your network for referrals.

- When you do, we suggest you follow the two-column format of the preceding letter. In addition, make certain you continue to keep the focus on what YOU can do for others, *not* on what you want them to do for you.

Here is a strategy for doing just that.

In many major cities, there is a weekly business newspaper that generally contains "*Business Journal*" in the name. Please see http://www.bizjournals.com.

Generally, each week a *Business Journal* publishes a comprehensive and well-researched list of the "top 25" or the "top 50" something – banks, or insurance companies, or privately-held companies, manufacturing companies – whatever the topic for the week - in their area.

One list a week, throughout the year.

Each list contains top-level information about the company: name, address, phone, website, the CEO, perhaps the HR director, key clients (if they wish to provide that information), relevant sales statistics and other information that is both interesting and useful to your search for new clients or work.

All that valuable information, right there for you. Each *Business Journal* complies their lists into an annual publication called *The Book of Lists*. (See http://www.bizjournals.com/bookoflists/.)

The Book of Lists may be in book format, downloadable or on a disk. Check the website to see what's available.

When I (Don) have been in the job market, I found the *Book of Lists* to be a phenomenal resource. I cannot urge you strongly enough to purchase the *Book of Lists*, or better yet, to subscribe to the newspaper in the cities of your choice.

Be Bold: The Spaghetti or the Meatball?

- **A strong warning:** This strategy is for those of you who are solopreneurs or working without a third party recruiter to find work.

- *If you are working with a recruiter or executive search firm and they are submitting your credentials to a company,* **under no circumstances** *should you go around them and directly contact the company yourself. Maintain integrity for the sake of your reputation. Recruiters network together!*

- **However,** if you are handling things on your own, with your new Professional Profile™ in hand (like the *Narrative* format, for example), and armed with an introduction to the top decision-makers found in *The Book of Lists* for the cities or regions of interest to you, you have the opportunity to take a bold step, moving from being spaghetti to becoming the meatball. Here's how:

- Consider sending your cover letter and Professional Profile™ directly to the decision-makers found in *The Book of Lists*

There is definitely risk in doing this. We know that.

Or you may look at it from this angle: You may be rewarded for your initiative, innovative thinking and the courage to stand out. You never know – the CEO may like what he or she sees and pass your Professional Profile™ to another decision maker for special attention. Or contact you directly. It happens. I know it happens. It happened to me.

I've noticed that frequently decision makers appreciate initiative.

I (Don) just finished a Professional Profile™ for another of our children. Not yet 40 and brilliant, he was unexpectedly urged to apply for a high-visibility Director of Engineering position with a prestigious company. His résumé was ... inadequate ... shall we say, and he needed to submit his credentials in less than 48 hours.

We got busy. He wrote his accomplishments essays, completed the skills analysis and began his cover letter. I polished the accomplishments statements, massaged the wording of the cover letter and formatted the final document. His mother proofed and edited the final packet – one-page cover letter and four-page Professional Profile™.

He went through three rounds of interviews, one of which was at Home Office and included the CEO. He got the job, winning over three others, all of whom were senior to him in age.

The point of the story is this: the CEO's strategy to lead the market is to be "disruptive" in all that his company does. His favorite word is "disruptive" and I am told that as he was looking at candidate résumés, when he got to our son's he exclaimed that it was a "disruptive résumé" and that he wanted to see the man behind it.

Two weeks later, the kid I taught to drive stick was named the new Director of Engineering.

That story contains a number of lessons for you in your search for new business or a new job.

Be the meatball, not the spaghetti.

I know from years of HR management experience that the HR department's primary function is to fill positions with the best-qualified people possible.

To do that, they strive to filter out the unqualified applicants while hopefully retaining the qualified ones.

Compounded by a difficult economy, staff cuts, computers and key-word searches, we also know that the purpose is laudable and the process is definitely an imperfect one. At times, technology designed to save time unfortunately filters out many well-qualified people who simply did not present themselves as effectively as their competitors, some of whom may be less qualified.

It is not an intentional thing; it is just the way it is. So one must do what they can for themselves.

It comes down to this: are you willing to be bold, to take a risk and step outside of the established process, or not?

To help you decide, let me tell you of a personal experience as a prelude to suggesting an alternative approach.

Some years ago, when the economy was in a slump, after only eight months on the job, I was one of 130 people who got laid off as my company downsized and my division disappeared. My position at the time was Divisional Vice President of Human Resources.

I received professional outplacement support, and for several months, I followed their guidelines. I did mass mailings like there was no tomorrow. I shot-gunned my résumé to lots of companies, going through the proper procedures and applying for specific positions as a Human Resources Vice President or HR Director.

I had been a Director for over ten years, and a VP for less than one year.

Several months into the search, I realized I was in a Catch-22. On one hand, I had not been a VP long enough to claim significant experience at that level. And on the other hand, a compassionate recruiter told me that when he shared my résumé with folks trying to fill a Director-level position, they arbitrarily decided that since I had been a VP, I would not want to take a back-step to Director, and so they stepped back from me.

Had I known then about the INNER GAME, I would have known that mine was in the pits. I spent a fearful and frustrating year watching my savings dribble away as I wedged myself again and again into the pack of applicants, all of us trying to squeeze in through HR's very narrow and quite inhospitable front door.

Following the outplacement company's generic process, I sent out almost 300 résumés, locally and nationwide. I went on three interviews. I got no offers.

During one of those three interviews, the senior vice president of human resources semi-jokingly remarked that I was better qualified than he was and if he hired me, he was sure his boss would replace him with me.

Catch-22 was alive and well. And it was a gift.

When I came across the ***Puget Sound Business Journal*** and its corresponding ***Book of Lists***, I had a flash of inspiration and I decided to be bold.

- I decided I no longer wanted to think of myself, or present myself, as a job ~~(applicant)~~ supplicant (the ~~line-out~~ is intentional).

- I decided I'd had enough of being spaghetti; it was time to be the meatball.

- Based on what the Senior VP had told me, I decided to see myself as senior vice president material. I put myself into the mindset of one executive-level professional asking a peer for assistance.

- If you're going to use this approach, I suggest you do the same.

- I immediately stopped using the outplacement company's templates and strategies, which of course did nothing to differentiate me from everyone else. Instead I created what I now refer to as a Professional Profile™, and using two particular sets of words I am going to share with you, sent my new cover letter and Professional Profile™ directly to the top people listed in several categories in the ***Book of Lists*** from the ***Puget Sound Business Journal.***

I sent out 100 letters to CEOs, General Managers, Founders, Presidents and Managing Directors. In my cover letter, I said I was going to be in Seattle exploring job opportunities over a specific three-week time period and I asked for the opportunity to meet with them. I didn't ask for a job.

GET THIS: <u>*Twenty of those 100 people responded with appointments or invitations to visit when I got to Seattle*</u>. A lot of them also made it a point to tell me they'd make sure I got a really good cup of coffee!

Can you believe it? *A 20 percent positive response!* **FROM C-LEVEL EXECUTIVES**

Four Magic Sentences for Your Cover Letter

After introducing myself, I opened the letter with these words:

"I am seeking referrals to people or companies where you think there might be a need for someone with my skills and experience. My résumé is attached."

Think about the first eight words of that first sentence.

To repeat: I was not asking anyone for a job. I was asking for *referrals.*

But wait! I wanted a J-O-B. Why did I ask for "*referrals*?" What's the logic here?

Let's assume a couple of things: You are the decision maker. You are a caring person, and your company is presently not in the market for an HR director.

If I tell you in my letter that I've been laid off and ask if you have a job for me and you do not, you'll tell me "no." And it's likely you'll feel moderate compassion for my situation and some regret having to say "no." And it's likely that you may also feel some personal discomfort.

- To avoid feeling uncomfortable, you will probably take steps to actively and quickly distance yourself from me, the cause of your discomfort.

- In other words, if I ask you for a job and you have nothing for me, the conversation is over, right there. Nothing personal – that's just human nature.

- However, I was not asking for a job. I was asking for *"referrals."*

Now what's the logic?

- With just that little change, I am no longer an applicant (supplicant); I am more like a peer. And I am causing you no discomfort.

You are still that same caring decision-maker. If you like my résumé and you think it's possible I might be valuable somewhere, even if you don't have anything for me at the moment, there is a good chance that you'll be a little bit curious, perhaps intrigued with my approach, and will invite me in for coffee and conversation. And you may see something you like and end up making space and offering me a job, or not.

HOWEVER, and this is the critical point, if you do *not* have work for me but like my cover letter and résumé, my request for *"referrals"* will have opened up an entirely different thought process in your mind.

Say these two sentences out loud and prove it to yourself. See if your thought process doesn't become narrow when you say, *"I'm seeking a job"* and expand when you say, *"I'm seeking referrals."*

Since people generally derive a warm feeling of satisfaction or pleasure when they can be helpful to someone needing assistance, or to a business colleague or friend, or stranger, the helpful thought process will likely continue.

I should tell you the results of my mailing:

I enjoyed a lot of great coffee during those 20 conversations, meetings and interviews.

I was given and followed up on a number of referrals.

I ended up accepting a consulting assignment from one of the original 20 individuals and he covered my relocation from back east to Vancouver, WA, where I remained for one year.

WATCH THE VIDEO www.YourProfessionalProfile.com/DonsVideos (*Be BOLD! Ask for Referrals, Not a Job*) for more on this story.

Before I finish up with the other set of critical words for the cover letter, let me give you another example of the benefit being the meatball, not the spaghetti.

When a company decided to do away with all of their field sales / marketing staff and go with distributor representatives, a number of people were let go, including a friend of mine and his boss.

Their company paid me to create Professional Profiles™ for both of them.

My friend enthusiastically embraced the concept of his new Professional Profile™ and applied his creativity to make it a truly personal and unique document.

His boss nit-picked me throughout the process and then nit-picked the end result. He nit-picked the nit-picks. He later redid his Professional Profile™ into something unlike anything I have ever seen. I don't know how to describe it but the term "train wreck" comes to mind.

My friend's boss took his new creation and began an intensive shotgun mailing campaign, sending his train wreck document far and wide, using traditional channels.

My friend did not. He used his time and energy to conduct a very focused campaign, *targeting only one company.* He knew where he wanted to work and knew with certainty they needed his marketing and sales expertise. *He knew he was the solution to the problem they had but did not know they had.*

- He analyzed their marketing practices, identified needs going unmet and created a unique marketing plan, just for them. He told them *what* needed to be done, but *not how* to do it. For the *how* part, they needed to hire him.

Keeping his focus clearly on them and not on himself, in his cover letter he made sure they understood that, even if they did not hire him, his marketing plan was theirs to keep.

It took him two weeks of focused effort to create that plan. Working intermittently on his Professional Profile™, it took me about two days to blend his input and mine, then polish both cover letter and profile to perfection.

When everything was ready, he completely bypassed the traditional HR channel and sent the plan, along with his new Professional Profile™ and a targeted cover letter to the senior vice president of marketing, and copied the CEO.

That was a very aggressive strategy and a gutsy move – sending his packet to his potential new boss, and to the boss's boss.

Remember my earlier comment that on one of my three interviews a VP of HR told me I was better qualified than he was and that if he hired me his boss would likely replace him with me?

By sending a copy of his packet to the CEO, he gently but effectively made certain that, should he want to, the VP of Sales and Marketing would be unable to simply toss his information in the trash.

(If you want to learn more about that approach, take a look at Michael Boylan's creative book ***The Power to Get In***.)

Three days after submitting his package, my friend was invited to meet with both executives. By the end of the following week, he had negotiated his package and was on board.

Total time: one month from lay-off to starting his new position.

Months later, I learned that his old boss was still flogging his train wreck of a ***résumé around the market.***

Focusing on the company rather than on himself, my friend presented himself as the solution to a need going unmet, and he was snapped up in a New York Minute.

His boss? Who knows? We both lost track of him.

What will it be: meatball or spaghetti?

Now, let's wrap it up.

- In our experience, people who shotgun their résumés out to a large number of companies in hopes of generating some interest almost never think in terms of the needs of the potential employer, and mostly *never offer the potential employer anything of value at the outset.*

We believe that is a mistake.

My friend offered something valuable and significant - a marketing plan - whether or not they hired him.

Earlier I said I changed my perspective *from* that of *job applicant asking for a job to* one *professional asking another professional for assistance.*

- Keeping that very different perspective in mind, here is the other set of important words, what I said in closing my letter to those 100 people.

- *"I view this as a request for assistance from one professional to another. I look forward to the opportunity to repay the favor."*

- Much as you need work, **your job search cannot, *must not*, be all about you.**

> **JOB SEEKERS AND SOLOPRENEURS**
>
> Much as you may need the work,
> **the focus of your cover letter and résumé must not be about you.**

Professionals reciprocate favors. I chose to elevate myself to the C-level of one professional asking a favor of another, and in so doing I obligated myself to each of them. A few asked something of me in return and I was happy to reciprocate. Most did not and just went about their business, content to have been of service. Please also pay it forward.

While I cannot prove it, I believe that using these two sets of words:

In the opening paragraph: *"I am seeking referrals to people or companies where you think there might be a need for someone with my skills and experience. My résumé is attached."*

And in the closing paragraph: *"I view this as a request for assistance from one professional to another. I look forward to the opportunity to repay the favor."*

I created a mindset in the recipients mind that helped set me apart from others in search of work. We urge you to consider using **the twin concepts of** *"seeking referrals"* and *"repaying the favor"* as you proceed with your search for new clients or a new job.

In Closing

We're done and you're on your way.

This book has been about getting your phone to ring with a recruiter or a new potential client on the other end calling you in for an interview.

> ***INNER GAME INSIGHTS:*** *At the end of each and every day you are seeking work, whether you won the position or the project – can you say you feel good about how you presented yourself on paper and in person? Can you also hope for the best outcome and be detached at the same time – in a healthy way? Can you acknowledge your efforts? We hope you are developing a confidence that is felt and heard and sensed and seen by those you interview with. Then when you win the assignment you desire, you can say to yourself, "Well done, Inner Game!" Once you have mastered the Inner Game, chances are you will find yourself attracting ideal assignments. And THAT is the point of the game!*

And PLEASE take advantage of the free training and orientation we are offering everyone who purchases the book. Join us for a free webinar that will jump-start the creation of your Professional Profile™. Please visit www.YourProfessionalProfile.com and click on "**I Bought the Book So Jump-Start Me**" to register for the next session.

In the future, we're planning three additional books to help you keep your career or your business moving forward:

- *Social Networking with Your Professional Profile*™
- *Interviews that Resume Careers* and
- *The Accomplishments-Minded Employee.*

We wish you all the best possible success in Winning the Inner and Outer Game of Finding Work or New Customers.

If you want to contact us, Deb (Deb@DeborahDrake.com) is your "go to" resource on playing a winning Inner Game, and Don (Don@YourProfessionalProfile.com) is the Outer.

We would appreciate your referrals as well as questions, feedback, suggestions for future editions of the book, and would love to hear how your search is going.

If you found the book helpful and would consider giving us a short testimonial for our website and future editions of the book, we'll say "thank you" with two special reports, ***"The Job Search From HR's Side of the Desk"*** and ***"Mastering the Inner Game in 12 Weeks (or less) For Good!***

And now, please check out a selection of other successful Professional Profiles™ including our own.

We hope they inspire you, filling your head with brilliant ideas that lead to wonderful things.

Warm Regards,

Deborah and Don –

P.S. Would you need or like some supportive structure and accountability as you take on creating your profile or refining the one you created while reading this book? *As a dynamite duo of Inner and Outer (with some tough love) and Honey and Vinegar (our inside joke), we offer One on One, Small Group and Self-Guided Coaching to assist you in getting started (the first hurdle), uncovering all your talents (the second hurdle), crafting crisp and vibrant essays (the third hurdle), and priming yourself for the interviews (the last and most critical hurdle to overcome.)*

Once you have your completed first draft of your Professional Profile™ in hand, you may decide you would like some editing and polishing and interview practice. If so, visit www.YourProfessionalProfile.com *and click on the **"SERVICES"** link to learn more about what levels of support are offered.*

APPENDIX

A Data Bank of Real Cover Letters and Real Professional Profiles™ that Got Real Results for Real People

Once Job Seekers and Solopreneurs liberate themselves from the box-like tyranny of generic reverse-chronological résumés and give themselves permission to embrace the flexibility and creativity of a Professional Profile™, the results can be breathtaking.

As we close the book on Professional Profiles™ (so to speak), we want to share a sampling of eleven actual Solopreneur, Job Seeker and Career Transition Profiles and cover letters.

The first thing you'll likely notice is that none of them are one- or two-page documents. Please get over that. They work.

The second thing you may notice is that their format probably does not look like what you are accustomed to. That's the point!! Please – Stand Up and Stand Out!

Strawberry, not whipped cream. Meatball, not spaghetti.

Our intent is to provide you with so many examples of accomplishments statements that worked for their users that you will have little trouble creating your own.

As you read the Profiles and cover letters, pretend you are the hiring manager, recruiter or potential client. See what catches your interest and makes you want to read more.

All eleven individuals read the book from cover to cover and completed all of the exercises. Three of the eleven created their own profiles with little to no involvement with us.

We would love to report that all eleven secured interviews. Ten did, and at the time of this writing, the eleventh, the Army Officer seeking a better civilian position, was not invited for an interview. He has put his job search on hold while he completes his MBA and gets married.

As you'll see, the Profiles run the gamut from serial entrepreneur to retail sales person to laid-off corporate executive to carpenter to a Baby Boomer caught in an acquisition.

Blue collar. White collar. Hourly. Management. Solopreneur. College graduate. Some college. Just out of high school. Loads of experience from the College of Life.

The point is this: the Professional Profile™ process can work for everyone who chooses to think in terms of what they have ACCOMPLISHED.

Our job was to help each person sort through their experiences, identify and clarify their accomplishments and skills used to achieve them, and present themselves in their own authentic "voice" so they stood out, like – well, you know.

We will preface each targeted cover letter and Professional Profile™ with a brief summary of the individual's situation and the results they achieved using their new tools. In the interest of confidentiality, we have honored requests and have removed information as necessary.

We affirm that what you'll read all belong to real people and that we have their permission to use them.

We will lead off with our **Professional Profiles™**

The Authors:
- Don's
- Deb's

And then you will find these summaries, cover letters and Professional Profiles™:

Job Seekers:
- Technical Trainer / Financial Services
- Director of Engineering / High Tech Manufacturing
- New College Graduate (Physics) / Seeking entry-level engineering position
- US Army Officer Transitioning into Civilian Job Market

Transitioning from Solopreneur to Employee:
- Self-Employed Journeyman Carpenter / Home Maintenance Expert to Employed Carpenter

Career Transitions:
- Commodity retail sales clerk to boutique Reservations Agent

Solopreneurs:
- Contract Producer of Educational and Training Videos
- Serial Entrepreneur (Start-up Specialist)
- Graphic Artist

Baby Boomers:
- Laid off Organization Development Manager repurposes contents of Professional Profile™ to become University Lecturer
- Laid off HR Manager in a for-profit company repurposes contents of Professional Profile™ to secure interview as HR Manager for municipal city government.

Don Burrows
PO Box 1800
Marysville, WA 98270
425.231.0085 Don@YourProfessionalProfile.com

FOCUS: Résumé Strategist for Job Seekers and Solopreneurs. Webinar/Workshop Leader. Author

CORE BELIEF: Think ACCOMPLISHMENTS! They will get you hired. Your chronological job duties will not

---

Job Seeker and Solopreneur Success Stories You'll Read About Here

JOB SEEKERS

- New College Graduate
- Career Transition
  - Hospitality Management to Newspaper Sales
  - Organization Development to University Lecturer
  - Self-Employed Financial Trainer to Metroplex City Government
- Military to Civilian
  - Enlisted - Navy
  - Officer – Army
- Senior Management
  - Mechanical Engineer
  - Systems and Sensor Engineer
- Middle Management
  - Electrical Engineer
  - Project Manager
  - Retired Boomer
- Non-Degreed
  - Food Server
  - Retail Sales

SOLOPRENEURS

- Project Management Consultant
- Video Producer
- Business Coach /Serial Entrepreneur

CORPORATE OUTPLACEMENT

- Multisite Custom Outplacement
- 90-Person Outplacement

SPECIAL SKILLS AND ABILITIES

- Creator of the **Professional Profile™ System** – flexible, customizable functional résumés that get people job interviews

- Expert at helping anyone – recent graduate, returning military, white collar, blue collar, degreed, non-degreed, entrepreneur, employee, Boomer, Gen-X . . . anyone . . . convert daily activities or job duties into measurable, marketable accomplishments

- Expert at helping clients authentically present themselves as an "ideal candidate" by customizing résumé and cover letter to the unique requirements of each job or opportunity

- Committed to helping clients realize and accept their greatness by identifying their *real* accomplishments

- Expert at helping job seekers and solopreneurs STAND OUT, like a strawberry on whipped cream

- All services available in Spanish as well as English

JOB SEEKER AND SOLOPRENEUR SUCCESS STORIES USING THE PROFESSIONAL PROFILE™ SYSTEM

JOB SEEKERS

New College Graduate (Entry Level Engineering Position). After three months of sending out countless generic résumés for an entry-level engineering position and going on no interviews, this 2011 graduate with a BS in Physics and I began working together. He quickly realized he could not stand out from his competition and memorably present himself as an "ideal candidate" if he continued to use of the generic reverse-chronological template his career development center recommended he use. Completing my process taught him to convert his school activities into relevant accomplishments while identifying the specific skills he used to achieve them. With that foundation, we developed customizable cover letters and résumés that focused on his accomplishments, resulting in three interviews in just under four weeks. Thinking now in terms of accomplishments rather than activities, his spirit and sense of optimism have taken a quantum leap forward.

Career Transition (Hospitality Management to Classified Advertising Sales). After seven years in her hospitality management position (her first job out of college) I helped this young woman create a broadcast cover letter and Professional Profile™ she used successfully to seek referrals from her network. Drawing from her data bank of over 20 relevant accomplishments and an equally extensive data bank of skills she used to achieve them, we put together a Profile of her favorite accomplishments and the skills she most liked to use, and a compelling cover letter. She conducted an effective email campaign resulting in a number of referrals, one of which led to her current senior sales position with her local newspaper. The format and content of her credentials made her memorable, and much to her surprise, people kept and circulated her résumé. For more than a year after she started her new job, she kept getting calls.

Career Transition (Organization Development Professional to University Lecturer). A Boomer with a successful 40-year career in Organization Development prepared the way for his successor and was then laid off when his company merged. Over six months he sent out hundreds of generic résumés and went on no interviews. After completing my Professional Profile™ process of identifying skills and accomplishments, we created a targeted cover letter and Profile for one particular position in one company. Ten days after submitting his credentials, the hiring manager called for a phone interview, then an all-day face-to-face interview. Unfortunately, my client came in second. **BUT WAIT!** Because of the thoroughness of his preparations, he was able to repurpose his accomplishments and skills into a teaching position at his local university. Both hiring managers raved about the thoroughness of his résumé, and neither objected to the *six pages of content*.

Career Transition (Self-employed Financial Trainer to Metroplex City Government). A victim of the economy, I helped this solopreneur financial trainer craft a referral request letter and Professional Profile™ that successfully made its way through a major metropolitan city's recruiting bureaucracy and won her an invitation to interview with the city's Human Resources Director. This was particularly rewarding to me because prior to becoming a solopreneur, this woman had been with her employer for 20 years and had significant accomplishments, which she downplayed as *"just doing my job."* The HR director disagreed with her self-assessment and was most apologetic that it had taken so long for her correspondence to make its way to his desk. Thrilled to hear that they liked her experience, she thanked him for his interest and declined the interview because in the interim she had been accepted into graduate school and was moving out-of-state.

Military to Civilian (Navy Enlisted / Information Technology). I helped a young Navy veteran who had been a LAN manager while on active duty (got his GED while in the Navy; no college degree) create the Professional Profile™ that earned him an interview at a prestigious engineering university. As we prepared his Profile I coached him to think about his professional time in the Navy not in terms of his day-to-day IT duties and responsibilities, but rather in terms of what he had actually *accomplished* and what his work meant to others. He got the interview and the position, beating some 50 other candidates, most with computer science degrees and more experience.

Military to Civilian (US Army Officer / Training and Development). I worked with a young veteran who graduated college and immediately enlisted in the US Army. Six years later (including an 18-month tour in Iraq), this decorated Infantry Captain completed his obligation and got out. He found work, but is underutilized. As we compiled his Professional Profile™, he told me the Army provided little in the way of effective career transition counseling or support to help translate his military skills and experience into applicable civilian opportunities. Calling upon my Army and HR recruiting expertise, I was able to help him translate his Army experience into civilian opportunities. He realized he had an interest and knack in training and development position. He has not yet landed, but is confident that he now has the tools to successfully transition into the civilian job market.

Senior Management (Mechanical Engineer. Career jump: Promotion from quasi-supervisory position to Director of Engineering). Invited to apply for a Director of Engineering position while they were still accepting applications, this engineer presented me with a significant challenge: update his current résumé, create a custom Professional Profile™ and targeted cover letter, within 48 hours. A premium service level, I: interviewed him and wrote up his new accomplishments; edited existing accomplishments to make them relevant to this position; kept him calm and focused while sorting through a myriad of engineering detail to get to the essence of the new accomplishments; organized his completed skills analysis; created a consistent format for generic "Part B" of his

Profile (work history, certifications, education, outside interests); and wrote his targeted cover letter. We met his deadline. Prior to his first, second and third interviews, I did interview training. The CEO, bored and unimpressed with the generic sameness of the other candidates" résumés, loved my client"s Profile, declared it *"disruptive"* (a good thing) and demanded to meet this *"disruptive"* engineer. He was the youngest of the finalists and won the job.

Senior Management (Systems & Sensors Engineering Manager to Director of Engineering). In his desire to transition from engineering team leader to director of engineering for a large division of huge multinational, I helped this gifted engineer prove to himself and others why he was ready to take on this new, highly-visible and critical position. I helped him expand his focus beyond the *numeric results* he had achieved to explain and present *what* he did, *why* he did it, and *how* he went about doing it. By coaching him to consider his accomplishments in terms of the additional three elements, we created a multidimensional Professional Profile™ that enabled him to stand out from his competition. He earned the interview and won the job. The function he took over was mired in traditional thinking of "not built here", and as a result they were paying the price for not having kept up with the intellectual times. His intellect and skills were just what they needed.

Middle Management (Electrical Engineer. Had to compete for his old job after a spin-off). During a spin-off when current employees faced job elimination and had to compete for positions in a newly-formed organization, I created a Professional Profile™ that enabled this engineer to successfully compete. With years of successful experience in the former company, I helped him sort through his many accomplishments and select and write up the most relevant ones, and identify the skills he used to achieve them. After he wrote his accomplishments essays I edited and tailored them to match the requirements for the position for which he was applying. Our final documents clearly showed him to be the ideal candidate for that position and he smoothly transitioned into the new company. He kept his same desk, at a significantly higher salary.

Electrical Engineer (MS degree. Picked his company. Identified Need Going Unmet. Created His Job). Using as his foundation the Professional Profile™ that we created, this eclectic, brilliant 4.0 electrical engineering graduate of a premier university created a job for himself where none had previously existed. Laid off from his technical sales job when his company changed business models, I was shocked to see that he was using a commonplace, boring, generic reverse-chronological résumé. We created a document and job search strategy to match his brilliance. He identified just one place where he wanted to work, researched that organization, identified new markets and needs going unmet. He prepared a marketing plan telling them *what* they needed to do, but not *how,* and we jointly created his Professional Profile Within a week they contacted him and one week later he negotiated a great package and was back to work. Total layoff time: one month.

NOTE: His former boss, for whom I also wrote a Profile, insisted on modifying my work to be more reverse-chronological and "normal." Six months after my client was hired, his former boss was still flogging his paper.

Middle Management (Project Manager with Master's degree and professional certification). After helping this project manager think beyond her job duties and activities to identify her major accomplishments and skills, I created an effective Professional Profile™ that gained her the interview she sought. After she wrote her essays and distilled them down to what she thought was the essence of her accomplishments, I asked, *"So what?"* a number of times until we *really* drilled down and truly identified the results, the essence of each accomplishment. In addition to creating a targeted Profile and cover letter, we conducted practice interviews, critiqued her responses, and practiced some more. She won the job.

Non-Degreed: Retired Boomer Back to Work (Former Office Administrator to Expert Gardener in a Big-Box store). I helped a woman substitute her lifelong passion / hobby for lack of credentials or paid work experience to land the job of her dreams. Retired after four decades doing administrative work and forced back into the job market by the economy, the thought of having to go back to her former profession depressed her to the point of physical illness. Her passion was gardening and she wanted to care for flowers in the garden shop of one of the big box stores. Using a résumé that focused on her admin background, she was summarily turned down when she applied for gardening positions. After attending one of my community workshops, she put together a targeted cover letter and résumé, and at my suggestion included a number of spectacular photos of her garden to support her expertise and offset her lack of credentials or paid gardening experience. She reapplied to one of the stores that had turned her down, was immediately interviewed and hired. She "blossomed." (☺)

Non-Degreed: Food Service Waitress (Twenty-five + years in the same job and restaurant. Laid off from one day to the next when owner closed business). A workshop participant, a waitress in her 60s, had been at the same Interstate exit restaurant for over two decades, was unemployed off from one day to the next when the owner closed at the end of her shift. When we got to the accomplishments part of the workshop, she said, *"I'm just a waitress. I don't have any accomplishments."* FULL STOP! I asked if she had experience diffusing angry customers and keeping them as happy ones? *"All the time. It was part of my job."* I said that each occasion was a separate accomplishment and her customer skills had value. I suggested she build her new Professional Profile™ around her ten most spectacular "guest saves." Two classes later she came back and about exploded with pride when she told us about her two interviews at the new casino, the 500 applicants (many much younger) whom she beat out, her wonderful benefits plan, and her tips (three to four times more than before).

Non-Degreed: Retail Sales / Motivational Speaker (19 years old. An author. A young man of integrity, providing financial help to his mom). I wrote a Professional Profile™ and targeted cover letter that helped an extraordinary young man move from a retail sales position to become a concierge in a luxury apartment. Just 19 at the time, he was a published author with a goal of becoming a motivational speaker and helping street kids either stay out, or get out, of gangs. But on his way to greatness, he needed a job to help take care of his mom and his cousin. After several discussions, he began to see himself in terms of his accomplishments and skills, and he realized they could be packaged and presented so he would be a viable candidate for higher-level jobs. The day after he submitted his package, the apartment general manager called and he went in for his interview. Within a week he was hired. (Please see his unsolicited video testimonial at www.ResumesThatResumeCareers.com/DonsVideos

SOLOPRENEURS (Using custom, focused content on social media profiles and websites)

Self-Employed Project Management Consultant with 40 years experience (Had gone two years with no new contracts). After 40 years of success as a self-employed project manager, this mid-60s man hit a two-year wall. His résumé was a disaster and his spirit and finances were in trouble. In the three days it took him to complete his prework, he told me had an epiphany: he learned more about himself then than he had over 40 years of work, and with excitement set to work identifying his accomplishments. When I gave him his completed Professional Profile™, he read it word-for-word and then sat in silence and stared at it. In a small voice of regret and sadness he said to himself, *"Where have you been all my life?"* In that moment, he realized all he brought to the „world of work," saw how his life could have been, and imagined how it would be when he got back on track. Which he did. We created new strategies and I wrote cover letters that opened doors to new clients; he regained his financial and emotional stability. Two years later, he died of a huge heart attack, and they were two very good years.

Video Producer and Project Manager (Starting a new business). This very experienced video producer and project manager with a track record of success working for large organizations used his Professional Profile™ to help establish himself as a solopreneur. After reading his generic résumé I asked him to identify and write essays about his most meaningful accomplishments. With no additional prompting, the flood gates opened and in short order he wrote over 20 essays which we then converted into accomplishments statements for his Accomplishments Data Bank. After completing the skills analysis of those accomplishments, he had filled his Skills Data Bank as well. With that as his foundation, we put together an exploratory cover letter and Professional Profile™ that caused recruiters and agencies to call him.

Business Coach / Serial Entrepreneur (Socially-motivated, in search of needs going unmet). This serial entrepreneur started his own insurance agency and ten years later sold it and no longer needed to work. But as a serial entrepreneur with a strong social conscience, he wanted to share his business-building skills with those who had a dream and not very deep pockets. Identifying an under-served market, he uses his new Professional Profile™ to set himself apart from his competition as he calls attention to himself and his services. As he reorganized his website, he gave his online Professional Profile™ prime placement, and reports that it has generated on-going interest, comments, calls, conversation and business from site visitors. He appreciates the power of the Professional

Profile™, particularly the ease with which the accomplishments and skills can be repurposed into any number of marketing formats. Most importantly, thanks to his new "accomplishments awareness" mindset he adds accomplishments to his data bank so he has a continual stream of fresh and relevant material.

CORPORATE OUTPLACEMENT

Supporting a Human Resources Vice President (Effective Multi-site Custom Outplacement). When a company had to lay off a number of long-service administrative employees in several of their branches in small towns from South Carolina to Pennsylvania, I traveled to client sites and provided custom outplacement services that were both effective and cost-effective. Knowing that good jobs were scarce in these small towns, the HR vice president wanted to go above-and-beyond generous severance and provide all possible reemployment help. I spent two days at each site where I created their unique Profiles, taught them to write their own accomplishments statements and targeted cover letters, developed individual job search strategies customized to opportunities available in each of their towns, and provided filmed and critiqued interviewing training. When I left each office, employees were confident they could find work. No one was angry at the company, nor did anyone bring suit.

CIGNA Worldwide Outplacement (Shut-down 90-Person Area Headquarters). When Corporate closed the Latin American Area headquarters in Florida, 90 people lost their jobs. As Latin American Area HR Director, I created and managed an in-house outplacement center. I trained everyone to write their own accomplishments-based résumés. Once they had written their accomplishments essays, I edited them into marketable accomplishments statements that they could use to customize the résumés they submitted. Over two months time, in between diffusing employee threats of job discrimination suits, I completed résumés and cover letters for all 90 people and conducted small group and individual video-taped interviewing training and coaching. We had no lawsuits and eighty-nine of the 90 individuals found new jobs that were equal to or better than the ones they lost. The 90th decided she wanted to take her new résumé back to the Caribbean and lay on the beach for a while, so she did. I consider my success rate to have been 100%.

Experience **Acorn Consulting Inc. Founder and Principal – (February, 1994 – Present)** / Marysville, WA.
- Enabling job seekers and solopreneurs to win interviews that can lead to new jobs and new clients
- Proprietary *Professional Profile™ process* enables users to make a complete personal inventory, then identify and speak authentically and with conviction about their business accomplishments and the skills used to achieve them. Their credentials will **Stand Out**, like a strawberry on whipped cream
- Author of *Résumés That Resume Careers*. Written in response to the economy, book and workshops offer job seekers and solopreneurs a proven process to stand out and win interviews by easily customizing credentials to unique needs of potential employers or clients
- Co-author of expanded second edition: ***Burn Your Résumé. You Need a Professional Profile™ - Winning the Inner and Outer Game of Finding Work or New Business*** (available 1Q12)

Chiquita Brands. Asia-Pacific Area Manager, Human Resources/Organization Development
Cincinnati, OH and virtual in Cary, NC. January, 1992 – January, 1994
- Created and managed combined Human Resource and Organization Development function for start-up joint venture and acquisitions in Australia, New Zealand, Korea, Japan and California
- Position eliminated as Corporate refocused on strategic objectives; declined transfer and new job in OH

Columbia Aluminum. Contract Organization Development Consultant
Vancouver, WA. February, 1991 – August, 1991
- Six-month contract to provide executive level HR and OD guidance to owner of privately-held company as he integrated four manufacturing sites in three states into one new organization

Dole Fresh Fruits. Vice President, Human Resources – Fresh Fruit Division
Boca Raton, FL. October, 1989 – May, 1990
- Responsible for full range of tactical and strategic HR planning and implementation of HR activities in the US, Central and South Latin America. Managed staff of nine
- Position was one of 130 eliminated in corporate consolidation

CIGNA Worldwide. Area Director, Human Resources, Latin America
Philadelphia, PA and Coral Gables, FL. June, 1984 – October, 1989
- Human Resources Director responsible for 1,300 employees in 13 countries in hemisphere
- Hired to provide Bi-lingual HR support of INA and Connecticut General merger in Central and Latin America
- Transformed admin HR function into one that made measurable bottom line contributions

Chicago Pneumatic Tools Company. June, 1979 – June, 1984
- **Division Manager, Professional Relations** (Jacobs Manufacturing), Bloomfield, CT
- **Division Manager, Compensation and Professional Development** (Tool Division). Utica, NY
- **Acting Industrial Relations Director, Europe.** (European Division), Geisenheim, W. Germany
- **Division Manager, Compensation and Development** (Tool Division) Utica, NY
- **Supervisor, Plant Compensation,** (Tool Division) Utica, NY

Marriott Hotels. Philadelphia, PA and Miami, FL. May, 1974 – June, 1979
- **Property Personnel Director, Philadelphia Marriott Hotel** (1,000 employees)
- **Property Personnel Director, Miami Marriott Hotel** (400 employees)

Education

Command and General Staff College, 1984, US Department of the Army

University of Maryland
- **Ph.D.** (Course Work Completed) 1974. College Park. Latin American Literature
- **MA** 1970. College Park. Latin American Literature/Area Studies. Photojournalism minor. Dean's List
- **BA** 1967. College Park. Latin American Area Studies. Dean's List and Spanish Honor Society

Military

US Army Reserves, Retired. 1970–1991. LTC. Civil Affairs, Latin American Foreign Area Officer and Military Intelligence

Publications
- *Résumés That Resume Careers* (Aviva Press, 2010)
- *Plan While You Still Can: 16 End-of-Life Checklists You Need Now* (Aviva Press, 2007)
- **People Prospectus™** Unique numerical people balance sheet identifying hidden people problems during mergers, acquisitions, joint ventures and as an internal organizational health check
- HR articles in *Mergers & Acquisitions* (October, 2002) and *HRMagazine* (September, 2006)
- *Area Study of Paraguay,* US Department of the Army (1988)

Deborah Drake
16203 NE 13th Pl, Apt F101
Bellevue, WA 98008-3666
425.223.5335 deb@deborahdrake.com www.AuthenticWritingProvokes.com

PURPOSE: Independent writing consultant, personal development mentor and marketing coach to solopreneurs and job seekers wishing to increase their business success, self-confidence and self-esteem by finding, developing, expressing and marketing themselves, their products and services in their own unique and authentic "voices."

CORE BELIEF: To mentor and share my gifts is to give meaning to life and to living

SPECIAL SKILLS AND ABILITIES:

• Strong listening skills to help clients sort through, crystallize and organize their ideas	• Agile mind; able to weave divergent ideas into creative and cohesive business initiatives	• Gently persuasive personal style that attracts commitment, rather than demanding it
• Developer of pragmatic, uncomplicated, easily implemented, effective marketing strategies	• A catalyst of ideas and people; holistically mentoring written and spoken authenticity	• Absolutely committed to the belief that "authentic writing provokes"

REPRESENTATIVE PROFESSIONAL ACCOMPLISHMENTS:

WRITING & COMMUNICATIONS CONSULTANT

- When it came to my attention that a Sports Psychology Consultant (who was scheduled to attend a conference in July 2011) was also sitting on a partial manuscript for which he had a publisher 32 years before, I suggested something "unreasonable. I proposed that he take me on as Writing Coach and we revamp and finish the manuscript, self-publish, and do so in time for the conference he was scheduled to attend. The greatest challenge would prove to be the competing editorial voices inside the author's head. My first objective was to get my author to channel the more encouraging editor in him and chuck the critical "English Teacher", which he did.

    He found his "voice" in a matter of weeks and in a blend of academic facts, humor and humility in recalling stories and illustrations. Between April and July I coached him in frequent laser coaching sessions nearly daily to maintain accelerated and continuous writing and editing for both the book and his blog. I served as developmental editor, motivational coach, muse, cheerleader and self-publishing consultant. In two and half months time 27,000 words were authored, edited, and then in two weeks was proofread and formatted. Between January and April he reported authoring 10 blogs. Between April and July he wrote 17. We produced his 168 page book, *The Athlete Within: A Mental Approach to Success in Sports and Business* in time to take to the conference and since the conference he has again résumé d his radio show of the same name and began booking speaking engagements with renewed enthusiasm. (I invite you to contact Mike Margolies: http://mikemargolies.com/. 425.241.6539)

- According to the Seattle Board of Realtors there are over 35,000 people competing to sell real estate in the area. Mark Beringer, a member of my Writers Circle, is one of them. When Mark first joined the group, he shared that he wanted to find a way to STAND OUT in a very crowded marketplace. He had never blogged and thought doing so might provide the solution. His website contained the usual realtor material that his competitors also offered.

    In my weekly Writers Circle sessions, I open with an icebreaker, and then gently guide the discussions that follow, letting the group pretty much determine the topics. One day Mark said he could see how he might use blogging to differentiate himself, but he did not know what to write about. Answering that question became the topic for the rest of the session. Someone asked him what his interests were, and from that unassuming question came his focus. In real estate terms, Mark is passionately interested in two topics: the history of the different neighborhoods in Seattle and the East Side, and birds. We batted that around for a while and someone suggested the title of his blog would be *"Real Estate for the Birds"* and that he write about the different species of birds found in each neighborhood. And just that quickly a blog theme and name materialized. Mark's site still contains the standard real estate data, AND it now stands out as a destination site for those with similar interests. He is gaining prominence as he posts several blogs a week and has begun to include video blogs as well. It is neither stretch nor exaggeration to say that we have a Magic Circle. (I invite you to contact Mark Beringer: http://realestateforthebirds.com & http://northwestlookingglass.com 425-283-8851)

PERSONAL DEVELOPMENT & COMMUNICATIONS MENTORING

- In March, 2010 I began a weekly writers support group and have been facilitating it ever since. Under the auspices of www.Biznik.com, it is called A Writers Support Group for Reticent Bloggers (http://biznik.com/events/a-writers-support-group-for-reticent-bloggers-aka-writers-68). We have consistently had stunning and inspiring conversations with 12 – 30 people who question the value of blogging. The dozens of people impacted by the weekly discussion who are now consistently, confidently and with strong sense of self blogging authentically on a topic they care about include: www.Realestateforthebirds.com, www.Northwestlookingglass.com, Singing Heart Coach, Redmond Rousers Rotary blog by Kelly Kyle, Susan Straub Martin of Strauberry Studios and Paul Zohav of Relationship Literacy to name but a handful. In July, 2011 I launched a community blog and began monthly writing challenges to provide a platform for sharing writing and developing our writing voice and skills. As of January, 2012 over 450 posts have been authored and the writing, SEO, and back links are impacting both the sites and the individuals Google Rankings positively.

- We have several entrepreneurs in the Writers Circle. Gerald Grinter, founder of The Twelfth Power Consulting, is one of our most prominent. Ten years after starting an insurance agency from scratch, he sold it and cashed out. A serial entrepreneur with a desire to both give back and do more, he became a mentor with Washington C.A.S.H. (www.washingtoncash.org), a non-profit Seattle-based microloan. Gerald brings his success and knowledge to teach what he learned to others. Many who apply to the microloan for assistance do not qualify, but they still need help.

    As serial entrepreneurs do, he identified a need going unmet and created his consultancy to address it. While networking is not the primary intent of the Writers Circle, it is definitely a by-product. After getting to know Gerald, I connected him with Don Burrows, who helped him create his Professional Profile (http://www.thetpconsulting.com/Professional-Profile.html). They clicked and are now learning about the Kindle book publishing process. The three of us are exploring opportunities to be of contribution to Washington C.A.S.H.. Gerald has always been a writer, and I am honored that he credits me and his experience in the Writers Circle with inspiration and ideas. Gerald has become a prolific blogger on his site and contributor to www.Biznik.com. He has at least three books in his head, and I cannot wait to see how he will change the world. (I invite you to contact Gerald Grinter: www.thetpconsulting.com. 206.650.4342.)

MARKETING COACH

- After providing Don Burrows, author of *Résumés that Résumé Careers* two hours of creative marketing brainstorming around what more he could do with his self-published book and the job search principles he writes about, he declared I had given him at least a year's worth of work to implement. He then designed a business plan for himself that included: custom résumé design, workshops, getting him approved as an Examiner (achieved in 24 hours after applying), offering corporate group packages, on-going mentoring and interview practice skills. Introducing the notion of the process applying to solopreneurs to better define themselves and raise confidence, he took it and ran with it.

    He determined a desire to come out with a second edition that incorporated my ideas around developing mastery of the inner game to go with the professional profile process and format. He requested I be his co-author for the revised edition to be titled ***Burn Your Résumé. You Need a Professional Profile™.*** How did I do this? In a hybrid approach of suggesting ways to repurpose his book and formats in which to do it, I asked him what would he be most likely to get excited about. He developed a game plan that had the potential for $300K in gross revenue to share with his partner, Me! We are targeting publication for 1Q12. (I invite you to contact Don Burrows: www.Résumé sThatRésumé Careers.com. 425.231.0085)

RELEVANT PROFESSIONAL EXPERIENCE

Authentic Writing Provokes. Bellevue, WA. July 2008 – present
A freelance marketing coach, writing consultant and personal development mentor and facilitator, I am a catalyst. Drawing on a number of skills and experiences, I holistically mentor and teach individuals to find and develop their own authentic voices to more effectively present and market their products / services. I have found that authentic self-expression is critical to my clients' business success and sense of self-confidence and self-esteem. On occasion I will partner with a client to help develop and implement a product or service that resonates particularly strongly with me.

Dale Carnegie Training. Bellevue, WA. November, 2009 – May, 2010
Training Consultant / Business Development
Divided my time between recruiting and pre-screening candidates to participate in the Dale Carnegie programs, and mentoring them before, during and in between training programs. I actively maintained contact with 100+ prospective students and dozens of enrolled students per month.
Reason for leaving: With a growing list of private clients, I opted to become full-time self-employed.

Crossroads Recovery Coaching, Inc. City, State. June, 2006 – present
Enrollment Counselor / Faculty/Webinar Facilitator
Crossroads Recovery Coaching's program has been certified by the International Coach Federation (http://coachfederation.org) as an approved coach training program. I provide marketing, facilitation,

mentoring and recruitment support to coaches, counselors, therapists and those in recovery desiring to acquire professional coaching skills.

InviteCHANGE – Academy for Coach Training. Edmonds, WA. December, 2007 – July, 2009
Business Development / Admissions Specialist
InviteCHANGE's coaching program has been certified by the International Coach Federation (http://coachfederation.org) as an approved coach training program. Working as an independent contractor, I provided a range of marketing, networking, business development, coaching and mentoring support to staff and students.
Reason for leaving: When it came time to renegotiate terms, I opted to not renew my contract.

Walden University. Baltimore, MD. July, 2006 – July, 2007
Field Recruiter for state of Washington
Recruited for graduate programs through on-site enrollment activities, information sessions, school visits, in-service programs. Developed and maintained a state-wide network of relationships with school administrators, teachers, alumni and current students. Attended local, regional and national K-12 conferences and events. Identified targets, set appointments and conducted 150 school visits yearly throughout Washington State.
Reason for leaving: I left Walden to pursue a contract with a Coach Training Program I wanted also to take part in.

The Wellness Institute. Issaquah, WA. August, 2004 – July, 2006
Enrollment Counselor/Business Development
Developed / maintained business relationships with prospective students and graduates. Contributed to marketing strategies, managed entire registration process and meticulously maintained data base of over 750 detailed client files.
Reason for leaving: Recruited by Walden University.

Contract Business Development Consultant. Bellevue, WA. August, 2002 – November, 2004
Two primary clients: Best Life Services and Peak Potentials Training
Provided a range of new business services including hosting open houses, cold calling, and development / presentation of custom proposals for groups and corporate clients. For **Best Life Services**, created initial community of 70 charter members in nine months time. For **Peak Potentials**, I recruited groups as large as 30 to workshops.
Reason for leaving: After completing projects and assessing potential for myself, I moved on to new assignments.

Washington CEO Magazine. Seattle, WA. August 2001 – July, 2002
Account Executive and Advertising Consultant
Reason for leaving: Paychecks kept bouncing

Palazzo de Mix (Now Palazzo Interactive). Seattle, WA. October, 2000 – July, 2001
Print Production / Account Manager
Reason for leaving: Lack of work

Bozell Worldwide. Seattle, WA. July, 1998 – October, 2000
Print Production Manager
Reason for leaving: Lack of work

McCann Erickson. San Francisco, CA. June, 1997 – June, 1998
Print Production Manager
Reason for leaving: Lack of work

EDUCATION

University of California – Davis. September 1983-March 1989
Bachelor of Arts in English/Creative Writing. Overall 2.9 GPA. In my major: 3.5 GPA

SPECIALIZED TRAINING AND CERTIFICATIONS

- Dale Carnegie: Sales Advantage Course, November 2009
- Dale Carnegie: Human Relations Course, March 2010
- Dale Carnegie: High Impact Presentations Course, April 2010
- Crossroads Recovery Coaching: Recovery Coaching certification
- InviteCHANGE : Living Your Vision certification
- The Wellness Institute: Heart-Centered Hypnotherapy certification
- Peak Potentials: Train the Trainer and Life Purposes certifications

LIFELONG LEARNING
Because I am committed to lifelong learning, not only will you have the benefit of my technical expertise, you will also have the opportunity to apply the knowledge of some of the best minds in the world. Here is a current list of professional and self-development programs whose concepts I'm prepared to apply to your unique situation and business challenges.

COURSES TAKEN
Peak Potentials Training (T. Harv Eker)
November 2002	Peak Potentials Training.	Millionaire Mind Intensive (3 day intensive)
March 2003	Peak Potentials Training.	Train the Trainer (5 day intensive)

Landmark Education
February 2003	Landmark Education	The Forum (4 days + 10 weeks seminar)
May 2003	Landmark Education	The Advanced Course (4-day intensive)
June-Sept 2003	Landmark Education	Self-Expression Leadership Program

The Wellness Institute
October 2004	The Wellness Institute	Hypnotherapy Training (6 days)

InviteChange
July 2008	InviteChange: Coaching	Living Your Vision (3 days + 10 weeks seminar)

Crossroads Coaching
2008-2009	Crossroads Coaching	Coaching Certification Program (42 weeks of 52)

Context International
April 2010	Context International	The Pursuit of Excellence (3 day intensive)
June 2010	Context International	The Wall (4 day intensive)

Dale Carnegie Training
Nov-Dec 2010	Dale Carnegie Training	Sales Advantage (7 weeks)
Jan-Mar 2011	Dale Carnegie Training	Effective Communication (12 weeks)
May 2011	Dale Carnegie Training	High Impact Presentations (3 day intensive)

COURSES TAUGHT

Approved Continuing Education by the International Coach Federation (http://coachfederation.org)
Recovery Coaching
Recovery Coaching Certification. (52 weeks). Virtual training.
Assistant trainer
    2009 Course: 11 participants started. 9 graduated
    2010 Course: 12 participants started. 10 graduated
    2011 Course: 10 participants started. 10 still enrolled

Coach and Grow Rich   Coaching Business & Practice Development (8 weeks).
Virtual conference call training
Lead Trainer
    January 2010: 9 participants started. 9 graduated
    September 2010: 9 participants started. 9 graduated

Writers Support Group
Founder and Lead Facilitator / Writing Mentor
Daytime Grassroots writers support group under sponsorship of www.Biznik.com
Weekly since March 30, 2010.
Started with six participants. Now over 100 and growing

Writers Supporting Writers
Evening grassroots writing laboratory, an off-shoot of the Writers Support Group
Weekly since April 2011 – Date
Participant level capped at five

Self-Publishing and Self-Promotion Salon
Creator and Organizer of semi-annual event
    September 11 2010
    October 31 2010
    January 11 2011
Average 20 paid participants and five industry presenters

OUTSIDE INTERESTS
- SEO and Social Media
- Astrology
- Long Distance Walking
- Travel and Travel Writing

TECHNICAL TRAINER – FINANCIAL SERVICES

This person had over two decades of domestic and international financial management and training experience – all with the same employer.

Before winding down her career with them, she acknowledged her entrepreneurial spirit and started her own financial literacy training business. Her intention was to bring her global skills and training to people in her local community.

Caught in the current recession, she placed that goal on hold and sought to return to a full-time position. At that point, we began to create her Professional Profile™.

She had never completed a comprehensive personal inventory of her accomplishments and skills, and she was surprised at what she learned and recalled about herself and her life to that point.

With ongoing coaching as the process unfolded, she realized that many of the "activities" she considered to be "just doing my job" were in reality significant and marketable accomplishments. That realization made it easier for her to recognize and surface other achievements she had forgotten.

She lived in a large metropolitan city and she cast a wide net. In addition to responding to specific openings, she sent targeted cover letters and her Profile to search firms and to her network. The following is the letter and Profile she sent to search firms. It led to a referral to apply to the city for a financial trainer position they needed to fill.

We created another cover letter customized to the requirements of that specific vacancy. She submitted it and her Profile. And waited.

Several months went by when suddenly the human resources recruiter called and enthusiastically told her she was just what they were looking for and when could she come in to interview.

Unfortunately, or maybe fortunately, during the interim, she had applied to and been accepted into a Master's degree program in another state, and when they called her, she was in the last stages of getting packed up to move.

She thanked them, wished them well, and was thoroughly delighted to know that her Professional Profile™ had successfully made its way through the bureaucratic process of big city government and made her STAND OUT and win an interview invitation.

Here are the cover letter and Profile she sent to recruiters.

NAME
Address
City, State, Zip
Cell: Email:

Date

Name
Title
Company
Address
City, State, Zip

Dear Mr. / Ms. XMXMX   IN RE: Corporate or Field Position
                                                    (domestic or international)

I imagine you are flooded with potential candidates whose cover letters and credentials focus on *themselves* and what *they* want. I believe this is an incorrect approach.

Rather, as a candidate, I believe I should tell you **what I am going to do** *for your clients*. The most effective way for me to do that is by telling you what I have done domestically and in the Far East for my previous employer, Company Name. I believe it is imperative for a Position to cut costs and increase profitability. Otherwise, what's the point?

As both an Position Title and Position Title, my intent was to positively impact my employer's bottom line. These are my primary areas of expertise where I have demonstrated success:

- increasing profitability
- increasing market share
- improving productivity
- reducing headcount.

I am just beginning my job search and am contacting a select group of search firms as well as applying for specific positions. Rather than using a generic, one-size-fits-all résumé , I will select from **my two data bases** my most relevant **accomplishments** and my **special skills and abilities** for each position for which I am applying.

The attached ACCOMPLISHMENTS-BASED RÉSUMÉ highlights my accomplishments in the above four critical areas. Other areas include Just-in-Time training, personal initiative, and community banking.

I'll give you a follow-up call ten business days to make certain you have received my information and determine next steps.

Thank you.

Name

1 incl: Résumé

Name _____ Address _____
      Home Phone: _____ Cell Phone: _____ E-mail: _____

OBJECTIVE: Full-time, permanent Technical Trainer position for a Financial Service institution that requires in-depth knowledge of banking practices, multicultural training expertise, professional platform skills, a love of travel and a welcoming training style that sets high expectations while putting nervous learners at ease.

PERSONAL TRAITS, SPECIAL SKILLS AND ABILITIES

- Hold high expectations for my own performance; strive for high levels of personal achievement

- Over 20 years experience developing and conducting financial management training in the US and overseas

- Confident when faced with learning new software and computer applications

- Happy person, committed to my colleagues and company

- Quick study; able to apply what I have learned and work effectively without supervision

- Unwavering work ethic; committed to achievement of goals – both business and personal

- Surging enthusiasm for life, and powerful desire to help others succeed by sharing my knowledge

- Committed to continuous learning and personal growth

- Committed to achieving and maintaining consistently high levels of client satisfaction

- Consensus builder; strong personal influencing skills; rapidly puts people at ease

- Strong sense of "community," based on belief in the value of helping others to help themselves

- Sense of adventure, love of travel and willingly embrace new cultures

REPRESENTATIVE PROFESSIONAL ACCOMPLISHMENTS:

DEVELOPMENT OF TRAINING MATERIALS

- Three of my colleagues from the Operations side of Company were scheduled to conduct Compensation training in Bangalore. When one of them was suddenly taken ill, four days before scheduled to leave for Bangalore, I was asked to replace him. Having managed that function previously, I was quickly able to create an effective training program, and was happy to be of service. I had been in Bangalore the year before and looked forward to returning. I effectively represented my colleague and communicated the material in a manner that was entertaining, involving, interesting and effective.

- When the second of the three Operations managers who were going to Bangalore to conduct Incoming Funds Transfer training learned that I was replacing their ill colleague and was developing training materials for the other person's sessions, he told me that he too had no training materials, and asked if I would develop his program for him as well. As I was already strapped for time to finish not only my own projects but my new Bangalore undertaking as well, I was tempted to say no. But having seen what can happen when Operations managers "wing it" when making both domestic and international presentations, I nonetheless agreed to help him as well. I met with him and his staff to learn what information they wanted to present.

    Then, using his guidelines, procedures and operations manuals, I quickly created a coherent, organized and effective training program for him. Knowing that he was not a trainer, I also coached him on how to present it effectively. He was astonished at the speed with which I put the program together, and was grateful for my willingness to help on such short notice. He expressed his gratitude by writing a letter to my manager and recommended me for an employee recognition award.

Page 2 – *Name // Cell Phone*

JUST-IN-TIME TRAINING:

- It is both critical and extremely difficult for banks to remain up-to-the-minute in the security aspects to prevent money laundering via US dollar funds transfers. As a Quality Assurance Technical Trainer at Company, on short notice, I chaired a joint team and developed and delivered specialized training for Compliance directors and senior managers and staffs for both ---- and ---- (confidentiality agreement prohibits further discussion.) My training enabled various levels within the bank to close loopholes, expedite processing, meet more demanding deadlines and reduce payment volume by approximately 30% because there were less payments stopping for repair.

PRODUCTIVITY IMPROVEMENT:

- It is difficult for call center customer service representatives to maintain productivity standards and provide excellent service to customers when they themselves are angry and feel unappreciated by their management. I was assigned the responsibility to correct that problem at Company. By sitting with and observing a cross-section of the reps, I saw their competency and dedication to their customers, and the basis for their frustration with management. Based on my analysis, I documented my findings, developed and submitted solutions and facilitated joint meetings. The net of my work was an immediately visible mutual change in attitude, and an increase in productivity from a daily average of 16 cases up to 22, and a significant decrease in errors as management took corrective action.

PROACTIVE RELATIONSHIP BUILDING:

- One aspect of my job as Negotiator was to track down and obtain overlooked or forgotten interest payments due us on bank remittances from other banks. This often involved large sums of money and banks are not required to voluntarily return the interest. Knowing that this would involve negotiations with a number of banks, I decided it would be more time-effective to establish business relationships with my counterparts in Bank, Bank, and other large banks at the outset, so that we could all save time and hassle in our future negotiations. My initiative resulted in improved business relationships among the banks, and spread to other types of payments. I never failed to regain the interest owed, always at least $5 million per month.

APPLYING GLOBAL BANKING SKILLS IN THE COMMUNITY

- Developed and conducted Financial Literacy Workshops within my community, some through churches and others through community centers. All have been very well received. In one case, a senior citizen retained my consulting services and after helping her complete her benchmark financial analysis, was able to help her to consolidate her debt, reduce it with a special debt consolidation loan, pay her credit cards to zero and have a $600 monthly surplus, which she will apply to her new loan balance and pay the loan off early. She is thrilled.

- For three years, as part of my duties with Company, I was a loaned executive to Operation Hope, Inc. As a Banker-Teacher, I taught a pilot program called "Banking On The Future." Aimed at young people in the Tri-State area, the program nurtured self-esteem while teaching these four modules: *The Basics of Banking, What are Checking and Savings Accounts? The Power of Credit, and Investment.* My participation was an additional duty, did not relieve me from any of my normal job duties and did add an additional 10 hours per week to my work load. The sacrifice was never too great because of the satisfaction I gained knowing that I may have helped at least one of my students escape the trap of debt or of living above their means.

PERSONALIZED CUSTOMER SERVICE:

- As a Position representative for Company, one of my clients was the Organization. The bulk of their retirees lived outside of the United States and many of the more elderly retirees would call or write each month with questions regarding their retirement deposits. While they should have directed their questions to their own bank and resolving their problems was not part of my job requirements, it cost me very little effort and time to be of service. Over that six year period, rendering the level of service that I would like someone to give to my elderly parents brought the bank and me a continual stream of favorable customer comments, and a number of new accounts whose total worth I estimate to have been $10 Million dollars.

PRODUCTIVITY PROBLEMS SOLVED WITH PERSONAL INITIATIVE:

- As a Position at Company, it soon became clear that throughout the company our internal clients were making the same processing errors and asking the same questions month-in and month-out. I decided to resolve the issue by creating and conducting a series of Brown Bag Lunch sessions and give them throughout the company. After "selling" my fearful manager, I wrote the training material and case studies, conducted the programs, resolved absolutely all the problems, and in the process made my manager look like a hero in the eyes of his boss.

PROFESSIONAL EXPERIENCE:

President, Company. City, State. **3/05 – Date**
Start-up financial literacy training and Consultancy Company offering workshops and 1:1 custom consulting to individuals, couples and small businesses. Began my own business while still employed at Company

Company. City, State. **9/82 – 02/06**
Quality Assurance Technical Trainer. 12/01 – 02/06
* Performed needs assessments and then developed and conducted customized financial, customer service and MIS training to resolve those business needs. Conducted programs either on-site or remotely throughout the United States, India, Singapore, Thailand and Malaysia
Supervisor, Money Transfer Compensation Unit. 3/88 – 12/01
* Supervised ten-person Ledger Liability Unit comprised of senior compensation analyst targeting collection of unjust enrichment in excess of $5M. Negotiation and technical training were integral components of my work
Customer Service Representative. 9/82 – 3/88
* Proactively resolve customer issues

EDUCATION:

Bachelor of Arts, Sociology/Psychology. University, City, State. **2001**
Associate of Arts, Liberal Arts. College. City, State. **1982**
NOTE: Completed degree while on active duty with Branch of Service at Post, City, State

ADDITIONAL SKILLS AND SPECIALIZED TRAINING:
- Design and layout of training materials
- Microsoft office: Word, Excel, PowerPoint, Paint Shop pro, NeatReceipts scanning tools

MILITARY:
Veteran, US ARMY. Sergeant E-4. Position. **1979 – 1982**
Honorable Discharge

OUTSIDE INTERESTS:
- Teach Sunday school
- Travel
- Reading and Personal Development
- Exercising and outdoor sports (Kayaking, mountain climbing)
- Retreats
- Financial seminars

DIRECTOR OF ENGINEERING - HIGH TECH MANUFACTURING FIRM. Division Level

This brilliant young engineer has a tremendously high energy level and can accomplish prodigious amounts of top-notch work in a short period of time. It requires a very special company and work environment to challenge his particular skill set and give him the opportunity to grow. Up to this point, none of his prior positions had challenged him at all. His abilities and his dream of making significant contributions were withering as his brilliance was made to conform to the lowest common denominator.

He learned of a Director of Engineering position, and had less than 48 hours to apply.

He had a résumé, but it was commonplace and offered no hint of his brilliance. During that very small window, we had to create a targeted cover letter and a custom Professional Profile™. Both follow.

After many hours of writing, phone calls and emails, we did it. He met the deadline and then we waited to see if he would move from applicant to candidate. Several days later, he called to advise that he was a candidate and would be phone-screened.

This was his first opportunity at an executive position managing a staff of over 20 professionals, many old enough to be his father or mother. Interview preparation and training were necessary, as was an introduction to interviewing etiquette.

We went through two rounds of interview practice / feedback, and developed interviewing strategies. He passed his phone screen with flying colors and a week later was invited in for an all-day round of interviews, including a group interview with his potential direct reports.

Being interviewed by his potential staff was a new experience for him. More coaching and more advice on the finer points of follow-up interview etiquette and writing effective and memorable thank-you notes.

Acing that round, shortly thereafter, he was invited to Corporate to interview with the C-level people: the CEO, the COO and the Corporate HR Director.

This was unusual in that Corporate generally did not interview candidates at this level. So why now?

The CEO's favorite word is "disruptive" and he wants "disruptive" people, particularly in critical positions like this one, because they will not accept mediocrity or business-as-usual. He had seen all of the résumés for this position and was not impressed. All were the same "spaghetti" résumés. None were "disruptive." No meatballs.

When he saw my client's Profile, he immediately declared it a "disruptive" résumé and said he wanted to meet the engineer behind it.

More interview strategizing, practice and post-interview etiquette, and shortly thereafter he was hired.

He is challenged and his star is on the rise. I now think of him as a "Disruptive Meatball."

NAME
Address
Cell:		Personal E-Mail:

Date

Ms. First Last
Position
Company.
Address
City, State, Zip

Dear Ms. Last Name,

Thank you for inviting me to submit my résumé for the position of Director of Engineering for Company's Product Name line. I am very excited, and the more I compared your requirements with my experience and interests, the more excited I became.

I want you to know right up front that I am not a plodding engineer; rather, I am a forward-thinking engineering leader with a proven track record for delivering high quality products on time and to standards. I have earned a reputation for innovation, rigorous testing procedures, a proactive and hands-on approach to cost reductions, meeting deadlines on large and small scale projects, and ability to lead and develop the engineers and technicians on my projects.

Here is how I compare in terms of what you seek for the position and what I offer:

YOU SEEK:	I OFFER:
1. Experience to direct all activities related to the research and development of hardware and software products, including creation, analysis, development, prototyping, testing and successful transition to manufacturing	• More than 15 years of experience leading product development teams in a range of industries – chemical, military, and medical – both domestically and internationally and success with transitioning designs from R&D to Manufacturing.
2 Manage the development of the division's full line of products, working with domestic and international operational staffs.	• Proven ability to manage the efforts of a diverse electro-mechanical product line. Strong ability to develop effective, lasting partnerships with all stakeholders with diverse backgrounds.
3. Review, validate, prioritize and allocate resources to manage and resolve problem reports	• Solid track record eliminating production delays without sacrificing quality, market reputation or product integrity while coordinating the work of as many as (12) business critical projects simultaneously.
4. Develop and implement new policies, processes, procedures and systems to ensure an efficient and effective product development.	• Drive to achieve innovation, measureable reduction in unit production cost and creative solutions to bottom line problems. A flexible approach to system design utilizing proven techniques.
5. Promote cooperation and communication between the various groups within the division to ensure operational efficiency and division profitability.	• High levels of commitment by all parties and highly successful projects both domestically and overseas.
6. Communicate performance metrics; evaluate performance, coach and counsel employees. Maintain harmonious employee/employer relationship	• A balanced left/right brain approach to managing employees developed over the years by mentoring from Engineering, HR and Organizational Development Executives. Proven ability to challenge other employees to achieve.
7. Promote the Division, its products, services and relationships with key and potential customers	• Effective and authentic company testimony to help win new business and maintain current clients

Please look over my professional profile. It describes in more detail examples of the results of the skills and abilities I bring to the table.

I'll check with you on June 1st to see about our next step unless you contact me first.

Thank you very much.

Best regards,

NAME
ADDRESS
CELL: PERSONAL EMAIL ADDRESS

OBJECTIVE: Director of Engineering for COMPANY NAME / DIVISION / PRODUCT, a position requiring significant project management, hardware and software research and development experience, metrics-based people management skills, and a deft touch to mentor and develop staff.

SPECIAL SKILLS AND ABILITIES:

Flexible managerial skills and experience to successfully guide, mentor, manage and develop a range of individuals of varying skills, education, age and temperament	Entrepreneurial mindset and the ability to balance multiple projects and priorities, carrying each through to successful completion	Strong sense of personal initiative to resolve bottom line problems, blending theoretical engineering expertise with practical applications
Accustomed to managing strict budgets, achieving results within time and budgetary constraints	Expert project management skills and corresponding experience to chart project's course, and adjust as needed	Broad range of engineering, computer, business software and peripherals

REPRESENTATIVE PROFESSIONAL ACCOMPLISHMENTS:

NEW PRODUCT DEVELOPMENT:
- Led a three-year engineering and design initiative for the major redesign of the Company Name / Product Name in-vitro diagnostic instrument. (Company)
    o Brought engineering and design efforts to completion 25% under budget; The unit price increase resulting from the product enhancements.
    o Based upon the perceived value increase, the team was able to sell the unit for 16% more and the sales increased by ~20%, managing customer expectations in the process.
    o Directly managed the contributions of six engineers and indirectly lead another 14 engineers and technicians. Partnered with an industrial design firm and manufacturers to reduce expected program costs by over $850K.
    o Led knowledge transfer teams from development to production with continued to support product through commercial sales.

- Over a five-year period, led over 30 project teams made up of internal engineers, component vendors and external consultants in development of new products from inception through commercial manufacturing. Developed and managed individual project budgets of up to $2M. Managed product sustainment throughout their lifecycles. In one case, product generated sustained 30% sales increase in its sector (Company)

- Demonstrated proficiency in development of proof of concept prototypes for mechanical, electrical (including power and PCB design), and embedded system programming. Championed projects through commercial implementation and initial production runs. Supported manufacturing during knowledge transfer phase, making myself available 24/7 by giving select manufacturing technicians my personal cell number. (Company)

Education
Advanced Special Student
Post Graduate Studies
27 / 33 hours of Ph.D. in Multiple Autonomous (Robotic) Systems
4 of 7 chapters of dissertation
U of STATE (6 hrs) and U of STATE (21 hrs)
GPA 3.5/4.0 GPA
Master of Science
Mechanical Engineering
University State Name. GPA: 3.5/4.0.
Bachelor of Science
Mechanical Engineering
University of State Name
GPA: 2.8/4.0
(GPA: 3.6/4.0 last 60 credit hours)
Dean's List last (5) Semesters

Computer Related Skills
Engineering/Technical
    Matlab
    Simulink
    LabView
    Maple
    CFDesign
    Programming:
    Visual Basic
    C/C++/C#

Productivity
    MS Office Professional
    SAP
    Modeling/Drafting:
    Solid Works
    Unigraphics
    Microstation
    AutoCAD

Additional Training
US Army Leadership Development
Design for Manufacturing / Assembly
Production Systems Modeling & Analysis
Project Management Institute PMP (174 PDU's)
Quality System Regulation FDA 21CFR820
EEOC / Ethics

Areas of Special Interest
System Modeling and Control
    (State Space, Classical)
Electronic Systems Theory and Design
Theory of Combustion
    (Slow Burn and Explosion)
Robotics (Controls, Modeling)
Mechanical Properties of Materials
(Materials Engineering)
Dynamics (Rigid, Multi-Body)

TOP SECRET Clearance
E.I.T. Certified

REPRESENTATIVE PROFESSIONAL ACCOMPLISHMENTS (continued):

EXISTING PRODUCT DEVELOPMENT
- As lead engineer for complex electro-mechanical products generating $1.7B annually, I was responsible for making the initial assessment of equipment problems referred to Engineering. I implemented a root cause analysis approach covering R&D to Implementation. After just two projects using this approach, the company realized over $100K a month savings. (Company)

- I was able to proactively identify obsolesce issues arising from ROHS and REACH legislation which may have prevented the selling of our instruments overseas. I generated a series of projects to address the future problems so that they could be solved in a non-crisis mode. (Company)

Page 2

RESOURCE MANAGEMENT
- Led program that reduced unit costs due to obsolescence and through product enhancements. Managed development costs and schedule for multi-year efforts, responsible for as many as 12 critical path projects simultaneously. My work saved the organization over $200K each month in ongoing bottom line costs for parts, labor and logistics. (Company)

- For the category of industry, I evaluated new software for use in electrical, instrumentation and process design. The proposed software required $100K in up-front costs and required $125k per year in licensing fees. After spending some time with the software, I found that, because of the overly complicated nature of the program, there was no productivity gain. I demonstrated some simple (and industry standard) techniques would yield significant productivity gains to my internal clients. After documenting the techniques, the company adopted my suggested processes. (Company)

INNOVATION, RESEARCH AND DEVELOPMENT
- Out of personal interest and curiosity, I developed a new manner in which to analyze military systems. My initiative resulted in an increasingly more realistic way to evaluate weapon effects. My research combined statistics, image analysis and materials engineering in a novel approach to the problem. This research attracted the attention of the US military branch leadership and I was asked to present my findings to the Senior Analysts Group (SAG) at the Pentagon and to senior researchers at the Department of Defense Research Centers across the US. The US military branch adopted this approach and it has become the standard approach to deterministically determine weapons effects. As a result of these efforts, I received an award from the three star Commanding General of the US Military Branch / Organization. (US MILITARY ORGANIZATION)

INTERDIVISIONAL COMMUNICATION
- For a production line update for the fiber industry, created an opportunity to automate the process due to structural symmetries. Working with a cross-functional team of engineers and designers, developed process through which a database and set of generic templates were used to automatically generate some 480 production drawings. Once the generic drawing template was agreed upon, the team only needed to input their equipment identification numbers into the database. The system would then generate drawings, and when requested, would plot them for review. This process yielded drawings with nearly 100% accuracy, and saved the project over 10,000 hours in design time. (Company)

MANAGEMENT AND POLICY
- Served as mentor, collaborator and support for peer, junior and senior engineers, providing developmental coaching and training in areas such as Lean Engineering principles and in the use of standard engineering practices. Initiated compliance paperwork to help projects in danger of missing milestones. Occasionally served as internal consultant providing software examples, prototype samples or solutions. These efforts have lead to four promotions. (Company)

- I started Name of Restaurant and Pub in City, State in 2007. Generating over $4M in sales in just 4 years, I managed a staff of 22, was responsible for all legalities of the business, financial reporting and building/maintaining solid government relations at the local, county, state and federal levels. After working a full day, I oversaw the night operations 6 days a week until closing. This work did not have a negative effect upon my engineering responsibilities evidenced by the promotions I received during this time. Sold the business to dedicate more time with family.

CUSTOMER / VENDOR RELATIONS
- I have learned the practical wisdom of cultivating a professional and mutually respectful relationship with my customers and vendors. It is well known that field engineers replace parts until problem goes away, guessing which part solved the problem. Generally, the engineering group receives only an incident report. I have found that through regular communication with field engineers, I could better understand what failure they observed and so could develop better designs. (Company, University of State Name, US Military Organization)

- I engage the fabrication vendors early on in the design process as a habit. In general, their personnel can provide advantageous input which can reduce cost and timelines. Further by getting their buy-in to the design and through regular communications with them, I am also able to negotiate better terms and, often times, receive prototype parts/assemblies at low or no costs with highly aggressive timelines. (Company, University of State Name, US Military Organization)

RELEVANT PROFESSIONAL HISTORY

US MILITARY ORGANIZATION, Location (Sept. 2009 – Contract End 12/11)
My work impacts on in excess $180M per year for infrastructure and $450M in development opportunities.

Deputy Manager / Senior Engineer – Infrastructure and Investment Management / Test and Evaluation
Providing guidance and oversight of US Military Branch test centers' investment and infrastructure planning. Providing technical guidance, planning, cost estimation, cost tracking and schedule oversight of major investments. Generating budgetary numbers for future costs. Inventory skills and capabilities of Department of Defense R&D test centers. Consult on and provide input to test activities to reduce timelines and costs. Engage in component- and system-level discussions to reduce timelines and assembly costs. Proposal development for new system development. Proposal writing and support to acquire new contract and development opportunities.

COMPANY (Formerly Company). Location (Sept. 2004 – Sept. 2009)
My work impacted on gross sales of over $1.7B per year based upon 2009 earnings.

Lead Engineer – Global Engineering Research and Development
Focused on troubleshooting complex electro-mechanical products. Managed interdisciplinary project teams in the US, Germany and an Italian contractor (Company – producer of automation solutions) to analyze causes of failures and the development of product and process enhancements. Also managed interdisciplinary teams responsible for new product development from inception to commercial manufacturing. Developed baseline costs and schedules. Developed pre-production designs for proof of concept efforts. Coordinated technical solutions with Supplier Operations, Marketing, Chemistry and Quality Teams to ensure availability and costs were in line with established standards and customer needs. Interfaced with customers to ensure their needs were understood and to set mutual expectations. Developed Failure Modes and Effects Analyses (FMEA).

Project/ Product Life Cycle Management. Oversaw quality assurance of medical device design (RA/QA). Maintained compliance with 510(k) submissions. Promptly completed Corrective Actions/Preventative Actions (CAPAs). Design validation, verification and reliability testing. Development of lean manufacturing SOPs. Development of laboratory capabilities. Developed junior personnel in skills and knowledge resulting in four promotions.

US MILITARY BRANCH ORGANIZATION. Location. (Aug. 2002 – Sept. 2004)
My work impacted $1.8B in materiel development projects.

Mechanical Engineer (GS-12+)
Simulation and modeling. Cost vs. Performance trades considered. Developed requirements for current and future systems, developed Key Performance Parameters (KPP) and developed Analysis of Alternatives (AoA). Worked with cross-military teams to develop Operational Requirements Documentation (ORD). Project estimation, planning and technical solutions.

University of STATE. Location. (Sept. 2000 –June 2002)
Research Assistant/Teaching Assistant
Designed and developed control systems and robotics systems. Modeling and simulation of the physical and electrical systems. Component design. Primary focus: Optimal Control of Multiple Autonomous Unmanned Ground Robots. Developed and executed tests for MAUGVs including cost tracking, schedule, analysis and report. Independent research in the areas of controls and nonlinear dynamics. Provided mentoring to over 80+ undergraduate students in the subjects of Statics and Dynamics. Planning and oversight of capital upgrades to laboratory infrastructure to generate additional capabilities for test and evaluation of research equipment.

COMPANY. Location. (Jan. 1999 – Sept. 2000)
Process Engineer (Reason for leaving: Began full time work on a PhD in Mechanical Engineering.)
Led a team of senior designers, PDMS designers and CAD draftsmen in the design and specification of chemical process lines and factory design. Managed an interdisciplinary team to improve communications and better standardization. On-site installation of equipment. Start-up testing and reporting of system functionality.

COMPANY. Location. (Jan. 1994 – Sept. 1999)
Electrical/Instrumentation/Mechanical Designer
Electrical, mechanical and instrumentation design. Designed automation systems to improve drafter productivity. Due to high energy and self-motivation, tasked to support projects in jeopardy of missing deadlines or exceeding personnel budget. Field testing and support of system start-up. Worked this position during my undergraduate education as an additional means of

support. During this employment, I transferred to the STATE NAME University to complete my education, after having made the transfer, I found that the College would not accept 40 credit hours. After completing a semester there, I transferred back to University of STATE NAME.

COMPANY. Location. (Sept. 1997 – Jan. 1998)
Site Lead/Designer *(Reason for leaving: Transferred from NAME OF STATE University to the University of STATE NAME to finish undergraduate degree.)*
In conjunction with plant engineers and technicians, designed the electrical and instrumentation systems of a tank farm for the on-site distillation of acetone and methanol. Appointed by the lead instrumentation engineer to direct the work of 25 electrical and instrumentation contractors.

In my Spare Time

RESTAURANT NAME. Location. (July 2006 –April 2011)
Managing Member/Owner
Managed a staff of up to 22 employees generating sales of over $4 million. Managed vendor interactions for advertising/ marketing, services, equipment and product. Developed and implemented Health, Safety and Environmental policies. Actively drove cost reductions and increased product quality. Developed and implemented HR policies. Developed and implemented Approved Supplier Approval policies. Developed and implemented procurement policy. Managed financial reporting from senior staff members. Managed government relations at the Local, County, State and Federal levels. Assumed legal responsibility for business. Developed and implemented a charitable giving policy which generated over $70K in donations to support research in Breast Cancer, Langerhans Cell Histeocytosis and Leukemia. Sold the business to dedicate more time with family.

OUTSIDE INTERESTS

- Family
- Soccer
- Chess
- Strategy games
- Reading – Control Systems, Math

NEW COLLEGE GRADUATE – BS IN PHYSICS / MATH

You'd think a graduate with a degree in Physics and Math with a specialty in laser optics would have an easy time finding an entry level engineering position.

Not in this economy.

This young man graduated with better than a 3.0 GPA from a well-respected Physics and Math program at an equally well-respected university.

His placement office did not encourage him to identify or think in terms of his accomplishments. Instead, they gave him a template with which to create a reverse-chronological résumé (that looked pretty much identical to his buddies / now competitors) and turned him loose on the world.

Several months mailing résumés later – nothing. He moved back home.

Like most people unaccustomed to thinking about their day-to-day activities in terms of accomplishments, when we first started working together he struggled to see the "accomplishment" in completing lab assignments or his senior project. To him, they were just activities, steps to go through to learn the material, pass the courses and graduate.

After some interesting conversations, he got the hang of it and began cranking out accomplishments essays.

Since he was not finding online openings for entry level engineering jobs in his field, we suggested he research and create a position description for one and include the key points in his cover letter following the YOU SEEK / I OFFER formula that has worked well for others.

Targeted cover letter and completed Profile in hand, we put him in contact with the new Director of Engineering whom you just met. They interviewed and the director is interested.

And in the meantime, as he networked and fine-tuned his Profile, two other interview opportunities have materialized. With a new tools and a plan, he's confident of finding an entry-level engineering position.

Here are his targeted cover letter and Professional Profile™.

Name
Address
Cell: Email:

Date

Mr. First and Last Name
Position
Company
Address
City, State, Zip

Dear Mr. Last Name,

First of all, thank you very much for the opportunity to meet with you during your recent visit to Seattle. As a new grad looking for my first "real job," I really appreciated your perspectives and your insights into COMPANY and what it takes to be a successful engineer in the "real world."

Since our meeting I have completed my résumé. While I see from your website that you do not at present have any openings for an entry-level Optics/ Laser Engineer, I've looked at some other postings and put together a summary of what I believe you would look for, and how I compare:

Entry-Level Optics/ Laser Engineer:

You Seek:	I Offer:
Bachelor or above in Optics, Laser, EE, or Physics. 1+ year hands-on experience on laser engineering	**B.A. in Physics, Minor in Mathematics. GPA: Physics:** 3.2/4.0 **Math:** 3.0/4.0 / Spent two years studying lasers and optics / **High School (Math/Science): Running Start Program** at City Community College. **Graduation GPA:** 3.8/4.0 from City High; 3.9 from City CC
Hands-on optical experience in one or more of these areas: • Research, develop, build and test lasers and optical amplifiers • Nonlinear optics / mode locked lasers • Short pulse characterization	**Senior project: Spatial-Spectral Hole Recovery**: Spectral hole burning with narrow-band laser holes in the characteristic absorbance pattern of a material at a specific frequency.
Someone who: • Is a self-motivated, energetic, positive, a quick study, willing, get-it-done team player • Effectively solves problems • Demonstrates strong personal commitment / focused work ethic • Has effective communication, presentation and people interaction skills	**At age 14, Eagle Scout project** was to plan and manage the restoration of native plants to a section of a wooded creek. Directed 28 Scouts and 6 adults / **Name Univ. Undergraduate Committee.** Finding gaps in the program and wanting to improve our education experience, I helped revise Physics curriculum / **Society of Physics Students - Vice President**: As graduating senior, left legacy for future students: plans to build a CO_2 laser and foundation for the advancement and continuation of SPS. / **Dean's Student Council (Letters and Science)** provided input and acted as liaison between Dean's office and Physics Department / **Various dormitory** volunteer and elected offices / **High School Student / Athlete** recognition

Thanks again for your time, Mr. Last Name. My résumé is attached and I have my fingers crossed.

Sincerely,

Name

Name

Address   Cell   Email

Education:
BS in Physics and Mathematics
Montana State University. 5/2011
• *Specialization:*
 • *Lasers and Optical Testing*

Testing Equipment:
Linear Actuator
Optical Power meter AD converter
Fabry-Perot Interferometer
Photo detector
Digital Oscilloscope
Stepper Motor
Acousto-optic modulator
Fast photo diode
Pulse generator RF Amplifier
Variable Angle Ellipsometer
Energy Ratiometer

Opticals Fibers:
Single-mode optical fiber (Fiber optics 630 HP),
Multi-mode optical fiber (3M optical fiber)

Lasers:
HeNe Laser
Pulse Beam Laser

Software:
Matlab-Mathworks
Maple15-Maplesoft
Cadense PSpice AD Advanced Analysis
NI Labview
MS Office

OBJECTIVE: Full-time permanent Optics/ Laser Engineer (laser technology / optical testing) position with Company, a company that values scientific rigor, intellectual curiosity, the optimism and enthusiasm of a new college graduate, and the uncompromisingly strong work ethic of an Eagle Scout.

MY PROMISE: To consistently deliver cost-effective, creative solutions while adhering to strict protocols designed to assure safety and precision in everything I do. I am constantly on time with project deadlines. I work to understand the parameters of all of the projects in which I am involved. My intention is to always to improve my work and be a benefit to my project group.

QUALIFICATIONS OVERVIEW:

• Strong academic experience in physics and mathematics
  • **Physics** GPA: 3.2/4.0 **Math** GPA: 3.0/4.0
  • **Senior Project: Spatial-Spectral Hole Recovery**: Spectral hole burning with narrow-band laser holes in the characteristic absorbance pattern of a material at a specific frequency. Spectrum Lab: Dr. Name Ph.D.
  • Consistently recognized for troubleshooting skills and resolving challenging technology issues with laser testing and calibration
  • Quickly learn-and master new technology; equally successful in both team and self-directed settings; proficient in a range of computer systems, tools and testing methodologies
• **Eagle Scout at age 14**. Embedded values of commitment, focus and goal attainment

SPECIAL SKILLS AND ABILITIES:

• Up-to-the-minute knowledge of cutting-edge Physics and Math research and practices	• Personal initiative to undertake and achieve stretch goals	• Demonstrated ability to succeed in both individual and team environments
• Planning, laying out step by step process	• Creative thoughts, solutions	• Developing and executing strategies
• Effective presentations holding listener attention	• Analyzing, comparing data	• Construction/deconstruction of instruments

REPRESENTATIVE PROFESSIONAL ACCOMPLISHMENTS:

RESEARCH, DEVELOP, BUILD AND TEST LASERS

Senior Project: Spatial-Spectral Hole Recovery: For my Senior Project, in conjunction with Spectrum Labs and using Maxwell's equation (Hilbert Transforms) I wrote a Matlab program that calculated the transmission of Chirp Laser through the absorbance patterns inside S2 crystals and through same material without any absorbance. I was able to predict a non-linear term from the difference in the calculations to cancel prior distortions, and further enhanced the algorithm to include phase noise and running comparison of the effects of phase noise processed with different filtering. The ultimate net effect will be the replacement of DVDs with a new generation of storage disc.

Research, Develop, Build and Test Lasers – continued Page 2

Stimulated Emission, Amplification of Spontaneous Emission and Dye Laser: Using another laser, I built a dye laser from scratch in order to study and quantify the phenomena that forms the physical bans of lasers. The most difficult part of the process was the alignment of the dye and the mirrors. To overcome this, I felt the best was to adjust the height against the black holder of the dye case and then move the light horizontally. By proceeding with patience and precision, my team and I were able to measure the beam waist, power and efficiency and ultimately calculate the properties of the laser we built.

Laser Light Show Driver: For the final lab project for our Laser class, my lab partner and I built two four-bit digital-to-analog converters which we placed in parallel formation to create an eight-bit circuit. Jointly we created the hardware needed to drive a laser light show. Specifically, the program presented the letter "B" – flying and buzzing the wall like a .... Bee! It had visibly-flapping wings, and after buzzing around, landed on a prism-shaped "land mine" where it exploded (transforming itself from "bee" to "boom").

Labview Driver: As part of my Senior Project (Spatial-Spectral Hole Recovery), as a check on the accuracy of the simulated results I obtained, I simulated white light and random noise inside an S2 crystal by changing a voltage across the crystal that can be easily controlled. After finding a complete Labview driver online, and then adding the ability to read text files of voltage outputs, I had it use the outputs to create an arbitrary wave and remove the not-required additions. Since this was the first time I had created a Labview driver on my own, I had to teach myself the programming and supporting subroutines. I was able to confirm that the data was being simulated correctly.

Optical Fiber: To learn how light propagates through optical fiber, I coupled a HeNe Laser into a single 100m single-mode optical fiber measuring the velocity of the optical pulse. To better understand this process I had to determine the maximum coupling efficiency of the optical fiber and discover the velocity with which light pulses propagates in the single mode fiber. I continued adjusting the x and y components to refine the process until I was able to precisely center the microscope objective (MO). My calculations were 100% accurate and I can use this knowledge in any number of ways to improve data communication.

SELF-MOTIVATION, FOCUSED WORK ETHIC

Awarded Eagle Scout at Age 14: My Eagle Scout project was to plan and manage the removal of an unwanted blackberry infestation and restore native plants to a section of a wooded creek near my home in City, State. I sought out and obtained donated supplies and over 150 plants from local nurseries, coordinated with the appropriate city and state authorities, and recruited and managed volunteers ranging in age from six to who-knows-how-old? (10 adults and 28 Scouts.) We replanted the area to City and State standards in 20% less time that had originally been budgeted, and Issaquah saved that money for other projects. I became the youngest Boy Scout in my troop to achieve the rank of Eagle Scout.

Student Athlete: As a simultaneous student-athlete at Issaquah High School and scholar in the Running Start Program at Bellevue Community College, I graduated with a 3.8 GPA from Issaquah High and a 3.9 GPA from Bellevue for my senior year. I played soccer throughout my high school career and was offered scholarships to play at six Division III colleges with academic student aide. Because of my desire to attend a top-rated university to study physics and math, I turned them all down and instead committed myself to repay student loans in exchange for a first-rate scientific education from Montana State University where I graduated with a 3.2 overall GPA and earned my Bachelor of Science degree in Physics with a minor in Mathematics. My GPAs in my respective specialties were 3.4 and 3.0.

Name // Cell

Representative Professional Accomplishments – continued Page 3

Student Involvement: When I was in my senior year at Name University, the Chair of the Physics Department had over 80 students he could ask to represent his department at a series of student-involvement conferences called by the Dean of the College of Letters and Science. My Chair selected me to represent him. I took my responsibility seriously. I researched the various issues the Dean put to us, and solicited, consolidated and presented input, feedback and suggestions from residents in my dorm, friends and as many other students as I could engage in conversation. I believe I was an effective liaison for the ongoing dialogues between the Dean, my Chair and my fellow students. Now that I have graduated, I'll be interested to see what the Dean will do with my recommendations.

Society of Physics Students - Vice President: At University, Physics students learned almost as much outside the classroom as in, and collaboration was definitely the name of the game. During my senior year, I was elected Vice President of the University's Society of Physics Students. The fact that this was my final year was weighing heavily on me, and I wanted us to leave a tangible, positive legacy for future Physics students. I coordinated the simultaneous research and development of detailed fabrication, assembly and budgeting plans for two ambitious projects: to build a CO_2 laser and a rail gun. Purely voluntary, this was in addition to keeping up with our regular class work. Ready to start building, we ran out of time, but the plans are there for those following behind us. I learned a good deal about project management and management in general, and take pride in the fact that I was motivated to give something back to others, not just gain knowledge for myself.

Education Is Paramount: When I decided to come to Name University, I turned down full-tuition soccer scholarships at several second-tier schools because I wanted a first-rate education in Physics and Mathematics. Finding gaps in the program and wanting to improve the education experience of incoming freshmen, I volunteered to sit on the Undergraduate Committee, made up to two undergraduate students and seven faculty members. It was an eye-opening experience for me in terms of how things work, and I'm proud to say that together we significantly strengthened the academic rigor of several critical courses. My personal contribution was this: One of the courses I argued for strongly to become a part of the professional degree program was thermodynamics. Thermodynamics was an optional class offered once a year. Arguably, many graduate programs were looking for this as part of the professional curriculum. The department adopted my recommendation and the course is now offered every semester.

EDUCATION:

University, City, State. May, 2011
Bachelor of Science. Physics w/minor Mathematics. GPA: 3.2/4.0

Community College, City, State. June 2006
Running Start Program. GPA: 3.9/4.0

High School, City, State. June 2006
National Honor Society. GPA: 3.8/4.0
Soccer 2004-2005

Relevant Professional History – continued Page 4

Name // Cell

RELEVANT PROFESSIONAL HISTORY:

Company, City, State. May 2006 – August 2009 (*Summers and school breaks*)
Machine Shop Operator
Trained to operate machine shop equipment: Arc Welder, Surface Grinder, CNC Lathes, Manual Lathe, CNC 3 Axis Mill, Drill Press, Manual Mill, Hydraulic Feed Metal Cutting Band Saw

PART-TIME STUDENT JOBS:
Cashier
- University **Ticket Office.** City, State May 2010 –August 2011
- University **Book Store.** City, State. Sept 2008 – May 2009 (Work/Study position)
- Name **Theaters – City, State.** May 2006 – August 2008

SERVICE/AWARDS:
- University Arts and Science Dean's Student Counsel   August 2010- May 2011
- Undergraduate Physics Committee   August 2009- May 2011
- University Society of Physics Students- Vice President August 2009- May 2011
- University Residents Hall Association- Social Chair   August 2009- May 2010
- Eagle Scout Award- Boy Scouts of America   November 25, 2003

OUTSIDE ACTIVITIES:
Fencing
Soccer
Photography
Reading
Long boarding
Hiking
Skiing
Video Gaming
Anime

TRANSITIONING FROM MILITARY TO CIVILIAN

Unfortunately, many of our returning veterans have difficulty finding fulfilling work in the civilian world.

My client, a young US Army Infantry Captain whose six-year commitment included 18 months in Iraq, was fortunate. He found a job, and he wants something more challenging and rewarding, one that will use his skills more effectively.

We connected through our alumni association and I agreed to help him translate the valuable skills and experience he acquired in the Army into civilian terms. Having been both an officer in the Army Reserves and a recruiter for my employers for many years was a plus.

After graduating with his Bachelor's degree, he enlisted in the US Army, completed his Basic training, then Officer Candidate School and was commissioned a Second Lieutenant.

The Army loves to train and develop competent people, and he fit the profile. Like so many who undertake the completion of the Professional Profile™ process, the challenge was to help him see the accomplishments inherent in completing his everyday duties.

One example. As a platoon leader, he told me about a multi-mission training exercise he and his platoon participated in, their final one before they were deployed to Iraq. The requirement would have been challenging enough had his equipment and platoon personnel levels been at 100%; both were in the 60% range. But since he is trained to get the job done with the resources available to him, adversity did not stop him; he succeeded. That mindset will be very valuable to the company lucky enough to hire him.

At first, he did not see that as an accomplishment; to him it was "just doing my job." However, to a former HR recruiter, his accomplishment demonstrated these special skills and abilities: planning and execution ability, commitment to find a way and succeed in the face of adversity, leadership, tenacity, team work. The list could go on.

Once he began to look at his work through a different lens, he quickly filled his data banks.

Having a natural bent for logistics and analysis, he thought an obvious direction would be financial analysis and he is enrolled in an MBA program. As we discussed his experiences and interests, it was clear that he was an effective trainer and I suggested he might also want to consider the training and development aspect of Human Resources. That was an eye-opener and he now sees he has an array of options to consider.

He found a position of interest and we crafted a targeted cover letter and Professional Profile™ and submitted it on-line. I'd love to say that his first application using these tools was a home run. Sad to say, it was not. But the good news is that, with his can-do attitude and his new-found knowledge, he has no doubt he will be successful.

Here are his targeted cover letter and Professional Profile™.

NAME
Address
City, State Zip
Email: Cell:

Date

Good afternoon, Company Name Recruiter

In Re: Posting # / Position Name

I am responding to your website posting for the above position. After comparing what I believe are the essential requirements for the position and my experience, I think I'm about a 95% fit, and believe we have reason for conversation.

YOU SEEK EXPERIENCE:	I OFFER:
• Creating and delivering SAP-based initiatives for adult learning solutions using cutting edge technology to support a growing organization	• Five years of ever-increasing responsibility in the continuous improvement training cycle of delivery / evaluation / adjustment / delivery using state-of-the-art US Army methodology/ equipment and civilian SAP-based initiatives
• Supporting and implementing end user training, analysis, development and evaluation of technology-based training to monitor and evaluate training effectiveness	• Numerous examples demonstrating computer-based analytical and project management skills and the taking of personal initiative to effectively apply, evaluate and adjust technology training solutions to business problems
• Partnering collaboratively with a range of project partners and stakeholders	• Demonstrated history of collaboration with stakeholders and end users; trained to assume effective leadership role as needed

In my first job out of the University of State was the US Army. Now, as a veteran of five years in the Army (18 months of which were in a combat zone in Iraq) and one year as a Position, I have developed my personal philosophy of work, summed up as follows: *"Judge by results. Often harsh. Always fair."*

This is not to say that I bring a harsh mindset to a job; rather that I am a results-oriented person.

I have admired Company for years, and have been a co-op member since 2006. As I said at the outset, on the basis of my experience and your requirements, I believe we will have a mutually worthwhile conversation. I look forward to speaking with you shortly.

Best regards,

Name

NAME
Address
City, State Zip
Email: Cell:

OBJECTIVE: Position Name at Company, a position requiring technology-enabled learning experience to analyze performance issues, develop and deliver effective training solutions, project management skills, and personal initiative, poise and physical "presence"

SPECIAL SKILLS AND ABILITIES:

• Planning, organizing and analyzing of performance and financial data in SAP environment	• Deal effectively in ambiguous situations where priorities are in flux	• Delight in planning strategies and then executing them with both enthusiasm and flexibility
• Strong attention to detail in order to customize training solutions to address specific performance objectives	• Significant experience in opening, maintaining and facilitating effective linear and matrix-based lines of communication	• Experienced multi-tasker, particularly relating to logistics and operations

REPRESENTATIVE PROFESSIONAL ACCOMPLISHMENTS:

NEW HIRE TRAINING:
- In my position as Title for the Renton District, I manage a team of 14 Clerks supporting three job title handling over 2,750 cases per month. Coming from a background where training is critical and a number-one priority, I was astonished to find that when I came on board, there was no formal, systematic training for new-hires – me or anyone else. My learning curve was just about vertical and it took me several months to feel both comfortable and effective in my job. Once I did, I created a comprehensive new-employee training program at my location. It is a flexible design covering a two-week period and includes a new-hire orientation, face-to-face meetings with job title and other key personnel, self-guided learning to understand our policies and procedures, computer training, and paired mentoring with a reliable and experienced clerk who has first-line responsibility to sign off when the new-hire is fully trained. I am ultimately responsible to certify their readiness to perform their job. Six new-hires have completed my program. Job title, administrative managers and supervisors have been quick to notice and enthusiastically comment upon the sharp decrease in clerical errors. We have a 100% retention rate of new hires during 2011, a first for my location.

SAP-BASED ADULT LEARNING SOLUTIONS:
- Training innovation and personal initiative are lessons the Army offers to teach both officers and enlisted personnel. As Position, part of my job entails an end-of-day accounting of all revenues received by each clerk, consolidation of their deposits and producing a daily revenue report. When I came on board and used the existing system, it took me between 60 and 90 minutes per day to complete that task. As the only one familiar with Excel in my location, I took it upon myself to create a very straightforward and user-friendly spreadsheet for each of the clerks to input their information as they went. Somewhat hesitant at first, all of the clerks came around and appreciated learning something new that has expedited their work. Seldom does it take me longer than 30 minutes per day to complete my report, a 66% time savings. My process is now in use throughout all seven locations.

COMMITMENT TO TRAINING:
- As an Army Infantry officer training with my platoon prior to deployment in Iraq, I focused every fiber of my being on learning all I could because when we arrived in-country, their lives would be in my hands, and mine in theirs. Our final training exercise prior to deployment was an Emergency Deployment Readiness Exercise. We were given just five hours notice to plan and execute our primary mission – to successfully raid an insurgent compound, and then be prepared for a follow-on mission. That would be challenging enough if my platoon and equipment was at 100%; it was not. My personnel strength was at only 60% and my available vehicles and equipment at 66%. Nonetheless, I have been trained to succeed with the resources available to me. I successfully planned and led the primary mission, and then three additional missions with little to no preparation time. Out of 20 platoon leaders in the exercise, I was one of only three who earned an "Excellent" evaluation rating, and was selected to serve on my Battalion Commander's staff.

BUILDING COLLABORATIVE RELATIONSHIPS:
- Upon graduating from Officer Candidate School, I was a Captain and went to Iraq. When I got there, bombs were still going off, people were dying, and I was assigned to advise the Iraqi Army. Unfamiliar with their capabilities, I quickly saw they were weak in operations planning and in the gathering, processing and dissemination of intelligence. Operations planning is one of my strengths and I was quickly able to help improve their performance. Identifying and addressing their intelligence needs took more doing. I prefer to understand how things are currently being done before suggesting alternatives. Therefore I began by befriending several Iraqi intelligence officers and sharing information with them. In relatively short order, they began to reciprocate and together we began to develop and conduct joint intelligence briefings. We were soon able to jointly identify patterns of enemy attacks, track and anticipate their moves. Over the first three months in that assignment, the number of enemy attacks on US and Iraqi forces decreased by 70%. I don't know what percentage of that drop was due to my efforts, but I claim a respectable amount of credit.

- Recruiting for the US Army on a college campus when the country is simultaneously engaged in two unpopular wars is difficult. After graduating OCS I was given an opportunity to go back to State for two months and help recruit ROTC cadets. I had not done ROTC, so I had to learn about how it worked and I had only been in the Army at that point for five months. I received a crash course in ROTC basics and was told to focus on recruitment at Name University. Operating largely on my own, I set up booths at school events and in the dining hall during lunches. In uniform, I walked the campus, engaging students in conversation and posting flyers. Since I had only been in the Army for five months, my perspective was fresh and new, and I could relate to them as students. I talked about the Army in general and never pressured them into ROTC. I generally achieved my personal goal of having at least five quality contacts daily. I signed up nine new cadets during my two months. Nine in two months may not seem like much, but it was significant to me, to them and to the Army. I achieved the Army Achievement Medal for my accomplishment, my first Army award.

MAINTAINING AND UPDATING TRAINING MATERIALS:
- One of my many duties in Iraq was serving as the Electronic Warfare Officer (EWO for short). I'm not an electrical engineer but I learned about and understand spectrum management, electromagnetic interference and why communication devices do not work and how to jam radio and cell phone communications. As part of my duties, I was responsible to over 100 pieces of electronic jamming equipment valued at more than $2.5M. My work was critical to the lives of both Iraqi and US troops because we used the jamming devices to block signals from the terrorists' home-made radio-controlled explosive devices (aka "bombs"). I was responsible for ensuring that our software was up-to-date and in perfect working order. In addition, my responsibilities included distance learning training of 16 other platoons how to properly use their jamming equipment to protect themselves from attack. I became the battalion's subject-matter expert for electronic warfare. Most importantly, we defeated all electronic attacks. During my 18-month tour, not one soldier within my area of responsibility, US or Iraqi, was killed or wounded by electronically-detonated terrorist bombs.

PROJECT MANAGEMENT:
- In comparison to civilian jobs, one of the distinguishing characteristics about the Army is that platoon leaders (junior officers) are often given responsibility far beyond their years, and are held accountable to perform successfully. At age 25, during my 18 months in Iraq, on ten separate occasions I signed for and was personally responsible for safeguarding and inventorying equipment (both secret and non) valued at just under $40 million. The inventory process was tedious and time-consuming because I had to read and insure the accuracy of serial numbers of hundreds of pieces of equipment. Platoon leaders were free to organize the inventory process as they wished. Based on how I organized and managed my inventory process, I completed my cycle in five days, typically a day or two faster than my peers. During my ten inventories, 100% of equipment was accounted and no losses were reported. There was no financial loss to the Army and no fear of our nation's secrets would be exposed. Additionally, because my system was faster than most, I could more rapidly release equipment for use in training, thus expediting training.

- After completing my tour of duty as an infantry officer in Iraq, I brought the knowledge and discipline I acquired there directly into an MBA program at Seattle University. Accustomed to creating complicated logistical Excel spreadsheets in Iraq, I thought I was pretty good with the tool. However, I was challenged to create a different kind of spreadsheet – one that will enable me to run a complete financial analysis on any company I choose. The essence of completing this project required a good deal of research to properly structure and input IF statements. Now that I have mastered the process, I can now quickly and easily perform a range of sophisticated financial analysis, well beyond the scope of simple formulas. I aced my project.

COLLABORATION AND PERSONAL INITIATIVE:
- Miscommunication in the civilian world can cost money. In the Army, it can cost lives. Due to a new security agreement with the Iraqi army, we were required to brief and get Iraqi approval of all patrols that US forces did in Iraq. As a young and newly-arrived Infantry Captain, I was given the responsibility of advising and training an Iraqi General's staff, and part of my duties required me to conduct daily briefings to secure that approval. My predecessor's practice had been to conduct these briefings using PowerPoint slides *in English* and have the interpreter sight-translate their contents into Arabic. I questioned the wisdom of this because I knew that we had lost American lives on these patrols due to miscommunication. To communicate as clearly as possible, I proposed we present the PPT slides in Arabic, not English. Bureaucracy, whether in a war zone or an office, is still bureaucracy, and I had to defend the soundness of my recommendation in the face of pressure from superior officers. I held my ground and my Battalion Commander authorized the change. The effectiveness of our communication and coordination immediately improved, and for the duration of my tour, the incident rate of conflict between our patrols and Iraqi troops dropped to zero.

RELEVANT PROFESSIONAL EXPERIENCE:

Organization, City, State. JAN 2011-Present
Position.
Manage administrative clerical staff of 14 supporting three position
- Primary focus: strict adherence to all local, state, and federal laws and guidelines. Liaison between clerical staff and position
- Use SAP's BusinessObjects to analyze and synthesize organization data into a presentable deliverable to upper management
- Use range of Microsoft tools (primarily PowerPoint, Excel, Outlook, SharePoint, and Word), to produce, analyze, and present a variety of reports, analysis, and information to diverse levels of government officials. Recipients include attendees of daily staff briefings

United States Army. JAN 2006 – JAN 2011
Status: Combat Zone Veteran / Honorable Discharge
Rank at Discharge: Captain
Operations Officer. Fort Lewis, WA. AUG 2010 - JAN 2011
After completing 12-month assignment in Iraq with the US Army 2nd Infantry Division, returned to Fort Lewis to complete my service commitment. **Responsible for:**
- Developing and conducting a range of training and briefing sessions to reorient and transition veterans returning home from serving in Iraq
- Contributing to development of long-term strategic operating plans for future worldwide deployment of US troops
- Advising new Commanding Officer of training facilities and resources available at Fort Lewis and Yakima Training Center
- Liaising between Headquarters and subordinate units to disseminate, coordinate and track status of projects, from inception to completion
- Using Microsoft Office (primarily PowerPoint, Excel, Outlook and Word), to produce, analyze, and present a variety of reports, analysis, and information to both higher ranking and lower ranking officers and senior enlisted personnel

Foreign Military Liaison / Operations Officer. 2nd Infantry Div. MAR 2009-AUG 2010
Baqubah, Iraq / Fort Lewis, WA
Rank: Captain
Managed a joint operations and intelligence center with the 18th Iraqi Army Brigade. Responsibilities included:
- Maintaining up-to-the-minute and as-accurate-as-possible real-time situational reporting on the battlefields for which we were responsible
- Briefing US and Iraqi military officers on current battlefield conditions
- Building stronger working relationships and trust with Iraqi military and government personnel by learning about their culture and being friendly
- Using Microsoft tools, produce daily morning meeting and a weekly executive status meetings for the Iraqi Army and US Army to share intelligence and coordinate separate as well as joint military patrols. (To reduce chances of US patrols being shot by friendly Iraqi forces, on my own initiative, successfully championed preparation of PPT presentations *in Arabic* rather than English to guarantee Iraqi understanding of where US patrols would be operating – a major accomplishment)

Anti-Armor Platoon Leader. Fort Lewis, WA. SEP 2007-FEB 2009
Rank: First Lieutenant
In preparation for assignment in Iraq, trained, led and managed a 12-man Anti-Armor Platoon. **Working with veteran Platoon Sergeant, was ultimately responsible for:**
- Planning and executing all tactical and skills training in preparation for being sent to Iraq
- Being fiscally responsible for $10 million worth of US government equipment

in Officer Evaluation Reports, ranked in top third of my peers in my battalion

Army Officer Student. Fort Jackson, SC/Fort Benning, GA. JAN 2006-AUG 2007
Commissioned as Infantry Officer in US Army
Rank Upon Entering Program: Specialist E-4
Rank Upon Commission: Second Lieutenant
Completed:
- US Army Airborne School on airborne operations and parachute techniques
- Basic Combat Training
- Officer Candidate School.
- Graduated Infantry Officer Basic Course

Primary elements of curricula were:
- Mission planning
- Military training
- Infantry tactics
- In addition to combat skills, trained to present information and analysis to a varied audiences from the rank of General on down, for both US and Iraqi military

EDUCATION

City University. City, WA.
MBA Program.
Current GPA: 3.2 / 4.0
- As of September 2011, have completed 12 credits of this 73-credit program.
- Working full-time job (45 hours per week) will graduate June 2014

University of State. City, State.
Bachelor of Arts. GPA: 2.6 / 4.0. DEC 2005
Major: Government and Politics. **Minor:** Criminal Justice
School Activities:
- Social **Fraternity**. Very active for all four years. Offices held / activities:
    - Fraternity President
    - Athletic Chair
    - Vice President, Alumni Relations
    - Fraternity representative to Inter-Fraternity Council
    - Intramural sports (football, basketball, baseball)

US Army. AUG 2007
- **Graduate. Infantry Officer Basic Course**
- **Graduate. Airborne School** (Airborne Operations and Parachute Techniques)

HONORS AND AWARDS
- Bronze Star Medal, 2010
- Army Commendation Medal, 2010
- Expert Infantryman Badge, 2008
- Army Achievement Medal, 2007
- Global War on Terrorism Service Medal, 2006
- National Defense Service Medal, 2006
- Army Service Ribbon, 2006

FOREIGN LANGUAGE PROFICIENCY:
- Learned enough Arabic for basic polite short conversations and working vocabulary of military terms

OUTSIDE INTERESTS:
During my free time (between full-time employment, my MBA classes and making plans to get married in August, 2012), I enjoy:
- Camping
- Hiking
- Jogging
- Running
- Working out in the gym

TRANSITIONING FROM SOLOPRENEUR TO EMPLOYEE:
From self-employed journeyman carpenter / home maintenance expert to employed carpenter

This is not a happy time for construction workers.

This man is a friend of mine (Don) and every now and again we hang out for coffee. He is a craftsman, a perfectionist on anything regarding home maintenance. Imagine Leonardo Da Vinci with a tool belt.

Some time back, when he was self-employed, I gave him a copy of my book, and our lives went on.

Out of the clear blue he sent me the following unsolicited email testimonial and the Professional Profile™ he created for himself that immediately landed him a job in Seattle's devastated construction industry.

Here is his testimonial. His targeted cover letter and Profile follow.

From: Name (email address)
Sent: Sunday, May 29, 2011 10:04 PM
To: Donald M. Burrows
Subject: Your letter of Recommendation Sir!

When I first heard of the "Accomplishment Based Résumé" I thought the idea was novel, but didn't think about it much, as I wasn't looking for employment. When I recently became unemployed, I realized with the unemployment as high as it was, that my résumé would have to stand out somehow. More importantly, I would have to show any future employer why I was worth the wages I was asking for. Trying to condense my skills and abilities into a chronological résumé was painful for me. How could I possibly show a perspective employer that one of my greatest strengths is thinking outside of the box to create real and lasting solutions, when a chronological résumé is exactly that. . . a box. The thought was depressing to me. Keeping in mind that pink stationary and scented envelopes are frowned upon in the construction industry, I turned to Don Burrows, who kindly gave me ANOTHER copy of his book (long story). When the student is ready a teacher will appear. Don Burrows' book outlines a process for controlling one's own career by removing the focus from titles and certificates and placing the spotlight firmly on what a person can do! Résumé s That Résumé Careers résumé d my career, but also helped me open doors that were not open with a chronological résumé. For example I have never officially held the title of a "Supervisor" but so much of what I have done absolutely requires the same skill set. So by using Don Burrows process, I was able to show perspective employers how my mind actually works. I was able to show how I would create a process to accomplish a goal, or how I overcome challenges and interact with people. The epiphany that I had accomplishments that would qualify me for multiple roles in multiple industries was absolutely delightful! The implications of this realization are far reaching for me and have changed the way I view my career. As cliché as it may sound, I am free, free from the box. I was now able to use my "Accomplishment Database" to submit a unique and polished résumé to companies in any applicable industry in minutes, thereby increasing my visibility and chances of an interview. The job seeking process became an adventure to me, but the adventure didn't last long. The direct result of following Don Burrows' process was securing an interview with my target company. I was unemployed for a total of 1 week. After I was hired I was told at a later date that my résumé was "the best résumé I have ever seen!" high praise from a former Panasonic Japan exec. This compliment amused me as I had gone from having the worst résumé to "the best" in the length of time it took me to read "Résumé s That Résumé Careers".

Don, Thank you so much for the book. Your work has truly impacted my life as well as my family. I am truly grateful. Attached is a copy of my résumé in the form of a pdf. I have to tell you that the cover letter was a major factor at getting the interview.

Sincerely,

Name and Phone

Date

Name
Company
Address
City, State, Zip

Greetings Name,

I am responding to the 3/15/2011 posting on Craigslist for restoration carpenter. Based on the requirements covered in the job posting, I believe I am an excellent match for this position.

Company Name **Seeks:**	*I Offer:*
• A highly qualified and presentable individual	• 17 years of experience in construction, and 10 years experience in restoring, remodeling and repairing residential and commercial properties
• Integrity, pride and love for one's work.	• Have earned the reputation of employers and fellow employees for being a knowledgeable, hard working individual who gains creative satisfaction for job completion.
• The ability to be a team player and work with others	• Ability to coordinate with team members in either a subordinate or managerial role. Giving and receiving feedback that is both constructive and polite. Amicably communicate processes and roles.
• Creativity, problem solving	• Creatively use or modify solutions from one problem to address another. Posses a wide range of task specific tools
• People skills	• Understanding that ours is a service oriented industry; therefore, I take pride in my interpersonal communication skills which have lead to excellent business and personal referrals.

Thank you for reviewing my credentials. I can be reached at Cell phone number.

Sincerely,

Name
Address
City, State, Zip
Cell
Email address

And the Professional Profile he created follows:

Name
Address
Cell

OBJECTIVE: Full time carpentry position with Company Name, a company that needs a highly skilled and presentable individual who takes pride and care in their work while maintaining excellent customer relationships independently or as a team member.

SKILLS & COMPETENCIES:

• Expect excellence in my own performance, incorporating feedback towards that end	• Focus for current task without losing sight of the larger goal	• Personal satisfaction from being a part of a team, working diligently to achieve individual and team goals
• Confident in my ability to learn, request assistance, and grow personally	• Effectively research solutions utilizing human, written, and online resources	• Creatively use or modify solutions from one problem to address another
• Politely communicate discovery of technical deficiencies; direct appropriate repairs safely and efficiently	• Ability to organize a flexible schedule to achieve daily and long term goals	• Quickly learn new software and computer applications
• Possess a positive work attitude and thrive on challenges	• Works safely and efficiently with no Worker's Compensations injuries for over 17 years	• Create repeat business by building and maintaining excellent relations with customers

REPRESENTATIVE PROFESSIONAL ACCOMPLISHMENTS:

Full bathroom design and remodel -
I interviewed the homeowner to discover his personal tastes in materials and gain an understanding of his overall goals for his bathroom. I then translated that information to the Auto-Cad Program "Chief Architect". Though I had no prior experience with Auto Cad type programs I was able to learn and utilize this program to create and submit three dimensional renderings, floor plans, material lists, and costs to the homeowner for approval. Once the project started I maintained an open and friendly dialogue with the homeowner, vendors, and subcontractors to execute the original schedule, and implement any unforeseen scheduling changes.

To minimize intrusion on the homeowner's living space, I designated and maintained operational, staging, trash and recycling areas to facilitate the full use of materials keeping the project clean and organized. During the course of the project I discovered multiple electrical code violations. I designed and installed a new circuit to IRC and UPC specifications by utilizing written and human resources. I inspected all work completed by subcontractors. In some cases I recalled subcontractors respectfully citing contractual requirements to repair rejected installations. This project was completed on time, within budget and surpassed all of the owners expectations, with no recalls. After the project was completed I established a yearly inspection of this bathroom to make sure all of the installations are functioning at 100%, and to make my services available for any other project the homeowner might have.

Secured Investment property after police action -
I received an emergency call to secure a property after police forcibly entered to resolve a hostage situation, resulting in the shooting death of the suspect. I immediately drove to the property and found that the door to the front of the house and the sliding glass door at the back of the house were destroyed. I arranged for a co-worker to keep the property secure while I purchased the appropriate materials to secure the property. I was able to obtain a matching pre-hung entry door for the front, but needed to order a new glass insert for the back sliding door. When I returned to the job site I replaced the front door and installed new locks. I installed a piece of plywood where the broken glass insert had been, keeping the door secure and functional. After I was satisfied that the property was secure, I cleaned all broken debris, and supplied the property manager with the new keys.

Repair of flooded residential ceiling -
I received a call describing "waterfalls, coming from a tenant's light fixtures". I informed the property manager that the tenant should not touch the electrical fixtures or switches, and that it was best to leave the apartment in case the ceiling collapsed. This particular apartment complex did not have individual water mains and needed to be shut off at the street. I quickly arrived at the complex and shut the water off, then shutting off the main power to that unit was able to make a quick assessment. The water lines were installed in the attic space of all 6 units and lacked insulation. An improperly installed fitting had decoupled and flooded the entire attic space of this particular unit. Many of the bays were still flooded.

As this was a very sudden leak, I determined that if acted upon quickly the sheet rock on the ceiling could be saved. I formulated and proposed a course of action to the landlord's insurance agent via the property manager. Upon receiving approval I drained each individual bay and vacuumed any excess water. I then treated the entire attic space with a mildew inhibitor. I isolated the leak and repaired the pipe. After the property manager made arrangements to temporarily relocate the tenant I rented two industrial de-humidifiers. I covered the eve and ridge vents and placed a de-humidifiers in the attic. I placed the other de-humidifier inside the unit, covering all drains to prevent the de-humidifier from removing the water from the p-traps. I drilled exploratory holes where the sheet rock was attached to the ceiling rafters, and tested for moisture, Once nominal moisture levels were achieved I repaired the drywall and replaced affected light fixtures. A follow up inspection revealed no mildew, and no delamination of the sheet rock, seams, or paint.

Home re-pipe with cross-linked polyethylene (PEX-A) -
Having never installed PEX before I educated myself with the abilities of PEX-A and its installation requirements utilizing human, written and online resources. I then trained myself to use and maintain the PEX-A expanding, crimping, testing tools, and PEX-A fittings safely and efficiently. To save time and material I drafted a diagram detailing the new piping system, which would provide maximum water pressure to the farthest drain fixture utility. I conducted an inspection and pressure test of each connection, manifold, and support per diagram, to insure full compliance with PEX-A, IRC, and UPC guidelines. The successful completion of this project gave the homeowners a clean, energy efficient water supply system with excellent water pressure.

EXPERIENCE:
Company Name, **Seattle, WA** May 2010 – March 2011
Remodeling Carpenter
Responsibilities: Completion of remodeling projects as instructed. Skilled laborer with the operation, selection and set-up of appropriate tools and equipment. Planning daily work to achieve company goals, homeowner satisfaction in the most unobtrusive manner as possible. Was responsible for a company credit card to acquire any materials needed. Inspected daily work for quality and functionality.

Company Name, **Marysville, WA** January 1999 – May 2009
Maintenance Coordinator & Carpenter
Responsibilities – Scheduled repairs with tenants. Consulted with landlords and investment managers. Managed the maintenance of multiple types of investment properties, private residences and appliances. Skilled laborer with the operation, selection and set-up of appropriate tools and equipment for each repair.

PERSONAL REFERENCES:

Name (Construction company Owner)
Company / Position
Phone number

Name (Very Happy Customer)
Author / Consultant
Phone Number

Name (Former Employer)
Company / Position
Phone Number

CAREER TRANSITION:
FROM COMMODITY RETAIL SALES TO BOUTIQUE RESERVATIONS AGENT

Eric Castaneda lives in Los Angeles. In a near-fatal case of mistaken identity, this extraordinary young man was in the wrong place at the wrong time and was shot. Five times. In the back. He was in a coma for months, and when he recovered had to learn to function all over again.

Once he had, rather than lock-and-load and go seeking revenge, he made it his mission in life to become a motivational speaker to help kids either stay out or get out of gangs.

When we met, Eric was 19 and writing a book (Action Mentality), that he has since finished and published (www.ActionMentality.com).

Lofty goals, and in the meantime he was going to school and working to help his mom and his cousin.

He was working retail and doing OK, but that was it. Eagle ambition and sparrow wings.

As we talked, he did not see that he had any accomplishments to be proud of, let alone write essays about. We had several interesting conversations, all aimed at helping him refocus how he thought about himself and his work, specifically what he accomplished on behalf of his employer and customers. This was a switch from "just doing my job."

Pretty soon he got the hang of it and wrote his essays. We created two impressive data banks – skills and accomplishments.

In preparation for attending a career fair, he put together his own Professional Profile™ that showcased the skills and accomplishments he wanted to highlight and distributed it at the fair.

Almost instantaneously it resulted in two interviews – one a sales position with a global multinational (car, expense account, bonus, generous salary) which he did not get, and another as concierge in a luxury high rise, which he did.

Two interviews, one on top of the other! He had an epiphany around his own self-worth.

And later came an opportunity to work with an exclusive, low-profile, stealth limo-service-to-the-stars. Again dipping into his data banks he selected the most relevant accomplishments and skills and put the following Profile together.

His Professional Profile™ blew the hiring manager away. He was quickly hired, and some two weeks after, he reported that she was still talking about it.

Eric became a raving fan of the Professional Profile™ process and Résumés That Resume Careers. He even sent me an unsolicited video testimonial that you can see on www.YourProfessionalProfile.com/interviews-with-don-burrows/

Here are the targeted cover letter and Profile he created. He has given me permission to share all of this information.

Eric Castaneda
2423 W. 78th Place
Inglewood, CA 90305
Cell: 323.424.8310 E-mail: ActionMentality@yahoo.com

January 27, 2011

TO: Avalon. Los Angeles, CA
SUBJECT: Reservations Agent

Dear Sir or Madam,

I am responding to your January 27th posting on Craigslist for a Reservations Agent

Based on the requirements covered in the job posting, I believe I am about a 95% ideal match for the position.

Your Position Requires: **I Offer:**

• Customer service skills	• Over three years of successful customer service
• Computer literate	• Years of experience with Microsoft Word, Excel and Outlook. Strong generalist computer skills
• Must be able to handle large call volume	• While working for an inter-national retail company answered a high volume of calls on a daily basis.
• Ability to multi-task	• While working for a national car company my multi-tasking skills allowed me to build relationships and increase my sales.

Thanks you for reviewing my credentials. I can be reached at 323.424.8310.

Sincerely,

Eric Castaneda

Eric Castaneda
2423 W. 78th Place
Inglewood, CA 90305
Cell: 323.424.8310 **E-mail:** ActionMentality@yahoo.com

OBJECTIVE: Full-time Reservations Agent position with Avalon, a company that requires excellent communication skills, customer service skills and an outgoing individual who will go the extra mile.

SPECIAL SKILLS AND ABILITIES

• Experienced in working with customers via telephone and in person	• Be detail-oriented and able to multi-task	• Data Entry Skills; both Alpha and Numeric
• Strong written and oral communication skills, both with team members and with customers	• Over three years of successful customer service	• Typing (40 wpm)
• Very flexible and able to adapt to change	• Very accurate and rapid data input skills; strong generalist computer skills	• Inbound and Outbound Call Center experience.

REPRESENTATIVE PROFESSIONAL ACCOMPLISHMENTS

A Commitment to Doing It Right
- While working at the respiratory care company, on some occasions customers would call and tell me that sleeping was even more difficult because their mask was bothering them. One customer in particular stands out. He had been adamant in his selection of an oxygen mask that went into the nostrils and now he complained that it hurt him. Without dwelling on his insistence on that model, I suggested that a full face mask that covered the nose and mouth would probably be better.

  We went online to our website and I showed him the full face mask we had available and he selected his new mask. I sent it to him and followed up shortly thereafter. He was delighted with the mask and with the good sleep he had gotten. By helping him find the right mask and not making him feel like he had made a mistake the first time, he signed on for a higher-priced maintenance program we offered, and referred others to us as well.

Accurate Data Input
- Part of my duties as a leads salesperson at a national cars sales company involved continual follow-up without client dealerships. For that to happen, I had to input accurate information into the Siebel Customer Relations Management System. I made detailed notes during all my dealership conversations, and immediately entered those notes into my computer. On average, I had over one hundred phone conversations per day, five hundred per week, week-in-and-week out. My compensation was based on the accuracy of the data I sold to dealerships. Fortunately for me, my note-taking skills, attention to detail, organizational and data entry skills were up to take and I continually increased my sales.

Page 2 – Relevant Professional Experience

RELEVANT PROFESSIONAL EXPERIENCE

Apple One Employment Services, Culver City, CA **September 2010- Present**
Customer Service/ Sales Temporary Jobs.
- Answered a high volume of calls in inter-national retailer call center.
- Recruited people to come to taste test for fast food restaurant.
- Organized customer information in order to conduct focus group study.
- Helped conduct study in focus group with prototype products.

Xbanker, Newport Beach, CA. **January 2009- March 2010**
 Customer Service Professional/ Sales Professional.
Scope of responsibilities:
- Business development with customers about building credit for their business
- Organizing customers information for effective follow-up
- Explaining the benefits of building business credit instead of using personal credit for their business
- Customer follow-up

Americare Respiratory Services, Los Alamitos, CA. **February 2008- January 2009.**
Customer Service/ Sales Associate.
Scope of responsibilities:
- Gather patients medical information
- Suggest and figuring out which machine and breathing mask would be best for the patient to get a good night's sleep.
- Send out machine and mask; follow up with customers to make sure they were getting proper results.
- Follow up with customers about progress made in helping them receive their equipment.
- Organize patient information to track progress.

Cars Direct, El Segundo, CA. **April 2007-December 2008**
Dealer Relations Representative - Call Center.
Scope of responsibilities:
- Work with 30 sales professionals in call center covering 50 states providing sales advertising and customer leads to dealerships nationwide.
- Support dealers in opening new accounts and upgrading existing service
- Quickly and effectively solve customer challenges
- Maintain quality control/satisfaction records, constantly striving to improve customer service
- Provide follow-up service to respond to customer concerns and to alleviate potentially difficult situations with professionalism and sensitivity.

EDUCATION
- **Continuing Education**: **El Camino College,** Torrance, CA.
- **Graduated Redondo Union High School,** Redondo Beach, CA. June 2006

OUTSIDE INTERESTS (In addition to motivational speaking)
- Reading
- Art
- Exercise
- Basketball
- Public Speaking
- Dogs

SOLOPRENEUR:
CONTRACT PRODUCER OF EDUCATIONAL AND TRAINING VIDEOS

Scott Bell is a Video Producer / Project Manager in Redmond, WA. His company website is www.MediaDesignSeattle.com. He gave us permission to present what you are about to read.

It is the Fall of 2011, the recession is still with us, and it is a difficult time him to start his business. One of his niches is producing educational and training videos.

He is a Solopreneur, and by definition he is self-confident, tenacious and sees opportunity where others may not. Scott persevered and his start-up is beginning to show results.

When we connected, he was using a generic résumé, and when he finished Résumés That Resume Careers he immediately grasped the concepts, wrote his accomplishments essays and filled his Accomplishments and Skills Data Banks in what is thus far the record - about three days.

Isn't it astonishing what we can achieve when we get focused, committed and determined?

Following one of the strategies in the book, he sent out a number of targeted cover letters and a tightly structured Professional Profile™ to several categories in the Puget Sound Business Journal's Book of Lists. He used one of our most effective strategies: he was not seeking work or a job. He was seeking referrals to people and organizations where the recipient thought there might be a need or an interest for someone with his skills and experience.

That mailing has begun to generate conversation with different companies. And having sent his Profile and a different cover letter to other sources, many search firms have contacted him regarding full-time film production positions. He is still getting calls from that initial mailing, a year later.

Here is his targeted cover letter to search firms and his Professional Profile™.

SCOTT BELL
11610 201st Place, NE
Redmond, WA 98053
425.922.0474 Scott@MediaDesignSeattle.com

March 31, 2011

Dear Ms. XMXMX,

I am a very accomplished and self-confident contract producer of educational and training videos. I'm seeking referrals to people or companies where you think there might be a need for someone with my skills and experience. My résumé is attached.

Making a strong and measurable impact on a company's bottom line is my top priority. Here is my comparison of what I believe companies expect of their contract video professional and what I bring to the table:

Companies Expect:	**I Offer:**
Revenue generation through improved knowledge and application of company processes	Proven success in turning procedural knowledge into revenue by effectively educating sales agents, management and employees
Sales Support: lead generation and closing sales by reassuring big-budget clients' buying decisions	Nearly two decades of success captivating the public with a wide variety of video products and information distributed through the internet, television, mobile devices, and DVD.
Technical expertise in all facets of video production	Professional-grade skills writing scripts, directing shoots, filming, editing and graphics.
Retention of clients and employees by educating them on their unique services and benefits	Proven ability to understand a company's proprietary tools and translate instructions into language and steps that non-technical people can understand and follow
Effective business relationship with contractor who works effectively at all company levels, stays within budget and timelines, and drives project from concept to completion	Sixteen-year track record of building relationships with a wide variety of people while immersing myself in deadline-driven creative projects that must be completed painlessly, accurately, on time, and on budget through my mastery of the video production process

I'll check with you on April 14th to make certain you have received my information.

I view this as a favor from one professional to another; I look forward to the opportunity to repay it.

Thank you.

Best Regards,

Scott Bell

SCOTT BELL
11610 201st Place, NE
Redmond, WA 98053
425.922.0474 Scott@MediaDesignSeattle.com

Specialized Industry Knowledge:
Computer and Information Technology, Broadcast and Production

Hardware:
Mac and PC, various decks, lights and cameras

Software:
Final Cut Studio (Final Cut Pro, Motion, Soundtrack, Livetype, Compressor, DVD Color, Studio Pro)
Photoshop
InDesign
After Effects
Adobe Encoder
Premier
Illustrator
Dreamweaver
Soundbooth
Camtasia
MS Office
Flip Factory
Autodesk Cleaner
Mpeg Streamclip
Lightroom
Cyberduck
Filezilla
Avery Products
Windows Movie Maker
Sharepoint
ScheduleAll
Google Earth
Avid Media Log
XDCam Clip Browser
P2Log
iDVD

Cameras:
Panasonic HVX200
Panasonic DVX100
Sony DSR300

Broadcast Equipment:
Multi-camera switchers
Audio mixers
Pinnacle Genie

OBJECTIVE: Contract producer of educational and training videos for Seattle corporations that require a proven track record of achievement, expert film, editing and script-writing skills, and a willing desire to mentor in-house staff as we complete projects.

MY PROMISE: I consistently deliver a cost-effective, creative solution to any kind of visual need. I work to understand and implement a client's vision. I am consistently on time, whether building a weekly TV show from scratch, uploading a national commercial to Direct TV, creating a huge training library on a short schedule, putting together a quick YouTube video or a large media campaign, or building an entire conference media package in record time. You can count on me.

SPECIAL SKILLS AND ABILITIES:

• Expert script writing and editing skills	• Strong listening and interviewing skills	• Expert producer of web-based training content
• Know or easily learn video & editing equipment	• Exemplary ability to turn concepts into reality	• History of being under budget / ahead of deadline

REPRESENTATIVE PROFESSIONAL ACCOMPLISHMENTS:

WEB-BASED TRAINING

- Faced with unacceptable turnover of new life insurance agents, I undertook an additional project within my regular job, and in only three months, I created and finalized all of the video and graphics content, and assembled all of the training modules, for a 12-week, 25 volume web-based training program for Altig (www.Altig.com). I hired and supervised two freelance video editors, interviewed and consulted with subject-matter experts, wrote scripts for the on-camera talent, ran the camera for videotaping, edited and distributed the raw footage to my freelancers, and seamlessly meshed everything in the GUI. Prior to creation of "Altig University," company turnover among new agents was hurting growth. One year after launching the universal training system for all offices in the US and Canada, new agent growth doubled, six+ month agent count increased by 50%, and profits rose by approximately 20%.

REVENUE GENERATION

- During my year with Comcast Spotlight, I generated the most revenue ($130,000) of any producer in Washington State. I accomplished this by always thinking ahead as I balanced multiple projects and internal and external vendors at any given time. I utilized my time with each client very judiciously, was hyper-aware of making budget, and continually checked with clients and my management to make sure nothing fell between the cracks. During that year, I produced well over two hundred commercials and two large Video-On-Demand projects.

Scott Bell / 425.922.0474

INCREASING SITE USAGE

- I support web functionality through content. In support of Altig's IT department's complete restructuring of the website www.PlanetAltig.com, I was responsible for understanding the beta version of each new tool and then writing the complete training manual for each one. I created multiple Camtasia screencast videos demonstrating the use of each of the new tool. I packaged the manuals and videos into web-based training modules, complete with landing pages and quizzes. Since I create my best work when I thoroughly understand the tools and how they work, I learned to use every part of six new tools. This was particularly necessary for me to create effective screencast videos. One of my strengths is being able to demystify technology for non-technological agents and managers so they can use technology to make their "numbers" and increase profitability. I was gratified to roll this training out two months before the site launched, and when the site did launch, usage increased by 200%.

CONTRIBUTING TO REVENUE

- As Creative Services Supervisor with Charter Media, I managed and/or initiated a number of revenue-generating projects using statewide Local Access channels. These projects increased local production revenue using a venue that was typically reserved for non-profit announcements.
    - **Storm Hockey broadcasts:** Supervised equipment set-up and directed live games, broadcast sponsor-driven content introducing Storm Hockey to 78,000 households. Increased Charter's annual revenues by more than $40,000.
    - **Reventon Musical:** Working directly with the creator of this Spanish music video show, I negotiated production costs, taped and edited the show, and created sets. Increased Charter's revenues by more than $8,000.
    - **Charter Kids Club:** Our sales manager charged us with creating an original kids show that would have a community outreach arm. I created 25 episodes that aired in rotation on weekends for one year. Partnership advertising for the Kids Club brought in approximately $25,000 in new revenue.
    - **Music Video Contest in partnership with KQKY Hits 106 and Computer Hardware Inc. in Nebraska:** I initiated the partnership. The station helped promote the contest by airing free promos; we ran the entries on our channel and encouraged viewers to vote for their favorites. Charter Media and the Computer Hardware provided the prizes. Contest sponsorships brought in approximately $12,000 in new revenue.
    - **Charter Social Awareness Project / Heart Month:** Building on the success of Breast Cancer Awareness Month, I partnered with the Nebraska chapter of the American Heart Association to create sponsored tags on promos encouraging people to be screened for heart disease. This generated approximately $8,000 in new revenue during a typically "down" month while increasing the public's awareness of the American Heart Association.

FILMING AND EDITING

- I am an extremely competent videographer and editor. In support of those two professions, I direct and edit local and national commercials, create DVDs, compress and upload video for websites and broadcasts. I use an in-house HVX200 camera, Final Cut Studio and Adobe CS5. I have excellent professional connections within the Seattle video community and can always provide expert freelancer support as needed. One area of specialization is the filming and editing of testimonials and in-house video content. I have been doing this consistently for Schick Shadel. The marketing team has appreciated the continuity of my efforts as they have quality marketing material from which to create new campaigns.

VIDEO-ON-DEMAND

- As a producer for Comcast, Schick Shadel Hospital was my most successful client undertaking. I wrote and directed their Video-On-Demand campaign (staying within their $10,000 production budget), as well as the commercials that supported the VOD. The key to a successful on-budget production is making all changes on paper before rolling the truck, and that is exactly what I did. Statistics confirmed that this was the most-watch VOD in Seattle for a solid three-month time frame. It is credited with increasing the hospital's patient count by 10% and remains the "gold standard" by which the Schick marketing people measure their success. NOTE: When I became an independent contractor, Schick Shadel became my first client.

Scott Bell / 425.922.0474

ON-TIME AND UNDER BUDGET
- Planning and budgeting over three years, I negotiated with vendors and bought seven new edit bays, cameras and media storage for three separate Charter Media offices, and trained all of our five producers on their use. Through market-based negotiating, I doubled our purchasing power over what colleagues in other companies were purchasing. As a result of my foresight and proactive mindset, we improved our space utilization and increased efficiency by at least 300%. One of my most effective efficiency solutions that my producers really appreciated was to make two of the seven edit bays laptop-based. Our producers could work from the road and did not have to bring piles of footage home with them. I accomplished all of this for under $200,000 over three years.

- Every week, like clockwork, Altig sent out one communication via three different methods: 1) new 20-30 minute episode on Altig TV; 2) update of www.PlanetAltig.com homepage with news, recognition and training, and 3) in-house email updates of TV and website information to agents and managers. Each week without fail for 18 months, I was responsible for completing all three methods. It was expected, to the point of being taken for granted, that the information would be available to the East Coast staff when they arrived at 8 am every Thursday. Over that time period, rain or shine, I never once missed a deadline.

ENTREPRENEURIAL ORIENTATION
- An entrepreneur sees a need going unmet and presents himself or herself as the solution to that need. While working as a fulltime Producer for Comcast, I was assigned to the Schick Shadel account. The client was delighted with the service I rendered. After I left Comcast, Schick Shadel was unhappy with their new producer. Inasmuch as the Hospital had already constructed their own studio with the intention of bringing video production in-house, I negotiated a contract and took over all aspects of Schick's video production responsibilities. They became my first client, and things worked out beautifully. They save thousands of dollars each year by handling their own production needs and get much more for their dollars as I build their video archives of testimonial content, create specialty DVDs and unique web videos.

PERSONAL DETERMINATION AND INITIATIVE
- I remodeled my 120 year-old house, including installing a completely new kitchen, new back porch roof, two bathrooms, and landscaping. I ran new wiring and plumbing, installed insulation, painted, and built shelves from scratch. When I needed to learn how to do something new, like install a new breaker, or put a light switch in the middle of a line, or install a shower, I looked it up on the Internet, or read the instruction manual, and just did it. *I promise you I will bring this kind of self-sufficiency and can-do goal-achievement attitude to your projects as well.*

PROFESSIONAL EXPERIENCE:
Media & Design, Inc. Seattle, WA. 3/10 – Current
Lead Producer / Editor. Write, shoot and edit all production work including web videos, DVDs, local and national TV commercials. Assemble online video training content. Write, narrate, record and edit Camtasia screencast videos. Write onscreen GUI text including headings, page descriptions, quizzes, supplemental instructions. Bid generation and client contact. Hire and manage freelance help as needed.

Altig International, Redmond, WA. 11/08 – 3/10
Media and Design Specialist. Produce, operate DVX100 camera, edit and encode weekly 20-30 minute web-based TV show. Create web-based video training segments to increase sales agent performance. Direct in-house talent during taping. Interview SMEs to effectively write, direct, produce and edit web-based video training library of on-camera talent, graphical slides, linked documents and narrated Camtasia screen capture recordings.

Scott Bell / 425.922.0474

PROFESSIONAL EXPERIENCE / Continued

Comcast Spotlight, Seattle, WA. 11/07 – 11/08
Producer. Produce local commercials and Video-On-Demand. Write scripts with clients to fit within their budgets. Manage three to five internal and external vendors to complete each project. Manage multiple collaborations in deadline-driven environment. Member of West Coast Think Tank, monthly WA/OR/CA brainstorming team for big-budget clients. Average project invoicing ranged from $2,000 to $10,000.

Charter Media. Kearney, Nebraska. 8/02 – 9/07
- **Creative Services Supervisor.** 4/05 – 9/07. Developed original programming and projects with organizations and community groups. Pitch and plan revenue-generating promotions. Plan purchases for cameras, editing, LAN back-up and set-up equipment. Rebuild state-wide editing suites and train others in their use. Produce and direct live, multi-camera sports broadcasts. Write, shoot and edit commercials in deadline-driven environment.
- **Producer.** 8/02 – 4/05. Work with clients to write, shoot and edit creative commercials under tight time constraints. Operate Sony DSR300 and HVX200 cameras. The "go-to" producer to "seal the deal" with bigger clients.

Contract Editor and Production Assistant. Los Angeles, CA. 7/01 – 8/02
Write original scripts. Shoot and edit videos for Sturgis Motorcycle Rally projects (Year of the Hog, Rumble in the Mountains, Sturgis Founders Video). Design artwork for POP displays. Assist on film shoots for students in the USC Peter Stark program.

Orange County News Channel, Santa Ana. CA. 8/99 – 7/01
Master Control Operator. Record live programming for playback. Dial in satellite and microwave feeds. Troubleshoot and train new master control operators.

Three entry-level positions from 5/95 – 8/99: Catholic Family Radio Network. Board Operator/Call Screener/Editor. **Cable USA.** Production Assistant. **KMOR KOAQ KOLT.** Radio Announcer

EDUCATION:
University of Nebraska, Kearney. 1996 – 1999
BA, Broadcast Production Management. GPA 3.2/4.0

Western Nebraska Community College, Scottsbluff. 1994 - 1996
AA, General Studies. GPA 3.2/4.0

OUTSIDE INTERESTS:
- Rotary – (Redmond Rousers Club)
- Redmond Chamber of Commerce
- Tossing the ball for my two Boston Terriers
- Play and school activities with my five-year-old son
- Gardening
- Riding bike, running, skiing, swimming, camping, exercise – just about anything outdoorsy
- Occasional cooking
- Backyard construction projects using "found" items (I created "the most uncomfortable bench in the world" from dead naturally-curved cedar limbs)
- Watching online video and graphics tutorials
- Industry and business reading

SOLOPRENEUR: Serial entrepreneur (Start-Up Specialist)

- Built and sold his insurance agency
- Started a small business coaching consultancy to teach others how to build businesses that could later be sold
- www.TheTPConsulting.com

Meet Gerald Grinter.

When we connected and decided to create a Professional Profile™ Gerald told us he has never had a résumé.

So we had a clean slate upon which to work.

Like many clients, when he wrote his first two or three essays, they were significantly short of the 250-word target. We invited him to not short-change himself and instead give himself the benefit of the opportunity to really think through what he had accomplished, how, why and the results.

As he really drilled down and thought about his accomplishments more precisely, he broke larger, more general ones into smaller, more pointed and powerful ones, and proceeded to write with great focus and intention.

In short order he created an Accomplishments Data Bank of over 20 accomplishments, and the companion Skills Data Bank as well.

In our experience, Solopreneur websites are frequently spaghetti sites - static, containing a generic list of services, perhaps names of client companies, and client-created testimonials that are often vague and superficial.

Nothing much pops. There's very little information on what the Solopreneur has accomplished for their clients – on the problems they have faced and fixed.

Gerald selected the accomplishments statements that were most relevant to his work and included them on his website, giving potential clients the opportunity to learn what problems he has faced and fixed for others, and a sense of possibility around what he could do for them. He also repurposed other aspects of his Profile to create a marketing flyer. Both are producing results.

He says that when he talks to visitors to his site, many of them appreciate and compliment him on his Professional Profile™

Thus far Gerald has not created a custom cover letter. Instead he repurposed his material and created a marketing flyer that he distributes at his events.

His flyer and Profile from his website follow.

The Twelfth Power Consulting

Gerald Grinter
Small Business Consultant / Coach

*"I'm permanently unemployable.
Therefore, I'm an entrepreneur."*

Sometimes as small business owners, we are often so intricately involved in many of the daily activities of our business we can't get out of our own way.

It's so easy to get thrown off by sudden and disruptive, emotional or family issues, lifestyle changes, personal fears and self-imposed limitations. As small business owners we have to adjust quickly, think fast and move faster.

If you are a small business owner, what you need is a fresh, practical, pragmatic and provocative approach to business planning... one designed to act as a catalyst for your ideas.

AS A SMALL BUSINESS OWNER WHO BUILT MY OWN INSURANCE AGENCY FROM SCRATCH AND TEN YEARS LATER **SOLD IT FOR MORE THAN I COULD EVER IMAGINE, I WANT TO SHARE SOMETHING WITH YOU!**

I can help you get out of the way of your business!

"There is nothing 'small' about small business. We put our hearts and bone marrow into our businesses. We care about people, the environment and our communities. We do not run our business casually".

OUR PRODUCTS

SMALL BUSINESS CONSULTING
Helping business owners get out of their own way and build businesses they enjoy owning that make money.

WORKSHOPS
Providing small business owners with tools and ideas to start run and grow their businesses.

BUSINESS PLANS AND INCORPORATION
Business and Marketing Plans and online Incorporation support in all 50 states.

WEB SOLUTIONS AND SUPPORT
Domains, Hosting, Web Design, Online Shopping Carts, and more...

Visit me @
thetpconsulting.com

CALL OR EMAIL
GERALD GRINTER
1425 Broadway Suite 114
Seattle, WA 98122
206.650.4342 phone • 206.650.4342 web solutions
thetpconsulting.com / washingtoncash.org

In the past, when I worked with people in the start up phase of my business I felt intimidated. With Gerald, however, I could talk openly about my ideas. After meeting with Gerald I felt empowered, invigorated and ready to pursue my dream.

Elena Nishizaki
Balanced Body Yoga
Yoga Instructor and Personal Trainer

Gerald is a professional with the knowledge and experience to easily handle any project you throw at him. He even took care of me with my dry sense of humor and lack of knowledge and business demands with the ease of a true professional. I highly recommend working with Gerald to help you with your business.

Erik Dow
Erik D. Plumber
Master Plumber

"Being a business means making money. If you have a business and are not making money, you are sitting up there on a rock. You need to put your money where your mouth is, get over your fear and get off the rock. My mentor told it to me straight and got me off my rock. I'll do the same for you. It's time to get off your rock."

Gerald Grinter

Two of my Small Business Accomplishments

They are called "growing pains" because they are painful. Between 2007 and 2008, my agency grew by 10%, largely due to adding commercial insurance to our book of business. However, neither my business partner nor any of my agents wanted anything to do with commercial, so if I wanted to grow, I knew I would have to leave and begin a new agency. So I did. Starting over gave me the perfect opportunity to take complete advantage of technology and go as paperless as possible. I formed business relationships only with companies that had similar values and business philosophies and leveraged technology to present a larger public footprint than I really had. Emerging as a reinvented agency, during 2009 - 2010, my business increased by another 11%. As it turned out, I had unintentionally created a valuable asset that would make money while not being at all dependent upon me as the source of that money. In January 2010 I sold my business for more than I ever imagined.

Two years before I sold my insurance agency, I taught quarterly classes on commercial insurance basics for aspiring business owners through the boot-strapping micro-loan non-profit **Washington CASH**. After about a year, I jumped at the honor and opportunity to step up my game when the executive director invited me to become a business mentor. I got to help my mentees write their business and marketing plans, develop and implement their new sales strategies, and was treated to a ringside seat as eight new businesses were born and took their first new steps. I now co-mentor and support fifteen new business owners.

CALL OR EMAIL
GERALD GRINTER
1425 Broadway Suite 114
Seattle, WA 98122
206.650.4342 phone • 206.650.4342 web solutions
thetpconsulting.com / washingtoncash.org

Meet Gerald Grinter

I can help you take the passion you have for your business and turn it into the rest of your life. I can help you turn your passion into money, so you'll work when you want to...forever.

Being a business means making money. If you have a business and are not making money, you are sitting up there on a rock. You need to put your money where your mouth is, get over your fear and get off the rock. My mentor told it to me straight and got me off my rock. I'll do the same for you. It's time to get off your rock.

The Twelfth Power Consulting was created to offer everything from incorporating your business online, business and marketing plans as well as other web solutions. It's a place where doing it yourself doesn't mean you have to do it alone. If you are a small business owner, what you need is a fresh, practical, pragmatic and provocative approach to business planning... one designed to act as a catalyst for your ideas.

They are called "growing pains" because they are painful. Between 2007 and 2008, my agency grew by 10%, largely due to adding commercial insurance to our book of business. However, neither my business partner nor any of my agents wanted anything to do with commercial, so if I wanted to grow, I knew I would have to leave and begin a new agency. So I did. Starting over gave me the perfect opportunity to take complete advantage of technology and go as paperless as possible. I formed business relationships only with companies that had similar values and business philosophies and leveraged technology to present a larger public footprint than I really had. Emerging as a reinvented agency, during 2009 - 2010, my business increased by another 11%. As it turned out, I had unintentionally created a valuable asset that would make money while not being at all dependent upon me as the source of that money. In January 2010 I sold my business for more than I ever imagined.

Two years before I sold my insurance agency, I taught quarterly classes on commercial insurance basics for aspiring business owners through the boot-strapping micro-loan non-profit **Washington CASH**. After about a year, I jumped at the honor and opportunity to step up my game when the executive director invited me to become a business mentor. I got to help my mentees write their business and marketing plans, develop and implement their new sales strategies, and was treated to a ringside seat as eight new businesses were born and took their first new steps. I now co-mentor and support fifteen new business owners.

AS A SMALL BUSINESS OWNER WHO BUILT MY OWN INSURANCE AGENCY FROM SCRATCH AND TEN YEARS LATER **SOLD IT FOR MORE THAN I COULD EVER IMAGINE, I WANT TO SHARE SOMETHING WITH YOU!**

I can help you get out of the way of your business!

Call or Email:
Email: startrunandgrow@thetpconsulting.com
Phone: 206.650.4342
Web Solutions: 800.335.2074
Mailing Address: 1425 Broadway Suite 114
Seattle, WA 98122
Follow us on: Facebook / Twitter / Yelp

SOLOPRENEUR: Graphic Artist

I tried to make **Résumés That Resume Careers** as much of a do-it-yourself book as possible so that readers could take the methodology and make it their own.

In the cover letter and Profile that follows, Bellevue, WA-based graphic artist Susan Straub-Martin did precisely that.

We have her permission to use what you are about to read.

Here is what she had to say about the process and the results she achieved:

My experience came with mixed emotions, some sad, some mad at myself and some, frankly mad at Don. "Just who was this guy and why was he making me think about painful things? I haven't done anything worthy of noting!" I kept going through the process and discovered more than I had ever thought possible. There I was writing these things about this person, that just happened to be me.

After I had completed the process I realized that I had more to offer than I had previously thought. When you put your life's work down on paper you get a real sense of who you really are. These are the experiences that have shaped you and your work. These are the things that set you apart from the herd. These are the things that the right employers are looking for.

Don's method is intense, the process gut-wrenching, but the results are truly amazing. I have had more views to my profile having gone through the process which is great! For me though, it cemented that I really want to work for myself. The process really became about my personal profile. Who I was and what I had to offer the world of business. You may not know what result you want going into the process, but when you come out the other side with Don's guidance you will see you are a better person for it. – **Susan Straub-Martin** - *http://www.strauberrygraphics.com*

Date

Contact Person
Company
Address
City, State, Zip

I am transmitting this cover letter & résumé to announce my interest in becoming a member of your design team. I am exploring new opportunities using my design & management talents to their fullest potential by aiding in the development and growth of your company, through design, client relations, and good business acumen.

Working in various types of companies throughout my career, I have garnered some unique experiences for a graphic designer. These experiences include designing for companies like Disney and Sunkist to client relations and brand building for Apple Inc. The experiences at Apple led to creating and designing curriculum for adult learners in the field of Graphic Design.

QUALIFICATIONS
Recent Career Positions
Sr. Designer / Art Director / Project Manager / Mentor / Graphic Design Instructor / Business Manager

Professional Strengths
• Freelance Graphic Designer - Print
• Freelance Art Director
• Award Winning Illustrator - hand drawing and computer
• Expert in Adobe Creative Suite® / Painter® / iLife and iWork®
• Apple Expert
• Proficient in Microsoft Office®
• Client Relations - Clients included SOHO (Small Office Home Office) to fortune 500 companies
• Account Management / Client Relations Management (CRM)
• Problem Solving / Client System Solutions
• Small Business Marketing Instructor - (Classroom and One-to One)

I am looking forward to our interview + portfolio review.
Please review my internet portfolio at http://www.strauberrygraphics.com
Thank you for all of your time and consideration.

Respectfully,

Susan Straub-Martin

Susan Straub-Martin
strauberry@mac.com
http://www.strauberrystudios.com

SOFTWARE EXPERT

- Expert: Adobe CS4 (Specialties Photoshop, Illustrator, InDesign), Elements, Painter
- Expert: iLife, iWork,
- Proficient: Flash, FinalCut Express, Microsoft Office®

PROFESSIONAL STRENGTHS

- Graphic Designer-Print
- Art Director
- WordPress Websites
- Award Winning & Published Illustrator
- Traditional & Digital Sketching / Drawing
- Social Media Marketing
- Branding
- Concept to Completion
- Presentation / Curriculum Design
- Client Relations / CRM
- Team Building
- Creative Thinking / Problem Solving

PROJECT TYPES

Branding, Social Media Branding (Custom Branded: Twitter, Facebook, YouTube, etc.), Web 2.0, SEO, marketing, Logo design, Business Packages (Business Cards / Business Stationary Custom email signatures, White Papers, Letterhead, Thank You Notes, Newsletters, Brochures), Custom Illustrations, Catalogs, Brochure, Posters, Promotions, Presentations (Keynote / PowerPoint), Book Cover Design

CURRENT CLIENT LIST

Diane Kern Feng Shui Consultant, Judy Dowling, Marilyn Mallet Contemporary Art, Divorce for Grownups, Northwest Looking Glass, Real Estate For the Birds, Singing Heart Coaching, Résumé s That Résumé Careers, IntelAct Consulting, Thought-Dog-Consulting, Yvonne Dalke, Terri Hermes, Larry Miller, I Am Sound & Video, Warner Brothers, Disney, Mondo Publishing, Intuit, Upper Deck, Sunkist, San Diego Zoo, Woodland Park Zoo, Immunex, Techno Divas, Fox-C Productions, Chinook Newsletter, Art2Arch.biz

FREELANCE PROJECTS AGENCY / IN-HOUSE - 5+ YEARS

Eddie Bauer - Catalog Design 2000
Washington Athletic Club - Anniversary Promotions Design
Hornall Anderson Design Works - Layout Design Print
Humongous Entertainment - Sell sheets for games
Pigs on Parade Seattle - Illustration for Pigs on Parade Celebration

Jenny Craig - Food Packaging
Grossmont Center Mall - Layout for advertising, mall signage, marketing pieces

PROFESSIONAL ACCOMPLISHMENTS

• Working with various agencies I gained a creative portfolio that consists of a wide range of projects. Most notable was a mall project that consisted of signage, print ads, and an 18 month campaign for the center. I created a series of icons for their smaller shops and worked with the two National Brands (Macy's and Target) that anchored the mall for a successful rebrand of the mall and a high ROI.

• I developed a line of greeting cards to benefit the CRES program through the San Diego Zoo. This line of black and white cards and limited edition prints were sold at the zoo and it's partner zoo; The Wild Animal Park. The limited edition pieces were auctioned at their yearly fund raising events. The results gained more recognition for the program and raised more funding for the cause.

• Working as a professional illustrator for 20+ years I have garnered international recognition, sold and created work for prestigious companies, plus created a signature style and product line. I researched and developed a line of plush toys based on my published children's book characters that I illustrated and authored. I have developed custom fabrics, ornaments, greeting cards and a full line of gift products.

• In a team environment I created work for multiple home developers and retail centers that included signage for the development, billboards, brochures, outdoor banners, and sales center materials. The original contract was for one week. In appreciation for excellent work, my contract was extended to over 18 months. I later returned to train their interior design department how to use Photoshop and Illustrator for their presentations to clients.

• Working with the marketing director for a local telecom company, I expertly branded their foray into the internet age, by creating a likable, friendly character to guide their clients into using the internet. This character became the company's portal and marketing for the project. I continued to work with the director on several other marketing campaigns.

• I have worked with brand standards to create packaging for Sunkist Fruit Gems. Working with Sunkist to create a produce type package design for it's "gems" of candy, gained the company a new area of the supermarket, the produce department. The packaging was so successful the original design is still in use today some 15 years later.

• I have designed curriculum for teaching adult learners in the field of "Marketing Your Small Business." for a local Community College. This lead to working with the Director of the Graphic Design department and additional curriculum designers to creating a new Graphic Design program for the college. Additionally I have lead the curriculum design for a new design class on Corporate Presentations in which students create an entire brand for a company over the course of the quarter, helping them build a real world example for their final portfolios.

CHRONOLOGY

Strauberry Graphic Design - San Diego / Seattle (August 1984 - Present)
Freelance Graphic Designer / Art Director

Project Types: Branding, logo development, graphic design for corporate clients, catalog, brochure, posters, promotions, boutique websites, marketing, presentations, illustration, gift items, greeting cards, children's book development, and commissions for artwork.

BRANDED WEB / SOCIAL MEDIA SITES

- http://www.singingheart.com
- http://www.realestatefrothebirds.com
- http://www.YvonneDalke.com
- http://www.TerriHermes.com
- http://intelactconsulting.wordpress.com
- http://iamsoundandvideo.wordpress.com
- http://thoughtdogconsulting.wordpress.com
- http://larrymillerre.wordpress.com
- http://www.nothwestlookingglass.com
- http://www.divorceforgrownups.net
- http://www.realestateforthebirds.com
- http://www.realfengshuisolutions.com
- http://www.Art2Arch.net

Bellevue College - Washington (May 2009 - Present)
Instructor

- Marketing Your Small Business
- The Business of Graphic Design
- Print Production / Portfolio Review
- Corporate Presentation Design
- Color in a Digital Age
- Graphic Design Basics

Apple Inc. - Washington (April 2003 - January 2009)
Managing Business Partner / Mentor

- Technical Advisor
- Project Manager
- Staff Mentoring & Training
- Instructor

Big Fish Promotions - Washington (June1997 - Nov2001)
Client Relations / Jr. Art Director / Graphic Designer

- Built strong client relationships.
- Provided clients with staffing solution recommendations.
- Recruited creative professionals plus reviewed résumé s and portfolios for presentation to clients.

5

- Marketing & Promotions
- Built strong client relationships.
- Provided design solutions.

EDUCATION
- University of California La Jolla
- University of Arizona

DOWNSIZED BABY BOOMER. Organization Development Manager

Repurposed his Profile to become a University Lecturer

I (Don) can't imagine how difficult it must be to have been proactive and successful in Corporate America for over 40 years, then be downsized and told I needed to submit a one-page résumé to be considered.

That's insane. And that's today's reality for thousands of Boomers, including this man.

Before we began working on his Professional Profile™, my client had been unemployed for six months, had sent out many generic reverse-chronological résumés and had gone on no interviews. His 40 years of experience and his generic credentials worked against him.

Unlike a lot of conventional current wisdom, we encourage clients, particularly Boomers, not to hide or withhold information or limit themselves to a finite time period – like only the last 10 or 20 years.

Why? Because I know from personal experience that we've learned and done a lot of good stuff that is relevant today. Rather than trying to appear younger, here's a more effective strategy to get an interview: complete the personal inventory that is the Professional Profile™, then customize our skills and accomplishments and present ourselves as very experienced solutions to specific needs going unmet.

Such was the case for this client. The first thing we did was winnow down 40 years of accomplishments to those of which he was most proud and would be relevant today - a BIG first step.

Once we had identified the accomplishments, his essays and both Data Banks quickly followed.

Then, since he embraced the concept of being the meatball rather than the spaghetti, we avoided the energy-sucking, debilitating, depressing and disappointing time-wasting trap of mass-mailing a generic document. We focused on one job he was interested and that matched his experience.

We created a targeted cover letter and dipped into his two data banks to create a customized Professional Profile™. We demonstrated to the company's recruiter and hiring manager why he was an ideal candidate, worthy of consideration and an interview.

His Profile, incidentally, was seven pages long. Gasp. Never mind.

A week later, the hiring manager called and they had the screening interview. During that call, the manager complimented my client on the thoroughness of his résumé, saying that because it provided so much information, it saved interview time so he could get to know the man behind the accomplishments. Then he invited my client to Corporate for the in-person interview.

Sorry to say, my client came in second. AND since one of the key benefits of using a Professional Profile™ is that it is easy to repurpose the information for other opportunities, he did so and is now a lecturer in organization development at his local university and is developing a curriculum proposal.

Here is the targeted cover letter and Professional Profile™ that won him his first interview in six months.

NAME
ADDRESS, CITY, STATE, ZIP

DATE

Name
Position / Company
Street Address
City, State, Zip

Dear Mr. Name,

I am writing in response to your announcement Number for an Associate Organization Development Director.

Based on my analysis of the major requirements of the position, I believe we have a lot to discuss.

YOU SEEK	I OFFER
• Proven expertise enhancing organizational and business unit effectiveness, and identifying / resolving business performance issues through the application of organization development and talent management. Work with limited guidance to achieve results	• Ten years OD Pharma experience (Company and Company). **Primary areas of demonstrated expertise**: business performance improvement, organizational needs assessment, culture change, change management, 360° feedback
• Provide management coaching to business leaders and managers to effectively meet business line/region goals	• Builder of trust and credibility to coach senior executives, department heads, managers and solo contributors, openly and as shadow coach
• Building leader and managerial bench strength, as well as supporting design and implementation of career development	• Built career determining organization's future needs, then assessing current bench strength and creating effective succession plans
• Consult with business leaders to identify on-going training priorities and develop initiatives aligned with business line / region goals	• Demonstrated history of jointly developing/co-training range of workshops and courses that achieve long-and short-term company goals
• Partner with regional / global staffing and training departments to enhance processes and implement talent-related projects	• Strong believer that training must be practical and relevant to the bottom line, and yield sustainable returns back on the job
• Gain support and work with regional business leaders to drive key OD/TM projects	• My professional philosophy is this: *OD must cut costs and improve profits. Otherwise, what's the point?*

While I did not see it in your position announcement, I wanted to let you know that, as a veteran of the Company cycle of mergers and acquisitions and the acquisition of Company by Company, I have acquired a whole new set of OD skills that may be of interest to you.

I still have my home in City and am planning to be there the week date. If you wish to contact me directly, my cell (number) is the most expeditious manner.

Thank you.

Sincerely,

Name

NAME
Address
City, State Zip
Cell: E-Mail

OBJECTIVE: Senior level Organization/Management Development Consultant position. Seeking a company requiring significant expertise in conducting and assessing organization needs, business performance improvement, change management, and an extreme ability to coach senior management to excel.

OD PHILOSOPHY: If OD doesn't cut costs and improve profits, what's the point?

SPECIAL SKILLS AND ABILITIES

• Significant grass roots OD experience positioning companies for growth during and after mergers and acquisitions	• Expert knowledge of a broad range of organizational assessment and feedback instruments	• Extensive experience in developing and implementing succession development plans and talent management strategies
• Demonstrated skill in successfully building and leading intact work teams to complete projects worth billions in revenue	• Expert design, facilitation and presentation skills. Adept at listening, drawing people out and helping people solve their own difficult problems	• Extensive hands-on OD experience helping senior management, work teams and individuals survive and thrive during mergers and acquisitions
• Notable success coaching senior executives and mentoring organization's future superstars	• Absolute desire to be held accountable by operations management to solve problems hurting bottom line	• Quickly and effectively build credibility and rapport with people at all organizational levels

REPRESENTATIVE PROFESSIONAL ACCOMPLISHMENTS

BUILDING SUCCESSFUL WORKING RELATIONSHIPS WITH ULTIMATE DECISION-MAKERS

- Company's senior vice president of Human Resources selected me to partner with him and one other HR colleague to design and implement a new cross-functional, consolidated function called the Office of Change Management (OCM), comprised of people of standing and influence in their respective functions. Our mandate was to comprehensively assess and then manage the organization's capacity and ability to address change issues on a company-wide basis. Additionally, I was partnered with the senior executive responsible for Managed Care to assess and implement cost saving initiatives and introduce efficiencies. After completing our analysis we combined a number of functions in the Managed Name Division and were able to contribute approximately $570 million in revenues the first year of its existence. (Company)

- To reverse a major profitability slide due to poor customer service, I conducted a needs analysis by introducing the use of 360º feedback to the 1,600-person Name Division / Company. Previous efforts to fix the problem had failed, due to a culture of corporate inertia and a compensation system that rewarded sales without regard for service. Using the results of my feedback assessments, I developed and implemented programs to address the identified issues. Empirical data indicated a significant reduction in customer service complaints and in employee relations issues. More importantly, prior to the initiative, divisional sales were about $5 billion; three years later, they were at $8 billion. While we did many other things to improve profits, my senior executive told me that our turnaround came when I willingly put myself "on the hook" with Operations to stop their profitability slide. (Company)

- While the Company City plant was always profitable, generally met all goals and were constantly being called on to test new processes, the Home Office held the perception that they did not "follow the rules" and they were frequently chastised for it. Confused about the basis for getting a "bad rap," the team suggested they seek external validation by competing for the prestigious All-Star Awards given annually by the City Society for Human Resources Management (SHRM). I was responsible for gathering and coordinating input from across all plant functions, and for writing the submissions. The site won Workforce Development Award in 2006, 2007 and 2008, the Diversity, Community Involvement and coveted Employer of Choice Award in 2009, and the Community involvement Award again in 2010. (City)

- As an OD partner in State for the merger of Company and Company, I had OD responsibility for a 22-person integration team. My mandate was to combine like functions where appropriate and to create new ones where needed in the newly-merged company. I was successful across the board, but my major contribution was in the design, development and implementation of the Marketing Analysis and Commercial Support (MACS) function. This new function was charged with eliminating what had become an unacceptable organizational norm in Company – **market analysis shopping.** My team ended market analysis shopping and caused product managers to be compensated based on actual sales of their products, not on their ability to find analysts willing to provide data that supported the optimistic sales projections they essentially paid for. We estimate that MACS saved the company $100 million in annual revenues (Company)

PROFITABILITY THROUGH TRAINING DESIGN AND DELIVERY

- Notwithstanding the fact that Company had always been compulsively focused on the bottom line, its internally-developed training seldom was. I championed the need to maintain focus on bottom-line relevancy of our "Teamwork" training and to avoid at all costs the inclusion of any fluffy feel-good components that didn't add to the bottom line and would be forgotten when participants returned to their offices. I led or co-trained over 25 sessions; of the 500+ managers I trained, I never received a rating less than 4 on a 5-point scale. Weeks and months after their sessions, participants continued to seek me out for coaching advice and guidance. (Company)

- Two years after Company and Company merged, I was hired to develop and apply creative OD tools, tactics and strategies to unify merged yet still alienated factions within five business groups critical to profitability. Beginning with the premise that becoming a successful team is a decision that individuals in a group make, I performed a needs analysis to determine deterrents to successful team work, gained senior management's commitment and then designed and conducted a flexible, customizable team development workshop that reinforced Company's nine core values. Over 26 intact work teams (>300 people) completed my workshop. Those teams began to "live" Company's core values, and the use of the values spread across the organization. My HR colleagues continually sought me out to use my process, and most teams kept inviting me back to work with them as they developed. (Company)

- At Company's City plant, I introduced a 10-step OD change management model that became the foundation for benchmarking practices of our High-Performing Work System (HPWS). Lack of a common language hampered our ability to meet our two primary goals: shipping product and being in compliance with Home Office and FDA/OSHA mandates. Under the umbrella of creating a unified plant-wide work system, I facilitated each of the 35 work teams (26 managers and >350 employees) to create their own complimentary processes to implement HPWS. My team facilitation and internal consulting resulted in more effective working relationships among Operations, Procurement and Quality Assurance/Control such that we met all of our Home Office obligations while being in full compliance with all government mandates. (Company)

- Company initiated a corporate-wide initiative to improve business performance by updating business practices and hired me as a plant OD Partner to help direct the efforts of a 14-person team to design, organize and implement a series of self-directed work teams under the umbrella of a High Performance Work System (HPWS) in a plant of 650 employees. The plant was charged with cross-training all operations staff on all production lines, upgrading the skills and capabilities of both the shop floor operations so they could trouble-shoot complex computer-controlled machinery, and train the mechanics so they could repair and maintain all of the automated systems. The plant achieved all goals within established time frames and budgets, and with no loss in productivity. (Company)

- When Company's senior management began the process of taking the company public, I was invited to be a member of the design team responsible for creating and conducting a management development training program - focused on "new rules of the road"; 360° feedback; silo busting and teamwork - for more than 500 senior managers from around the country. In addition to facilitating iterations of the program, I created and facilitated the wrap-up final half day of the four-day workshop. Everything I did in that module enabled participants to return home with concrete, immediately-actionable plans for facilitating feedback and fostering cross functional cooperation. Operations management monitored progress and commended me on the success. (Company)

IMPROVING RESULTS THROUGH EXECUTIVE COACHING

- As an interim step to appointing a new Managing Director for the Company's City plant, Corporate created the temporary position of Associate Managing Director. In addition to mastering plant operations, the incumbent had ultimate responsible for creating and implementing a High Performance Work System. In addition to my OD responsibility for the implementation of the HPWS, I was given liaison responsibilities to facilitate his transition to Managing Director in the plant. Thanks to the competency of my HPWS teammates, I was able to dedicate most of my time to coaching, counseling and guiding the Associate Managing Director, sometimes visible in my role, and other times being a shadow coach and sounding board as he mastered his new role. Together we established new levels of trust and accountability with each other and throughout the plant. (Company)

- When making changes at the senior management level, Company-Corporate named several women to the City Plant Leadership Team (PLT); I was asked to coach and facilitate their entry into their new positions. For years the PLT had been all male and employee perception was that they did not want women in any senior positions. That perception made it difficult to achieve gender and racial diversity at lower levels within the plant. Using a range of recognized assessment and feedback instruments, I enabled all members of the Plant Leadership Team to learn how their peers and subordinates perceived them, and how they themselves contributed to those perceptions. All members of the PLT opted for self-disclosure, leading to open discussion and ultimately enhanced mutual trust and openness. With intentional nurturing, those behaviors began to trickle down to other levels within the plant. (Company)

ESTABLISHING CLEAR LINES OF ACCOUNTABILITY AND COMMUNICATION

- Company's Plant Leadership Team was so pleased with the results of the assessment and feedback sessions I led that they asked me to take the process to their direct reports and to the next level as well – an additional 54 people. This time, the focus was to enhance teamwork, identify development needs and continue to promote necessary cultural changes. I managed interactions, monitored relationships and intervened as needed. I augmented assessments and feedback sessions with a comprehensive mentoring program, which I anchored with the establishment of "learning contracts." Our stated goal at the outset was to eliminate the need for a formal mentoring structure and to make mentoring a cultural norm throughout the plant. We achieved that goal, and mentoring became an integral part of plant life. (Company)

NAME / Phone Number

- As a contracted consultant with Company I was responsible for leading the development and implementation of an OD strategy to fix documented and highly visible customer complaints. Not wanting this to be a unilaterally developed Human Resource initiative without Operations support, I recruited one person from each of the four Company Operating Groups to be members of the design team and presenters of the series of custom workshops we developed for each of the Operating Groups. Within six months, we achieved a 31% drop in customer complaints and a 48% increase in our internal employee satisfaction surveys. This translated into approximately $300K in annual savings in responding to service complaints. (Company)

APPLICATION OF FEEDBACK AND ASSESSMENT TOOLS

- When I was brought into City's Department of Juvenile Justice, a staff of 600 was responsible for the supervision of some 660 inmates incarcerated in the City's only secure juvenile detention facility and

  the administration of the agency. Employee and inmate morale was horrible. In the two years before my arrival, the jail had documented 202 successful escapes. Citizens and politicians were screaming for change. With the full support of the Department's new Commissioner, I introduced into this heavily politicized, unionized and deeply entrenched civil service environment a number of methodologies and strategies from the private sector. Based on my guiding principle *"If you have the problem, you have the solution,"* I created a training solution that incorporated: corrections procedures, basics of adolescent development, safety procedures, and facility management.

  My prime strategy to get people to open up to me took everyone – staff, guards and inmates – by complete surprise: I spoke with them courteously, politely, and respectfully. I listened to what they had to say, and I treated them as competent, responsible individuals, as adults or young adults, as professionals. This was a "first" in that environment. For the first time in decades, supervisors, managers and counselors began to feel valued and respected as professionals. As they began to treat each other with respect, they began to act as professionals, and this showed in their relationships with the juvenile inmates. When I left four years later, conditions in the detention center were such that inmate escapes were down by more than 60%, and the press the agency received went from anger to approval. (City Department of Juvenile Justice)

PROFESSIONAL HISTORY:

Company, City, State. 6/05 – 6/10
My efforts impacted on $800M in gross revenue
Note: Company acquired Company in October, 2009
Senior Organization Development/Human Resources Consultant. 9/08 – 6/10

- **Scope of responsibilities:** Internal consultant, coach and program manager providing Organizational Development and Human Resources support for individuals and groups throughout the City Facility, with emphasis on the development and implementation of High Performance Work Systems (HPWS) in an approximately 900-employee manufacturing/packaging environment. Primary products include Product, Product, Product, and Product
  Volume of annual business supported: $800 million. This plant led all of Company's plants (five in North America and two in Puerto Rico) in all profit indicators over the last four years
  Reason for leaving: As a result of company merger I spent my final four months providing OD and HR support to senior management, staff and employees in preparation for acquiring company to shut the plant

Senior Organization Development Consultant. 6/05 – 9/08
- **Scope of responsibilities:** Internal consultant, coach and program manager providing Human Resources business partner support for client group of 350+ in this facility of 600+ hourly and 260+ salaried associates
- Firmly aligned with Operations and willingly made myself accountable with managers with P&L responsibilities to identify business problems that threatened the bottom line, then developed and implemented OD solutions to resolve those problems and achieve business objectives
- Volume of annual business supported: $800 million
- Reason for leaving: promoted to current position

Company. City, State 2/03 – 6/05
Lead Consultant: - Offered clients an array of strategic and tactical organizational and human resource development options, including access to a network of HR professionals with wide-ranging expertise.

- Industry focuses: pharmaceutical, manufacturing and technology
  Consulting specialties: Strategic Human Resource Development, Organization Management, Team Development, Effectiveness and Tuning, Internal Consulting Competence and Leadership/ Management Development.

- Consulting assignments included: Design and facilitation of a four day world-wide Marketing and Sales meeting for an RTP-based technology firm; design and facilitation of off-site meetings for a product development team, a pharmaceutical support function, teambuilding for a corporate media buying team. Coached executives in mid-sized and small firms on a variety of leadership issues and initiatives.

- Representative assignment included: Team building sessions for a major manufacturer of power transmission and distribution products; creation and facilitation of a sales strategy simulation during the global management meeting of a company creating data management solutions for service providers of mobile data traffic and multimedia applications; individual coaching to managers, executives and team leaders in the pharmaceutical industry.

Company. City, State 1/01 – 2/03
Senior Manager Organization Development
My efforts impacted on $5B in gross revenue
- **Scope of Responsibilities:** OD lead for the Office of Change Management in US Pharma that included: Organization Development, Project Management, Financial Management and Resource Management mandated to comprehensively assess and then manage the organization's capacity and ability to address change issues company-wide.

Company. 7/97 – 1/01
Manager Organization Development Consultant –
My efforts impacted on $1.2 B in gross revenues
- **Scope of responsibilities**: Primary OD support for several business, product and service units in US Pharma including: Marketing Analysis and Commercial Support, NeuroHealth and the Customer Response Center (CRC)
- Reason for Leaving: Position elimination with the Company/Company merger.

Company. City, State. 2/96 – 7/97
Manager Employee Development and Organizational Effectiveness (Consulting Assignment)
My efforts impacted $135M in gross revenues
- **Scope of responsibilities**: Creation and implementation of employee development strategy, including management/supervisory development, performance management, technical and customer service skills, 360° assessments and feedback, organization development.
- Reason for Leaving: End of consulting assignment

Company, Division. City, State. 2/93 – 3/95
__Director/AVP - Executive Development & Succession Planning__. 2/94 – 3/95
My efforts impacted $750M in gross revenues
- **Scope of Responsibilities:** Creation/implementation of development strategy linking sector, division, and firm-wide strategic objectives. Critical components included: 360° assessment / individual feedback; personal strategic development action plans; in-place professional developmental assignments.

__Manager, Executive Training & Development__ (Division Name)   2/93 -2/94
- Reason for Leaving: New COO took control over a major portion of my development and succession planning responsibilities; I requested and received a severance package.

Company / Division. City, State. 9/88 – 2/93
My efforts impacted $750M in gross revenues
__Management Development Consultant__ -- Division. 9/88 – 8/91
__Senior Management Education Consultant__ -- TRS Corporate. 8/91 – 2/93
- **Scope of Responsibilities**: Managed / facilitated various corporate management, technical and performance skills development programs. Created and implemented development process linking individual performance goals and strategies to those of their Division business units; utilized process in various divisional business units with a total population of over 6000. Introduced 360° feedback instrumentation in Division
- Reason for Leaving: Company offered an opportunity to expand my skills in strategic organization development.

Company. City, State. 9/83 – 9/88
My efforts impacted on $75B in gross revenue
- *__Communication & Training Consultant.__* (Company). 11/85 – 6/88
- **Scope of Responsibilities**: Partnered with executive management in an intensive company-wide culture change initiative.
- *__Management Development Consultant__*. Employee Development Office/Corporate Headquarters 11/83 – 8/85
- Reason for leaving: Chose not to relocate to City, State.

COMMUNITY RELATIONSHIPS AND TEACHING EXPERIENCES

I continue to acquire additional skills and knowledge in order to put them to practical use, both for my own benefit and that of others because I am committed to sharing my talents and knowledge with others. Some of my current and past projects are noted below. You are free to contact each person listed to discuss real-life applications, methodologies and successes.

- FM Radio Station. City, State. - From 1997 until 2005 I was a volunteer at this Public Radio station located on the campus of University. In 1998 I began hosting a weekly jazz program that focused on educating listeners and primarily playing traditional jazz of the big band and Be-bop genres. In addition, I created weekly three-minute educational spots for the *Jazz Artist of the Month* segment.

- STATE **MUSEUM OF LIFE AND SCIENCE.** City, State – from 1998 - 2005 I became a member of the Board of Directors of this nationally-known institution and held various committee assignments including Chair of the Strategic Issues Committee and member of the Search Committee. In addition, I provided – pro bono - ongoing leadership and management development training workshops to the museum's management team

- **EXECUTIVE SERVICE CORPS.** Emeritus Board Member

- **NATIONAL BLACK MBA ASSOCIATION.** Lifetime Member

NAME / Phone Number

- **CITY BLUES FESTIVAL.** Volunteer/Emcee

- **UNIVERSITY GRADUATE SCHOOL OF EDUCATION.** Adjunct professor in program for educators serving at-risk high school students

- **COLLEGE OF CITY.** Designed and delivered a course on intervention strategies for elementary school educators

EDUCATION

University	University
City, State	City, State
M.Sci. /Adult Education HRD *1982*	BA Communication Arts *1970*
GPA: 3.8/4.0	

CERTIFICATIONS

- MBTI Myers-Briggs Type Inventory
- SkillScope ® and Profilor ® *360°* Feedback Instruments
- LIFO ® Life Orientations Model
- IMA/Accelerating Change ®

OUTSIDE INTERESTS

- Jazz
- Community service
- Voice-over recordings
- Reading
- Exercise

NON-DEGREED BABY BOOMER HUMAN RESOURCES MANAGER WITH TEN YEARS EXPERIENCE AT THE SAME COMPANY. Used her new Professional Profile™ to win an interview as municipal government HR Manager

I (Don) believe the Universe brings people together for a reason, as was the case here.

Off and on for several years I had been gently lobbying my wife to see if I could get her to want a Doberman Pinscher, my favorite dog. She stalwartly resisted my best efforts. All that changed in 2004 when she was diagnosed with Stage III breast cancer. For a while things looked iffy and she told me to go ahead and get my Doberman. She said that if she died, there would be someone there to love me.

Pause for eyes to refocus and lump in throat to subside.

Once I recovered, I flew back to a Doberman rescue website where I had a seen a photo of a black and tan Dobe named Ruthie. She was "grinning" and the caption said she was a grinner and was good with cats and kids. Perfect! We had cats and the neighbors had kids.

I contacted the owner of the rescue (let's call her "Connie") and made arrangements to meet Ruthie at her foster home.

Long story short, we brought Ruthie home and a week or so later Connie came to do a home inspection to make sure her girl was coming to a good home.

Direct-spoken and fearlessly blunt, Connie is 158% dedicated to protecting her dogs – loves them dearly, passionately committed to their wellbeing. I appreciate that kind of passion and for some reason I cannot clearly define, she and I "clicked" and Ruthie was ours.

Over the years our friendship has deepened as my wife and I have supported her Doberman rescue and Connie has told me more than once that I have become an HR mentor to her in her HR manager role.

Throughout my career I have observed that owners of small and unsophisticated family-owned businesses in small towns often think of HR as the "Personnel Department" from the 1950s – a superfluous cost center of administrivia, payroll-and-picnic. A waste of money. A luxury.

It's a dedicated HR professional of special character and integrity who remains in that Catch-22 environment – valued by her employees but not by her management – in a small town of limited professional HR opportunities and where her Doberman rescue is firmly established.

Fast forward to December, 2011. Connie is 65 years old and learned of this opportunity. We tailored her cover letter and Profile to the requirements of the job, and within ten days they had called her and booked an appointment. Her cover letter and Profile follow.

Quite simply, she is spectacular and has earned this chance to be appreciated for all she does and all she is. Whether or not she is hired, she sees herself and her work differently and can now see potential opportunities with greater clarity.

Name
Address
Cell and Email

December 12, 2011

City of Name
Attn: First and Last Name of Person
PO Box Number
City, State Zip

REF: Human Resources Manager

Dear Ms. Last Name,

I am a 12-year resident of City and am currently the Human Resources Manager at Company. After reviewing the requirements for the HR Manager position, I believe I am about a 96% perfect fit.

You Seek an Experienced:	I Offer:
• Technical resource to supervisors and employees in recruitment, selection and orientation	• Ten years of multi-site experience recruiting, selecting and orienting new hires from entry-level to senior management
• Administrator of fringe benefit programs and related issues	• Fully experienced in all aspects of benefits management including vendor selection / negotiation
• Drafter, interpreter, administrator of personnel policies	• Have always written policies with an eye toward having to defend them
• Administrator of classification, pay and appraisal systems	• Fully experienced in these three areas, and believe in pay-for-performance
• Specialist in employee relations management and grievance resolution	• While I am management, have earned the respect of all levels within the organization and have a reputation of fairness
• Forward-looking person to develop, implement and maintain new programs and processes	• CORE BELIEF: *Human Resources must cut costs and improve profits. Otherwise, what's the point?*
• Compliance watchdog for all applicable Federal, state and local laws, policies, procedures	• Fully responsible for compliance with all applicable Federal, state and local DOT, HazMat, EEO, WC, Unemployment Compensation laws, policies and procedures. View Compliance as source of indirect revenue by never getting fined
• Person of independent judgment / initiative to do what needs doing	• PERSONAL BELIEF: *"Judge by results. Sometimes harsh. Always fair."*

Ms. Last Name– at the risk of sounding trite, if your first question would be *"Why do you want this job?"* my answer would be this: *"City has been good to me and I would love the opportunity to give something back."* Corny? Perhaps. True? Definitely.

My cell is xmx.djd.jjgg. I look forward to speaking with you.

Best regards,

First Last Name

Name
Address
City, State Zip
Cell: xmx.ddd.erer **Work (with discretion):** dkr.ttt.wera
Email:

OBJECTIVE: **City of** Name **Human Resources Manager**, a position requiring demonstrated expertise in all aspects of recruiting, compensation and benefits management, policy administration, employee relations, compliance, and a strong sense of pragmatic personal integrity and spirit of innovation

SPECIAL SKILLS AND ABILITIES:

Quick to learn new tasks and resilient when faced with challenges	Self-taught in disciplines of web creation / management, transportation management, human resource practices, accounting	Capable of working independently, with minimal guidance and supervision
Particularly adept at learning and understanding new software applications and applying them to automate everyday tasks	Database management; Creation of interactive Web pages using DreamWeaver and Excel	In order to bring out the best in employees, am sensitive to understanding and adapting to their needs, rather than forcing them to adapt to me
Understand techniques of computer animation and cascading style sheets for Web page creation	Solid, practical experience in all aspects of business accounting, including payroll and depreciation	Strong degree of business ethics and personal integrity in working with senior management, peers, and employees

REPRESENTATIVE PROFESSIONAL ACCOMPLISHMENTS:

- As newly-hired manager, performed initial procedures audit and discovered over 50 infractions of Federal Highway Administration interstate commerce regulations. Had the Federal DOT found the violations, the company would have been placed on the Federal Watch List, severely limiting its ability to secure future contracts. Also, at $2,500 per infraction, fines could have been in excess of $250,000, and company would have faced lawsuits and other punitive sanctions that could have led to bankruptcy.

  Convinced owner and operations management of the need to establish and maintain effective processes and procedures to ensure compliance. Worked extensively with owner, operations manager and field management in seven sites across five southeastern US states to educate them regarding current regulations, and helped them reverse 12 years of neglect. Can affirm with certainty that my actions enabled the company to remain in business. Four months after completing training and records update, company received "FULLY COMPLAINT" evaluation in DOT spot audit.

- Upon assuming new position, found that company's SAFERSYS experience rating was 23% lower than national average of "fair," or 75%. Educated owner and operations management staff regarding existence and importance of SAFERSYS and how much their infractions, and ultimately their performance rating, was costing the company by being "targeted" by DOT. Initiated scheduled review of all logbooks, developed and conducted extensive accident prevention training among managers, drivers, and warehouse staff, trained and followed-up to insure proper completion of all manifests and bills of lading, and implemented "driver attitude readjustment" to insure they dealt professionally and politely with police when stopped. Net result: after two years of effort, SAFERSYS experience rating is now in the top 5% percentile of "in compliance" carriers.

- Saved company in excess of $10,000 per unemployment compensation insurance claim by teaching managers how to effectively and legally document issues of poor performance in order to successfully deny unemployment compensation to employees terminated for cause. Estimated annualized savings are in excess of $280,000.

- Using and then modifying off-the-shelf templates, created company's first-ever Human Resource database covering 47 employees in two sites in two states. Database includes all payroll information, EEO data, all personal contact data, performance history, skills profiles, verbal and written warnings, attendance, compensation / benefits, training / testing. Have documented the entire process for future use and users. Creating the database myself enabled me to create a completely customized database, and saved the company in excess of $25,000.

- Applied Excel to streamline inventory management, order processing, and billing for 27 stores in seven states coast-to-coast. Result provided management with real-time snapshot of all pertinent aspects of performance bicycle business, enabling nationwide business decisions, including tailored advertising programs, to be made and implemented daily, rather than weekly. Estimate that new process increased market share by 15%.

- Saved company approximately $300,000 annually in nationwide service charges while improving store manager satisfaction regarding HVAC servicing. Negotiated more responsive and effective servicing relationships with purveyors in 27 states; enlisted support of store managers to define needs and expectations, then established and communicated processes and expected levels of performance to selected HVAC vendors; took active role to follow up on performance.

PROFESSIONAL HISTORY:

Company. City, State. 2001 – Present
Current: Human Resources Manager
- **HR Specialist.** Responsible for human resources for 50 employees in State and State exempt and non-exempt employees for both states. Created and manage company's first-ever full-function Human Resources department.
- **Transportation Specialist.** After 9/11/2001 I was the only one in the company with experience to determine the Company's DOT and FMCSA compliance. Oversee fleet of work vans and box trucks. Brought and maintain company in compliance with DOT and FWHA regulations

Company. City, State. 1997 – 2001
Director of Administration
Responsible for: payroll, payroll taxes, contractor settlements, A/P, A/R, HUT, IFTA, all DOT-required documents for HAZMAT transportation company

Company. City, State. 1994 – 1997
Administrative Support to Human Resources for Retail Stores
For 27 stores nationwide, created and managed range of daily, weekly, monthly, quarterly, and annual reports for retail store revenues, expenses, payroll, and various accounting analyses. Taught WordPerfect, MS Word, MS Excel, Lotus, and various applications

Company. City, State 1993 – 1994
Environmental Monitoring Technician
Performed pre-operational and long-term monitoring field activities; maintained requisite equipment and prepared necessary records; fielded landowner complaints and performed community relations

Company. City, State. 1992 – 1993
Richmond County Field Site Secretary
Reception and administrative duties during Characterization of the State Low-Level Radioactive Waste Disposal Facility Potentially Suitable Site

Company. City/State and City/State. 1981 – 1992
Co-Owner and OTR Driver
Managed A/P, A/R, collections, State and Federal tax filings. Applied for and gained Interstate Commerce commission authority as Contract Carrier. Obtained leases for equipment, permitted equipment for 48 states and Canadian operations. Tracked and filed highway and fuel use taxes. Handled DOT audit, all business documentation, and review of drivers' logbooks.

Company. City, State. 1978 - 1981
Terminal Manager. City, State
Supervised 35 employees. Managed dispatching, trip leasing / permitting, sales for freight services.

EDUCATION:

University of City. City, State. 1966 – 1968
Major: Microbiology; Minor: Business

University of State. City, State. 1964 – 1966
Major: Veterinarian Medicine/Animal Husbandry; Minor: Business

INTERESTS:
Doberman rescue, computers, new computer applications

The Epilogue

a life can change in a tenth of
a second
or sometimes it can take
70
years.

>   -Charles Bukowski
>   you tell me what it means
>   The Flash of Lightening Behind the Mountain

Change.

Specifically, changing your behaviors and changing how you see yourself.

We have space for one more quick story.

For the first couple of decades of my life, I (Don) bit my fingernails. No, actually, I gnawed them pretty much to my wrists.

One hot and sweaty summer day I was crawling around in the dirt out in the woods with my army unit. My scalp itched something fierce and I removed my helmet to really scratch my head. With no nails, all I got was an unsatisfactory fingertip rub.

I remember really looking at my fingertips and thinking how useless my nails were to me at that moment, and how disgusting they looked, and how much I really wanted to scratch my head.

In that instant, I CHANGED. I realized I wasn't going to gnaw on them anymore. I decided.

That was over four decades ago. I have nice and useful nails now.

SO WHAT?

So permanent, significant change can happen in a tenth of a second, or decades, or happen never.

Over the course of our time together, you've changed.

Please compare the résumé you were using before you read the book, and your new Professional Profile™.

Big change, we would imagine.

Please recall how you were feeling about your chances of finding new business or your job search prospects then, and how you are feeling now.

Another big change – yes?

If you have really applied yourself to writing your accomplishments essays and then:

- distilled them to their essence in a very focused manner,
- thoughtfully identified your transferrable and motivated skills, and
- effectively compiled Part B of your professional profile,

we are certain something you were not expecting has happened to you.

We believe your self-opinion, how you really see yourself, has changed for the better.

If you began the book thinking, "I'm just a ….,." we believe you have now discarded that notion forever and replaced it with this idea: "Damn, I'm good!

If you began the book thinking you had no accomplishments, we are sure you have now discarded that opinion and have opened your eyes to the truth, and that truth is, "Damn, I'm good!"

If you began the book thinking there was no reason for you to have a Professional Profile™, we believe your self-awareness and self-worth has increased to the point that when you think of yourself, you stand a little taller and your first thought is, "Damn, I'm good!"

And if you began the book thinking that résumés based on accomplishments were only for managers and executives, we believe you have dropped that like the wrong idea it is, and have replaced it with, "Damn, I'm good! And I've got the Professional Profile™ to prove it!"

(your) "… life can change in a tenth of a second"

We believe that at some point as you were reading the book, you had a little inkling. Something moved inside you, and the real you began to awaken, to emerge, as you changed.

You began to see yourself in a different light, see yourself as a different person.

Maybe you saw yourself as more capable.

Maybe you began to trust yourself more.

Maybe you felt an increase in your self-confidence.

Or perhaps you could actually "see" yourself doing the work you always thought was beyond you.

Or, maybe your subconscious grabbed on to the idea that you ARE the solution to some company's need that is going unmet

And you listened to your little voice inside you as it thundered out, "YES! I CAN!"

Whatever the change, please continue to blow gently on that little flame, feed it and nurture it until it grows into a bonfire that will consume all self-doubt and take you and your life where you want to go.

Good luck.

And, one *last* request from us: When good things happen to you we'd love to hear about it that we can share in the happiness you may be feeling as you start a new career or new job or a great new project! Drop us a note via email or contact us through the blog! We will virtual high five you!

Not that you'll need it, because as you have discovered:

"DAMN! YOU'RE GOOD!"

Do you know job seekers or solopreneurs who need to read

Burn Your Résumé. You Need a Professional Profile™ ?

Please send them to
www.YourProfessionalProfile.com

For volume sales to corporations, libraries, government, or to assist our military to transition into civilian jobs, please go to:

www.YourProfessionalProfile.com/buybooks

For additional information, please call 800.597.9972

How Can We Be of Service?

Gainfully and happily working or in transition, we believe every job seeker and solopreneur needs a flexible Professional Profile™ "at the ready" to be able to quickly and easily respond to opportunities to present themselves as the ideal candidate.

In addition to specialty options, we offer four levels of coaching, guidance and support:

Done BY You - For the Do-It-Yourselfers.
You receive:
- a copy of **Burn Your Résumé – You Need a Professional Profile™**
- online access to White Papers on tips and tactics on playing and winning the Inner and Outer Game of Finding Work or New Business
- free attendance at our overview introduction-to-the-process training webinar and
- free access to our monthly "Open Mike Q & A Sessions" on the Inner and Outer Game

Done WITH You - For those wanting step-by-step help to create their Professional Profiles™ on-line
You receive:
- Everything in **Done BY You**
- Membership in a four-week four-session on-line webinar where you and your cohort will:
    - learn the Professional Profile™ methodology
    - incrementally create your own unique Professional Profile™
    - learn to write a targeted cover letter
    - receive one professionally-written cover letter
    - participate in community brainstorming
    - sharpen your "accomplishments awareness" with access to our growing Library of Accomplishments Statements
    - receive one hour of Inner Game telephone coaching with Deb
    - receive one hour of Outer Game telephone coaching with Don
    - Three months membership to our "Cohort Community" Check-In Calls and website (www.CommunityCohortCheckInCalls.com)

Done FOR You – For those wanting personal attention and custom service done for you by us.
You receive:
- Everything in **Done BY You** plus an in-depth personal inventory / intake interview with Don and Deb to help you identify/clarify your:
    - Goals, aspirations, unique talents, vision, ideal customer/employer, ideal product or service, work you love and work to avoid at all costs
- A process customized to your personal requirements that will expedite completion of your Professional Profile™ and three targeted cover letters
- Two hours of 1:1 Inner Game coaching with Deb
- Two hours of 2:1 interview coaching / critique / practice with Don and Deb
- Two hours of customized strategy planning
- One year of open access to our evolving Library of Accomplishments Statements to continually sharpen your "accomplishments awareness"
- Six months of "Members-Only" Quick-Access to us for continued email / phone support

6-Pack of Custom Cover Letters – An option for those who have completed **FOR**, **WITH**, or **BY**.
You receive:
- Six cover letters customized to the position you are applying for
- Written as needed, based on job requirements
- 24 hour turnaround (and we mean 24 hours!)

Please check www.YourProfessionalProfile.com for additional details and current fees.

If You Want Interview Opportunities Use These Tactics!

Over a four month period, I (Don) as HR Director managed the shutdown/dismantling of a divisional headquarters, laying off 90 professionals. **What happened next?** *I personally wrote 90 custom functional résumés / cover letters, and provided videotaped / critiqued interviewing training.* **The end result:** *All 90 employees got new positions equal to or better than what they lost.* **May we do the same for you?**

Here are some of the many "Tactical Nuggets" I learned, and the rationales for each. Please don't ignore them. If you can't get the interview, how can you get the job?

 # 1: BE ORIGINAL: *Avoid fill-in-the-blank templates.* **WHY? You want your résumé to be an accurate reflection of the authentic "you," not read like a bunch of Mad Libs strung together.**

 # 2: BE YOURSELF: *Know that looking for work or new business is like dating.* **WHY? The *"date face"* is superficial and tiring. Throughout the hiring process, show employers the authentic "you".**

 # 3: BE PERSONAL: *Stop mass mailing your generic résumé hoping to get lucky.* **WHY? Companies receive thousands of generic résumés like yours. The odds of someone selecting yours are horrible.**

 # 4: BE THE MEATBALL: *To STAND OUT, customize your cover letters and résumés for each position's specific requirements.* **WHY? Be the IDEAL CANDIDATE, not a generic applicant.**

 # 5: BE A CONTRIBUTION: *The focus of your cover letter and résumé should not be on what YOU want.* **WHY? Potential employers and customers want to know what *you* can do for *them*.**

 # 6: FIRST THINGS FIRST: *Put your most relevant skills / accomplishments on the top half of Page One of your résumé.* **WHY? You've got between five and seven seconds to hook the reader's interest.**

 # 7: BE A SOLUTION: *Use this process to identify your <u>Representative Professional Accomplishments</u> and <u>Special Skills & Abilities.</u>* **WHY? Employers want to interview "unique solutions" to their needs.**

 # 8: BE DISRUPTIVE: *Put yourself in the hiring manager's shoes.* **WHY? Which cover letter/résumé would you read first: generic chronological job duties or skills/accomplishments targeted to you?**

 # 9: BE IN INTEGRITY: *Don't mislead by trying to appear younger.* **WHY? Effectively presented, your accomplishments speak for you. Be authentic. Deceit is unnecessary and unworthy.**

 # 10: BE STRATEGIC: *Stop making it easy for them to say "NO!"* **Why? Let them fall in love with your accomplishments before you present potential negatives like gaps in your job history.**

 # 11: BE CONGRUENT: *Imagine having a résumé that gets you an interview but giving an interview that makes them wonder why they invited you in.* **WHY? Be the same person on paper, in person and on Day One at work.**

Just so you know... Tactical Nuggets 1 and 11 come to you courtesy of my co-author, Deborah Drake. Deb teaches clients how to play an authentic *Inner Game* (maintaining your spirit, self-esteem and authentic self*)*. I'll teach you to play an effective *Outer Game (*cover letters and résumés).

Welcome to **Your Professional Profile™ - Winning the Inner and Outer Game of Finding Work or New Business.**

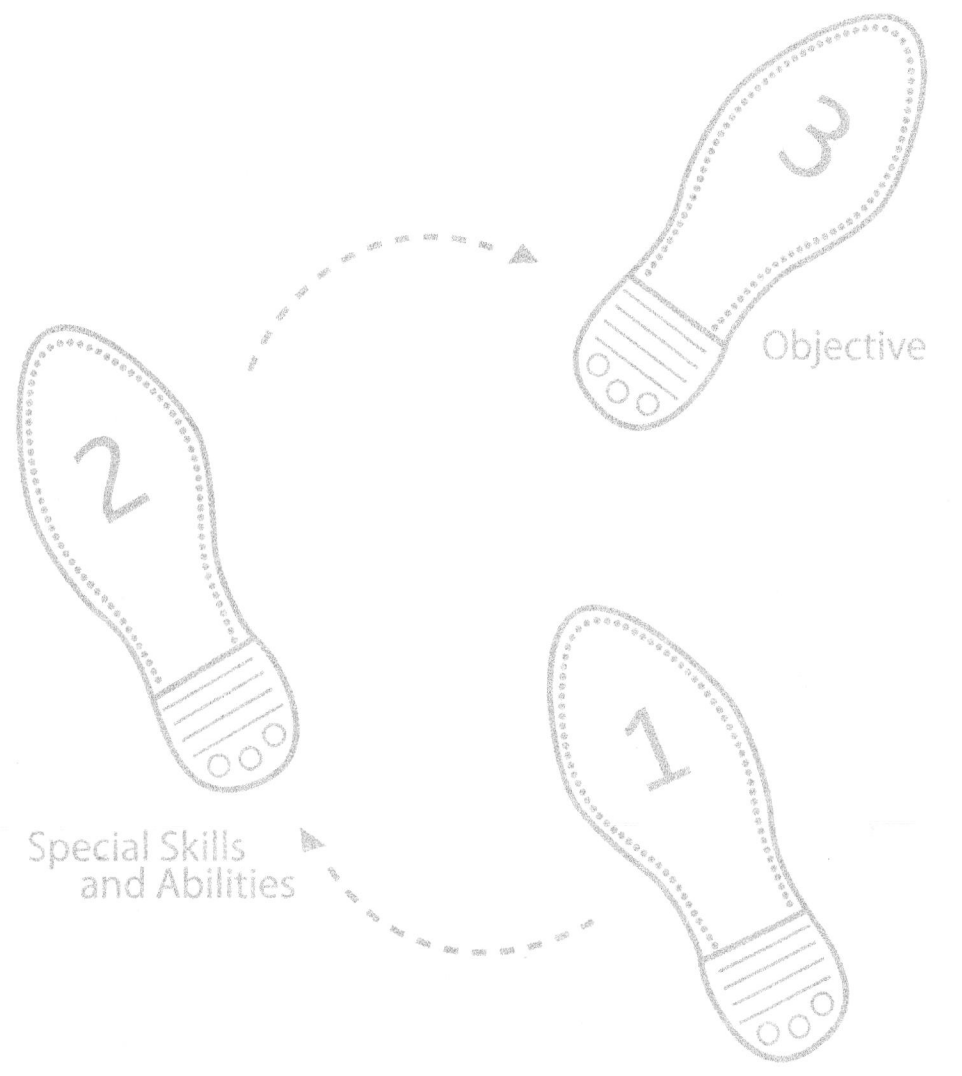

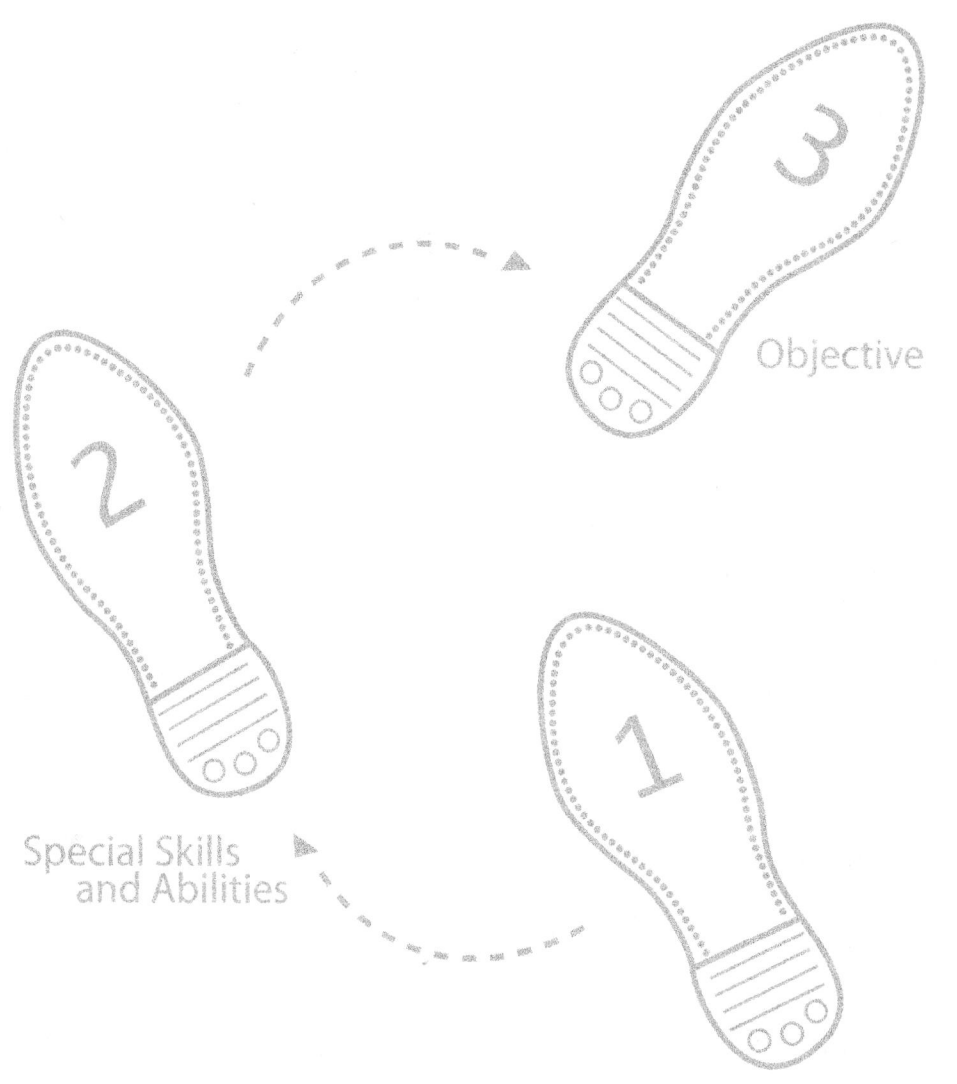